PLAYS WELL WITH OTHERS

PLAYS WELL WITH OTHERS

The Surprising Science Behind
Why Everything You Know About
Relationships Is (Mostly) Wrong

ERIC BARKER

HarperOne
An Imprint of HarperCollinsPublishers

HarperCollins books may be purchased for educational, business, or sales promotional use. For information, please email the Special Markets Department at SPsales@harpercollins.com.

FIRST EDITION

Library of Congress Cataloging-in-Publication Data has been applied for.

ISBN 978-0-06-305094-5
ISBN 978-0-06-325287-5 (ANZ)
ISBN 978-0-06-326703-9 (Intl)

22 23 24 25 26 LSC 10 9 8 7 6 5 4 3 2 1

To all the relationships I've screwed up.

(I'd list them, but I only get one page for the dedication.)

Henry Thomas Buckle once said:

"Great minds discuss ideas; average minds discuss events; small minds discuss people."

I'm here to discuss people.

CONTENTS

CONTENTS

INTRODUCTION

Nobody's been shot yet. Yeah, I know, those aren't the most re-assuring words you've ever heard, but from where I'm sitting, they're downright optimistic.

Two guys tried to rob a convenience store, but the cashier hit the silent alarm. Police arrived, bad guys went barricade and took the cashier hostage. The Emergency Services Unit—a fancy way of saying SWAT—is now stacked up outside. NYPD's Hostage Negotiation Team has established contact.

Oh, and HNT has a special guest today. That's me. Hi. For most of my life I've been afraid of getting emails that read "From Detective Thompson, NYPD," but I wanted to write a book on dealing with people and this seemed like a fun way to learn. Now I'm *here*. "Fun" is not the first word that comes to mind. SWAT teams are mobilized, lives are on the line, and I'm wishing I had opted instead to spend the weekend at some new-agey relation-ship seminar where fewer guns are pointed at people. I do all my own stunts, folks. The next five minutes are going to be the most stressful ten years of my life.

Oddly, the guy on the other end of the phone seems pretty nice. But it's way too early to feel any kind of good about things. The first half hour of a hostage negotiation is the most dangerous. There's no rapport, no transference, no anything to act as a buffer if things go sideways. Just adrenaline and fear.

As the negotiator starts talking with him, I quiz myself on proper procedure: *Slow it down. Use active listening. Voice tone is important. Remember that your actions are contagious.* But the single most important thing right now is: *keep them talking*. Because if they're talking to you, they're not shooting people. Unfortunately, he's no longer talking to us. The line just went dead. Things cannot get worse . . .

So, of course, they do. He calls back. But it's not the same *he*. It's someone else. Someone who's speaking quickly and cursing a blue streak. I can't even follow everything this guy is saying. I do catch references to being an alum of the penal system, and killing two people years ago, along with a Whitman's Sampler of other felonies.

"Don't freak out," I tell myself, totally freaking out. At the end of movies they always say, "No animals were harmed in the making of this motion picture." My disclaimer might have to read, "Very *few* people were harmed in the writing of this book."

The negotiator responds to the suspect: "Sounds like you're frustrated." Yeah, that's an epic understatement, but it's also a fundamental active listening technique: labeling. Giving the hostage taker's emotion a name. Neuroscience research by Matthew Lieberman at UCLA has validated that labeling dampens powerful emotions. It also builds rapport by showing someone you're on their wavelength.

"I *am* frustrated! You got an entire SWAT team out there?!? My nephew's scared to death!"

"Nephew?" Mirroring. Another pillar of active listening. In the form of a question, repeat the last thing they said. Keep 'em talking. And all the while you're getting more information and building rapport.

"Yeah, you just talked to him . . . Look, I can't handle being out of prison. But I don't want that for him."

"Sounds like you're concerned. For his future. You want him to get out of there safely." More labeling. More rapport. And slowly inching him in the direction you want this to go.

As they keep talking, the tone gradually shifts. The hostility starts to dissolve, and it's almost like they're working together to solve this problem. It's not long before the suspect sends the cashier out. Then his nephew. And soon after, he's surrendering.

Seeing the power of active listening in action hits me like a Frisbee to the face. I feel like I just watched a magic act, but instead of the magician reaching into the hat and pulling out a rabbit, he pulled out a Lexus. This method not only changes minds, it gets people to drop guns and accept prison sentences. I'm thrilled. Thrilled that I have the key to my next book and thrilled that it wasn't me on the phone.

The negotiator turns to me: "Eric, your turn to be on the phone."

Oh, did I forget to mention that this was a training simulation? Oopsie. (Please don't call me an "unreliable narrator"; it'll make my mother think I'm an author who doesn't pay his rent on time.) Despite this being "fake," there's a good reason my adrenaline was spiking. The NYPD's training facility is spectacular. It's the size of an airport terminal and reminiscent of a Hollywood studio backlot. There are realistic sets for the most common hostage incident locations: a bank lobby, a police intake unit, a rooftop jumper scenario, and a convenience store (complete with Oreos). Professional actors play the roles of perpetrators and hostages. They take this more seriously than I've ever taken anything. And rightfully so. (In fact, at the request of the NYPD, I altered some elements of the scenario to keep their training protocols confidential.)

After a generous dose of simulated terror, I couldn't feel better. I climbed the mountaintop to study with the Zen masters of people skills and achieved relationship enlightenment. I'm still over the moon as we're hanging out after training. I found the skeleton key to human communication: active listening. Now I know what everyone needs to improve their relationships at home . . .

"By the way, this stuff doesn't work at home." It was one of the negotiators.

Huh? I think my heart just stopped.

"With your spouse. These techniques won't work at home with your spouse." Another negotiator nods and chuckles as if to say "Ain't that the truth." My jaw drops. Along with my will to live. So this incredible system for dealing with people won't work when your wife is angry or your husband is being a jerk? It can save a life but not a marriage? I want to scream at them: *Don't you realize I have a book to write and need answers that make for good sound-bites?*

But I don't. I take a deep breath. I may not know a lot about dealing with gun-toting bank robbers, but I know a fair amount about psychology. And pretty much every form of marriage therapy recommends active listening during conflict. I go back to my hotel and double-check. And I'm right. It *is* recommended by everyone . . .

It just doesn't work. Every marriage therapist (and me) is wrong. The hostage negotiators are right. John Gottman, professor emeritus of psychology at University of Washington, actually put it to the test. Active listening sounds great. And it works well in scenarios like hostage negotiation or therapy where the practitioner is a third party and has some distance from the problem. But marital arguments are different; they're about *you* not taking out the trash. Mirroring, labeling, and accepting all emotions when you're being screamed at by your spouse are about as natural as telling someone not to run away or hit back when physically assaulted. Gottman found that people just couldn't do it in the heat of the moment. And in follow-up studies, with the few couples who actually could actively listen, it showed only short-term benefits. Couples quickly relapsed.

In hostage negotiation short-term benefits are fine. Works long enough to get the guy in handcuffs? Perfect. But in a marriage that will (hopefully) last longer than hours or days, it's a disaster. Therapists recommended it, but until Gottman, nobody had actually *tested* it. Except the hostage negotiators. Maybe that's why research shows that only 18–25 percent of couples report any improvements one year after marriage therapy.

Note to self: something designed for terrorists and emotionally disturbed people isn't perfect for your family. (Okay, maybe something designed for terrorists and emotionally disturbed people is perfect for *your* family, but I'm not going to assume.) Humans are complex. Three-dimensional chess complex. And it was naive of me to think that something so complex would have a simple skeleton key.

What I assumed about dealing with people was wrong. What all the marriage therapists believed was wrong. And a lot of what *you* think you know about relationships is wrong. Relax, it's not your fault. We've been getting conflicting information all our lives:

○ Do "clothes make the man"? But they told me "don't judge a book by its cover"?
○ Do "birds of a feather flock together"? Wait, I heard "opposites attract"?

○ You should "just be yourself." Or is it "when in Rome, do as the Romans do"?

Of course we're confused and believe silly things. How could we not? But this is vitally important stuff. And I don't mean in some saccharine Hallmark card sorta way. Consider this: the Grant Study at Harvard Medical School has been following a group of 268 men for over eighty years. The amount of data accumulated on them could fill rooms, and the insights about what makes for a long, happy life are plentiful. Yet when George Vaillant, who led the study for much of his own life, was asked what he learned from decades of studying these men, he replied with one sentence:

That the only thing that really matters in life are your relationships to other people.

It seems absurd that so much research could be reduced to a single sentence. But it rings true. We spend so much time chasing the shallow things in life. But when tragedy strikes, or late at night when your brain asks too many questions, we know it's the relationships that matter most. *Whom can I trust? Does anyone really know me? Does anyone really care?* If you think of your happiest moments, they will be about people. The most painful moments will too. Our relationships to others make or break our lives.

So humans have been dealing with humans for thousands of years—and we still can't get it right. How do we not have good answers to this stuff? The single most important thing in life is left to innate ability, hearsay, and the little insight we can slowly grind out learning brutally through pain and rejection. Some might say that there are plenty of texts on the subject, but the words *relationship book* are usually muttered in the same tone as *infomercial*. We know full well that most of those are specious opinion at best, with a Magic-8-Ball-level of scientific accuracy. We need real answers.

Sigmund Freud said, "Love and work are the cornerstones of our humanness." My first book was about work. I played *Myth-Busters* with the maxims of success we all grew up with to see if they were really true. (Luckily, that book was a bestseller, because if you write a book about success and it's not successful, well, I can't think of any greater proof that you don't know what the hell you're talking about.) And now, here, we're gonna cover the first half of Freud's statement. Relationships.

This book is about what we get *wrong* when it comes to relationships and how we can be a bit more right. We're gonna test those maxims we grew up with and see if they hold water, scientifically:

o Can you "judge a book by its cover"? Or is that something only Sherlock Holmes can do on TV?
o Is "a friend in need a friend indeed"? And what does that phrase really even *mean*?
o Does "love conquer all"? Or are divorce rates so high for a depressingly accurate reason?
o Is "no man an island"? (I have always felt that I was more of an archipelago, honestly.)

We'll leverage the best evidence available—no platitudes or magical thinking. (I don't believe in blowing on the dice for luck before you roll. I believe in card counting.) And we'll look at *multiple* sides of the issue before we render a verdict. What we'll find is surprising and counterintuitive. It's gonna shake the Etch A Sketch on conventional wisdom. We're gonna bust the myths, get the real answers, and then learn how we can use that information to live lives filled with love, warmth, and kindness—all without choking anyone in the process.

I've spent the past decade studying the science of human behavior on my blog, *Barking Up the Wrong Tree*. I've earned a bunch of fancy degrees, and I even survived growing up in New Jersey. But those aren't the reasons you should trust me to be your Virgil on this tour of the relationship Inferno.

I've been called a lot of things in this life, but "a people person" isn't one of them. Agreeableness is among the five fundamental traits that psychologists use to evaluate someone's personality. On that attribute I scored a four . . . out of one hundred. Oof. Relationship-wise I have been driving through life with the parking brake on. One reason I started studying social psychology is that I have never been good with people and I wanted to understand why. So this is not a *I'm a guru, do what I do* book. This is a *I had no idea what I was doing so I talked to a lot of people way smarter than both you and me to get some solid information* book. However much you may feel that you need these answers, however much you may have failed with relationships, been a loner, an outsider, or just someone for whom it all just never clicked—I am right there with you. We're going on this journey *together*.

We'll see that the fundamental core of relationships is the stories our brains weave to create identity, agency, and community—and how those stories not only bind us together but can tear us apart if we're not careful.

And then I'll explain the meaning of life. Seriously. (Let it never be said that Patricia Barker raised an unambitious son.)

Relationships bring us the highest of highs and the lowest of *oh-my-god-I-never-guessed-it-could-get-this-low* lows. We all fear being vulnerable or embarrassed. At times we wonder if we're cursed or broken. We cannot stop the waves, but we can learn to surf. Whether you're already good with people or you're a socially anxious introvert, we can all build better friendships, find love, reignite love, and get closer to others in this age of increasing emotional distance and loneliness.

Often our problems with others start with our inaccurate perception of them. We've all gotten burned trying to judge people's character. Can we learn to size up people accurately? To know what's on their minds—scientifically? To detect lies? Read body language? (And cover it all in under sixty pages?)

Simply put: Can we "judge a book by its cover"?

Let's start there . . .

PART 1

CAN YOU "JUDGE A BOOK BY ITS COVER"?

1

His eighteen-year-old daughter had vanished a week ago, and the police had nothing.

On February 13, 1917, Henry Cruger's daughter Ruth had gone to get her ice skates sharpened and never returned. Despite assurances from the highest levels that the case was a priority, police leads had immediately gone cold. And as if that weren't enough pain, the newspapers were in a feeding frenzy. A girl from a prominent, wealthy family had gone missing? The media couldn't get enough.

His wife would wail at night. Not that he had been sleeping either. But Henry Cruger was not the kind of man to give up. He was wealthy. He was powerful. And he knew he would find his little girl. Because he had just hired the greatest detective there was.

This man wasn't a police officer. This man's detective work had recently saved someone from a death sentence. This man was a master of disguise. This man was a former US district attorney. And this man had done all of this while facing opposition and challenges that no man in 1917 faced. Because at the beginning of the twentieth century, the greatest detective in America was no man at all.

Her name was Grace Humiston. And it wouldn't be long before New York's newspapers were referring to her as "Mrs. Sherlock Holmes." Comparisons to that fictional character were all too apt—because her life sounds straight out of a detective novel. Grace only wore black. She took all cases pro bono. Since the law schools at Harvard and Columbia still didn't accept women, she went to NYU. There were only one thousand female lawyers in the US when she passed the bar in 1905.

Grace established her own firm that represented poor immigrants, helping them fight employers and slumlords who exploited them. She received death threats as often as you get junk mail. When immigrant men desperate for work began vanishing in the Deep South, she went undercover and exposed a peonage conspiracy that led to a national scandal. At twenty-seven she became the first female US district attorney. Not bad for someone who, as a woman, still couldn't even vote.

But with the Ruth Cruger investigation, Grace would have her work cut out for her. Not only had the case gone cold but so had the story. The newspapers had exhausted their scandalous speculation and turned their focus to World War I, which was raging in Europe. There would be no help coming. But even Sherlock needs a Watson.

It was while working for the Department of Justice that Grace met "Kronnie." Julius J. Kron had a reputation for being a tad too aggressive—and maybe a tad too honest—for a government job. That suited Grace just fine. A former Pinkerton detective with a deep facial scar, he was never without his revolver. And Kronnie was quite good at ensuring the death threats Grace frequently received remained just that—merely threats. As for the Cruger case, Kronnie was the father of three girls himself. He didn't need any convincing. They got to work.

The two checked every hospital and morgue in the city but came up empty. The only thing remotely resembling a suspect was Alfredo Cocchi. He owned the store where Ruth had gone to have her ice skates sharpened the day she vanished. The police interrogated him but discovered nothing. They had eliminated him as a suspect. Twice, actually. As a recent Italian immigrant,

Cocchi feared that a mob would come for him and had returned to his home country. There just wasn't much to go on. They went for five weeks without so much as one new lead.

But Grace wasn't giving up. She was convinced the police had missed something. She and Kronnie split up to redo the *entire* investigation. Kronnie took his "persuasion" abilities to the street to find out more about Cocchi, while Grace reviewed every shred of evidence there was about the case until she knew it inside and out.

Talking to locals, Kronnie found out there was more to Cocchi than the police had discovered. His shop had been a hangout for gamblers and lowlifes. And Cocchi liked girls. A lot. He would lure them down to the cellar for after-hours drinking sessions. It was rumored he arranged "meetings" between young women and his clients. And there had been assaults. Nobody said a word to the police because they didn't want their daughters' reputations sullied.

Meanwhile, Grace reviewed the police files and found something that had never hit the papers: when Cocchi first spoke to the cops, his face and hands had fierce scratches on them. That was the final straw. She'd never laid eyes on Cocchi, but Grace knew he was the one. She would have to get into that cellar to prove it.

But Mrs. Cocchi wasn't having it. She had resisted every new attempt to search the store since her husband fled. She even threatened Kronnie with a hammer. Since the police had already searched the shop, there was no way Grace could get a warrant, so instead she got a *deed*. Working through an intermediary, she actually purchased the store from Mrs. Cocchi. And there was no way to block the new owner from checking out her own cellar.

Grace, Kronnie, and a few workmen descended the cold, dark steps. For a workshop, it was eerily empty. There was only a single piece of furniture: Cocchi's workbench. The workmen heaved it to the side. Beneath it, the floorboards had been ripped away.

Embedded in the concrete was a door. Kronnie opened it and looked down into the darkness. It was like staring into ink. There was no way to see what was down there. He didn't hesitate. Kronnie jumped down into the darkness and landed on . . . something.

A body. One so badly decomposed it was impossible to identify. Limbs bound. Head caved in. And then Grace saw them . . . a pair of ice skates. Crusted over with dried blood.

On October 29, 1920, in his native Italy, Alfredo Cocchi was convicted of the murder of Ruth Cruger. Grace never even met Cocchi, but she knew he was the one and proved it. She must have used Sherlock Holmes–style deduction, right?

Wrong. According to Brad Ricca, author of *Mrs. Sherlock Holmes*, Grace laughed at the suggestion and replied, "No, I never read Sherlock Holmes. In fact, I am not a believer in deduction. Common sense and persistence will always solve a mystery. You never need theatricals, nor Dr. Watsons, if you stick to a case."

So the real person most similar to Sherlock Holmes didn't need people-reading skills to solve her toughest case. She never even laid eyes on the perpetrator. Does the ability to accurately size people up exist only in fiction?

No, but before we learn how to do it right, we need to discover the secret behind what we've been doing wrong . . .

*

Who has to analyze people's personalities with very little information when the stakes are ultra-ultra-high? What do we consider the gold standard of breaking people's behavior down when you don't have their cooperation and lives are on the line?

I'd say profiling serial killers. No small investment of time, energy, or money has been put into building this system of personality analysis. The FBI's Behavioral Science Unit has been working on this stuff since its inception in 1972. Sounds like a great starting point for learning how to judge a book by its cover, right? There's just one minor problem . . .

Profiling doesn't work. It's pseudoscience.

You'd probably do just as good a job yourself with no training. In 2002, work by three researchers, Kocsis, Hayes, and Irwin, showed that college chemistry majors produced more valid profiles than trained homicide investigators. Ouch. A 2003 study gave one group of police a real profile done by professionals and another group of police a fake profile of a fictional offender. Nope—they couldn't tell the difference. And a 2007 meta-analysis (a roundup of all the research on a topic to get a big-picture view) said: "Profilers do not decisively outperform other groups when predicting the characteristics of an unknown criminal."

The UK government looked at 184 crimes that leveraged profiling and determined that the profile was helpful just 2.7 percent of the time. Maybe you're wondering why an American author is citing British stats? Because the FBI refuses to even provide this type of data. How often does profiling work for them? They won't say.

Despite all this, people think profiling is useful. In fact, 86 percent of surveyed psychologists involved in legal cases do. You probably thought it was useful until five minutes ago.

How could a system so relied on at the highest levels for something as serious as murder be almost useless? How did we all get fooled? Turns out it's not as big a surprise as you might think. A lot of people get fooled by astrology and fake psychics, right? I know, you're probably thinking, "That's totally different." Actually, no. It's the same. *Exactly* the same, in fact.

In psychology it's known as "the Forer effect," or by the more telling name, "the Barnum effect." Yes, after P. T. Barnum, the infamous huckster. In 1948, Bertram Forer, a college professor, gave a written personality test to his students. A week later he gave them each a custom profile describing their unique personality based on the results. Forer asked them to rate the profile between 0 and 5, 5 being most accurate. The class average was a 4.3, with only one student giving it less than a 4. And then Forer told them the truth . . . they had all received the exact same profile. Yet every one of them had looked at the dossier and said, "Yup, that's uniquely true of me." Know where Forer got the profile from? An astrology book.

And the Barnum effect has been seen again and again in studies. It's a common error our brains make. Noted Cornell psychologist Thomas Gilovich defines it: "The Barnum effect refers to the tendency for people to accept as uncannily descriptive of themselves the same generally worded assessment as long as they believe it was written specifically for them on the basis of some 'diagnostic' instrument such as a horoscope or personality inventory."

The key issue here is what statisticians call "base rates." Simply put, base rates tell you how common something is on average. The base rate for "having made a phone call" is absurdly high. The base rate for having completed a spacewalk for NASA is extremely low. So, knowing that someone has made a phone call isn't very helpful in narrowing a group of people down, while knowing someone has completed a spacewalk could take the population of the planet and reduce it to just a few people.

Police profiles (unintentionally) leverage high base-rate statements, just like the Forer experiment did. If most people want to be liked, telling someone they want to be liked has a high likelihood of being correct, but isn't terribly insightful. Want to make a legit-seeming criminal profile? Take some high base-rate facts (75 percent of US serial killers are Caucasian, 90 percent are male). Then throw in some unverifiable stuff where you can't be wrong. ("He has deviant sexual fantasies, but may be reluctant to admit it.") Finally, add a few random guesses. ("He still lives with his mom and always dresses casually.") If you're wrong on those guesses, they'll be glossed over—but if you get lucky, you look like a genius. And a 2003 study found exactly that. Researchers created a profile consisting of vague assertions to deliberately leverage the Barnum effect. Police officers judged it to be as accurate as a real profile.

Forer fooled his students, and it turns out criminal profiling has been fooling us all. When we're told some vague quality with a high base rate conveys a relevant story, we want it to be true. In fact, we look for evidence to *make* it true. And we have a strong bias toward remembering things that confirm our beliefs and forgetting things that don't.

People turn to crystal balls and tarot cards not for hard answers but for a story that gives them a feeling of control over their lives. Phony psychics and stage magicians use a system called "cold reading" that leverages the Barnum effect and base rates to make it seem like they can read minds and predict the future. And our minds conspire to make the stories they tell us seem true. The mentalist Stanley Jaks demonstrated this by reading people's fortunes and telling them the *opposite* of what standard palm reading would have said. The result? Didn't matter. People believed it just as much.

As Malcolm Gladwell explained in a 2007 *New Yorker* piece,

that's basically what profiling is: unintentional cold reading. Laurence Alison, one of the leading researchers on the ineffectiveness of profiling, even quotes a study on psychic readings comparing it to profiling: "Once the client is actively engaged in trying to make sense of the series of sometimes contradictory statements issuing from the reader, he becomes a creative problem solver trying to find coherence and meaning in the total set of statements." We're not objectively evaluating what we hear; we're active participants in trying to make the puzzle piece fit. Rationalizing. Excusing. Accepting something vague as "close enough."

Maybe you think anyone who believes in tarot cards or crystal balls has a hockey score IQ, but we're all affected by this bias to one degree or another. There's a fundamental reason why astrologers outnumber astronomers. As Gilovich explains, humans are prone to seeing meaning where there is none. Emotionally, we want a feeling of control over the world around us. We desperately need the world to at least *seem* to make sense. And for that we need a story, even if it's not true: "Oh, my relationship ended because Mercury is in Gatorade."

The real challenge in analyzing people often isn't with them; it's with us. Yes, decoding the behavior of others is difficult, but the hidden problem, the one we rarely realize and never address, is that our own brains are often working against us. We think the secret to reading people is learning some special magic indicator in body language or lie detection. But the primary thing we have to contend with is our own cognitive biases. That's what we really need to overcome . . .

2

In 1891 Wilhelm von Osten realized his horse, Hans, was a genius. Okay, okay, not *Albert-Einstein-genius* but genius for a horse. Hans would become one of the most famous horses ever and be responsible for a tremendous advancement in the history of science . . . but, um, not in the way von Osten expected or desired.

Von Osten deeply believed the intelligence of animals had been underestimated. He was so serious about this that he began teaching math to his horse, Hans, using sugar lumps and carrots as rewards for correct answers. He would do this every day . . . *for the next four years.* (And you think *you* have crazy neighbors.) But could a horse really learn like a person? Or was this all as ridiculous as it sounds?

Well, after four long years of training, von Osten held his first public exhibition of Hans's skill. A crowd was gathered in front of the stage. Von Osten turned to Hans and said, "What's two plus one?" Hans stomped his foot three times. Smiles of amusement throughout the crowd. "What's the square root of sixteen?" Hans stomped four times. The smiles were replaced by surprise. "What day of the month will this Wednesday be?" Hans stomped nine times. Gasps from the crowd.

And then they did fractions. Hans told the time. He counted the audience members. He even counted the number of audience members wearing glasses. Some would later estimate that Hans had the math skills of a fourteen-year-old human. And he didn't merely respond to verbal commands. Von Osten wrote the number "3" on a blackboard, and *stomp-stomp-stomp* was the reply.

By coding the alphabet to numbers (A = 1, B = 2, etc.), Hans was able to spell words and answer questions. He could identify colors, playing cards, and people in the crowd. Play a song and he could name the composer. Show him a painting and he named the painter. Hans wasn't perfect, but he was correct roughly nine times out of ten.

It didn't take long for word to spread about the horse dubbed "Clever Hans." Von Osten took him on tour, and soon he was stomping for bigger and bigger crowds every week. Hans became a sensation. And people far beyond Germany's borders started to take notice. But there were skeptics, of course. Was von Osten giving him the answers? Was the whole thing rigged? Finally, Hans became so famous that the government stepped in to test the miracle horse.

In 1904 Germany's Board of Education formed the Hans Commission. And, as the *New York Times* would report, the commission found no fraud. What was most convincing to all was that Hans displayed his amazing abilities when von Osten was not present. After this, the Hans legend exploded. Some now believed that the horse might be able to read minds.

But not everyone was so sure. Oskar Pfungst, a young scientist and member of the Hans Commission, wanted to do further testing. He asked a wider range of questions and tested far more variables than the previous study had. Hans still performed with flying colors, but Pfungst noticed two irregularities that made him curious.

First, while the commission had done an excellent job of controlling distractions for Hans, no one had considered what the horse paid attention to during the study. Pfungst made a note that

Hans "never looked at the persons or the objects which he was to count, or at the words which he was to read, yet he nevertheless gave the proper responses."

Second, nobody ever focused on the *wrong* answers that Hans gave. Yes, he was correct the vast majority of the time, but when he was incorrect, his answers were so off base, it implied he really didn't "understand" the question. His wrong answers were the wrong kind of wrong.

So Pfungst decided to try something new: he put blinders on Hans so that the horse would be unable to see the questioner. Whammo. For the first time, Hans became aggressive. He forcefully resisted, straining to see the questioner. Finally, they managed to get him to complete the test with blinders on. His accuracy rate plummeted from 89 percent to 6 percent.

Pfungst was still confused—but he knew he was getting closer. This time he took the blinders off so Hans could see the questioner, but Pfungst made sure that the questioner didn't actually know the answer himself. Again, Hans's performance was terrible, going from 90 percent to only 10 percent accurate. If Hans couldn't see the questioner or if the questioner didn't know the answer, the horse's IQ suddenly plummeted.

Pfungst finally understood. Hans wasn't a genius. What Hans could do was read people extremely well. Research shows that horses are able to detect head movements in humans as small as one-fifth of a millimeter. Sufficiently motivated by a tasty lump of sugar, Hans was picking up on unconscious cues that questioners would make when he performed the correct number of stomps. Hans was just a regular horse, motivated by food, responding to stimuli. When he got startled, he didn't stomp out, "Wow, that sure was surprising, huh?" No, he would whinny and bite someone nearby, like horses always have. After Pfungst released his results, von Osten did the rational, objective, scientific thing: he got totally pissed off, refused further testing, took his horse, and went home.

But Hans would have an enormous impact on not only psychology but science in general. Textbooks today still refer to "the Clever Hans effect," which is also known as "the observer effect."

If you've ever heard the term *double-blind study*, you can thank Hans. He led to its creation, which had a profound impact on how research is done. Normally medical studies give half the participants the active drug and half a placebo. But let's say that as the experimenter, I know which one is the placebo, and whenever I give it to someone I snicker and roll my eyes. Just like with Hans, the experimenter knowing "the answer" can consciously or unconsciously inform the patient and reduce the objectivity of the experiment. So studies are done "double blind"—neither the patient nor the experimenter knows which is the placebo. Like putting blinders on Hans.

Hans wasn't a genius—but he could read people. And if a horse can learn to read what's on someone's mind, certainly we can too . . . right?

*

Would you like to be able to read the minds of others? To know what those around you think and feel? Of course you would. We're not crazy for wanting this ability. Research shows even a slight edge here is quite powerful. "Accurate person perception" has a conga line of personal and interpersonal benefits. Studies show that those who possess it are happier, less shy, better with people, have closer relationships, get bigger raises, and receive better performance reviews. When we look more specifically at those who are better interpreters of body language and nonverbal communication, we see similar positive effects.

Wow. Sign me up. Right? Only one problem: *on average, the vast majority of us are absolutely horrible at these skills.* I mean, comically bad. University of Chicago professor Nicholas Epley has found that when you're dealing with strangers, you correctly detect their thoughts and feelings only 20 percent of the time. (Random chance accuracy is 5 percent.) Now, of course, you're better when dealing with people you know . . . but not by much. With close friends you hit 30 percent, and married couples peak at 35 percent. In school that's an F. Actually, it's probably closer to a G. Whatever you think is going on in your spouse's head, two-thirds of the time, you're wrong.

Yet here's the truly funny part: *we think we're awesome at reading others.* Again, that pesky brain is telling us flattering stories. Ask people to rate their partner's self-esteem, and they get it right 44 percent of the time. But they're confident about their guesses 82 percent of the time. And the longer you've been together, the more your confidence goes up. Accuracy? No, that doesn't improve. But you sure do get more confident.

How can we be so off base? And yet so confident in our inaccuracy? The technical term is *egocentric anchoring.* Epley says we're too caught in our own perspective: "Survey after survey finds that most people tend to exaggerate the extent to which others think, believe, and feel as they do." As with profiling, we're too trapped inside our own heads and stories. Even when we try to take the perspective of others, studies show our accuracy doesn't improve. Yeah, it reduces egocentric bias, but what we replace it with isn't any better. When we ask others questions, our accuracy goes up, but we don't do that enough. Usually, we just play in our own heads with our own stories and replace bad assumptions with different bad assumptions.

So who *is* notably better at passively reading the thoughts and feelings of others? If I was forced to give an answer in one word, I'd say *nobody*. That's not true, strictly speaking. Obviously, some folks eke out an edge. But there seems to be a hard ceiling—and a rather low one at that. Mental health issues can confer superpowers in one area but are often balanced out by deficiencies in another. We're all just pretty bad at this—while remaining blissfully unaware of our poor showing.

I know what some people are thinking: "Whoa, whoa, whoa. Aren't women more accurate people readers than men?" Oh boy. Time to play hopscotch on the third rail. Political agendas and gender debates aside, in your heart of hearts, do *you* think there's a difference between males and females when it comes to reading people? And what do you think a dump truck full of scientific studies says? (Drum roll, please.)

Yes, women are better. Female superiority in detecting nonverbal communication is well documented. It's only about a 2 percent edge, but it's very consistent across ages, testing methods, and cultures. That said, it's not uniform. Women are no better at lie detection than men. The advantages are more pronounced in detecting facial expressions and in emotion recognition.

So why do you think women are better at this than men? Turns out it's not the direct result of biology. It's actually due to one of the things that can make *all* of us better mind readers: motivation.

When studies dig deep to look for the underlying cause, what many find is that women, on average, are more motivated to read people accurately than men are. They are simply more interested and try harder. A 2008 study by Geoff Thomas and Gregory Maio really drives the point home. What happens when researchers inform guys that being empathic will make women more interested in them? Bingo. Male motivation increased as did men's ability to accurately perceive thoughts and feelings. Just like Hans wanting those carrots. Of course, there's a flip side to this: when motivation drops, so does accuracy. Husbands in unhappy marriages can read random women's nonverbals *better than those of their wives*. Oof.

To neuroscientists, all of this is totally unsurprising. They know just how lazy our brains are most of the time. Motivation is almost a neuroscientific panacea. Giving a crap makes our brains better at almost everything because our default is barely paying attention to anything. Michael Esterman, a professor at Boston University and cofounder of its Attention and Learning Lab, says, "The science shows that when people are motivated, either intrinsically, i.e., they love it; or extrinsically, i.e., they will get a prize, they are better able to maintain consistent brain activity, and maintain readiness for the unexpected."

When people are judging romantic partners, accuracy goes up. And by the same token, when a study had anxiously attached women eavesdrop on their boyfriends talking to beautiful female researchers, guess what happened? Yup, their ability to correctly predict his answers to questions increased. But when there's no loss or gain, our brains just idle along.

In this kind of book I'm supposed to coin catchy names for core principles, aren't I? You know, like "The Five Second Rule" and all that. Wouldn't want the genre police coming after me. I hereby dub this **The Lazy Brain Axiom**™.

So the first step to being better at reading people is to be curious. Even better is to provide yourself with some sort of external gain or loss that motivates you.

Problem is, even when sufficiently motivated, we can improve our skills only so much. We're just naturally not that good at reading people. Motivation improves accuracy, but only with people who are sufficiently expressive and readable. If you're dealing with someone who has a Botox-level poker face, motivation won't help much. This leads to our second big insight: *readability is more important than reading skills.* People-reading skills aren't that variable, but how readable people are ranges widely. Most of the reason we're able to read people isn't that we're skilled; it's that they're expressive.

So as far as reading people's thoughts and feelings goes, if "judging a book by its cover" means only *passively* evaluating people, then the myth is already pretty close to busted. We'll give the maxim a fighting chance and assume that's not what it means. But it still seems like we're stuck. Should we just accept that we're going to routinely misinterpret others and there's not much we can do about it? Nope. To graduate first in my class, I can either improve my grades *or* make everyone else do worse. We're going to focus on the latter, just like I did in school. So we'll call this **The Eric in High School Theorem™**.

Since we can't improve our people-reading skills that much, we have to focus our efforts on making others more readable.

Instead of passively analyzing them like Sherlock Holmes does on TV, we need to *actively* elicit stronger signals to get more telling reactions. The first and easiest method is to manipulate context. Would you learn more about someone over a cup of tea or by playing football with them? The first might get you more information (if you can trust what they say), but the latter would organically show you how they make decisions and strategize, and whether they bend the rules. The wider the variety of stimuli you expose them to, the more facets of who they are will become clear.

Bringing other people into the mix is powerful too. Having third parties present can show different sides of someone. (If you only dealt with someone in the presence of their boss, would you think you were seeing the full them?) And don't talk about the weather. Emotional reactions are more honest, and "safe" conversation topics turn people into politicians, conveying little of substance. When researchers had people on first dates talk about STDs, abortion, and other taboo topics, they not only learned more about the other person, they reported enjoying the conversation more.

And as we've established, our own brains are often the problem here. We have a tendency to pay attention to the wrong signals. Which brings us to the issue of body language. And everybody just *loves* body language. But the literature is consistent—the value of consciously analyzing body language is grossly overrated. There's a reason nobody has ever created a "Body Language Rosetta Stone." Nonverbal cues are complex, context dependent, and idiosyncratic. We can never be *certain* what is causing what. Yes, they're shivering, but you can't be sure if that's because they're nervous or because they're cold. And this point is critical: *body language is utterly useless without a baseline.* Some people always fidget, and it means nothing. Other people rarely fidget, and it's very telling. But if you don't know their default, you're just letting your brain spin fanciful stories again.

Truth be told, if you wanted to focus on something, skip body language and laser focus on their speech. When we can hear someone but not see them, empathic ability declines only about 4 percent. When we can see someone but not hear them, the drop-off is a whopping 54 percent. Pay less attention to whether they cross their legs and more attention to when their voice changes.

So the science says reading the minds of those around us isn't something we're naturally good at, but it does give us some tips on how we can be better. But what about when we meet someone new?

Ready to learn the real deal about how first impressions work—and how we can get better at them? (Stomp your hoof once for yes or twice for no, Hans.) First impressions are a critical part of "reading a book by its cover." But to really get at the core problem we have with them, we need to take a quick detour through the world of memory . . .

3

"I have a problem with my memory" is what the email said. And James let out a tired sigh. All the time. He gets these emails all . . . the . . . time.

James McGaugh is a professor of neuroscience at UC Irvine and one of the world's leading experts on long-term memory. But one downside of his status is an awful lot of email from strangers who misplace their keys one time and immediately assume they have Alzheimer's. So he replied to this latest email the same way he has to all the others, referring the person to a clinic where they can be tested if they're really concerned there's a problem.

But Jill Price immediately wrote back saying no—she needed *him*. James rolled his eyes. But Jill followed it up with something that made him pause, something he had never heard before. Jill repeated that she had a memory problem . . .

But her problem was that she never forgets. "She's probably nuts," he thought. But what the hell. So when Jill came in for her appointment, James took a book from his shelf. It was one of those reference books that lists all the big events of the past century. He flipped to a random page and asked, "Rodney King was beaten by LAPD officers on what day?"

Jill did not hesitate. "March 3rd, 1991. It was a Sunday." One after another, she answered flawlessly. James was surprised. The answers just popped out of her the way you'd reply if I asked your name. He'd never seen anything like this . . .

But then she got one wrong. James relaxed; this wasn't as weird as it seemed. "Sorry, Jill, the Iranian Hostage Crisis happened on

November *5th*, 1979." But Jill shook her head. "No. It was on the fourth." So James checked another source.

And Jill was right. The book was wrong. James would come to realize that Jill effortlessly remembers where she was, what she did, who she was with, and how she felt for nearly every day of her adult life. But Jill's near-perfect memory is only autobiographical. She only remembers what happened to her directly. She doesn't remember everything she reads or learns and, frankly, didn't do all that well in school. But because Jill is a news junkie, she was able to remember the events in James's book.

He had never seen anything remotely like this. In 2006 he published a paper, "A Case of Unusual Autobiographical Remembering," about his work with Jill. Initially he named her condition "Hyperthymesia," but it later came to be known as HSAM (highly superior autobiographical memory).

The study received a crush of mainstream media attention. Millions of people heard about HSAM, and thousands began contacting UC Irvine saying they had it. James began testing them, and one after another he realized that they were mistaken, crazy, or lying. But three were not. James was thrilled. Now he could start to uncover the mystery of HSAM . . .

Their memories were, on average, 87 percent accurate for claims that could be third-party verified. Imagine someone asking you to remember a specific day from twenty years ago, and nine times out of ten you could say what you did, who you were with, and even how you felt. How HSAM worked started to become clearer to James—and it was the *opposite* of what he had expected: they aren't better at remembering. They're just bad at forgetting. Our memories fade with time. Theirs don't. Every day stays as clear as yesterday is for you now.

And he discovered the warm upside of having such an incredible memory. HSAM folks described "traveling"—revisiting their perfect memories like watching movies, almost traveling back in time. Jill's husband had passed away. But with no exaggeration she says that "she will never forget a moment she had with him." Pretty enviable, right? Or maybe not . . .

When asked, James said he would not want a memory like this. *Huh?* You see, dear reader, when Jill sent that first email to James, she was not contacting him to talk about her "gift." She was contacting him about her *curse*. She wanted a cure. She wanted it to stop.

For decades, Jill's perfect memory has plagued her. It's like a demonic involuntary search engine, flooding her with results. She hears a date mentioned on TV, and *boom* she's there. A torrent of memories she cannot stop. Breakups. Bad decisions. Regret in all its flavors. Over a lifetime there are many, many things it is good to forget.

Our brains have biases. And sometimes those are for our own good. Many assume memory operates like a perfect video camera, but the truth is, memories warp with time. We forget details, reconstruct things, or change the narrative so we're the righteous hero or the innocent victim. We forget the bad and remember the good. This helps us to heal and to put things behind us. But Jill cannot "put a new spin on things." Her mind *is* that perfect video camera. She cannot rationalize, forget the details, or shift the blame.

And that doesn't even seem to be HSAM's worst curse. What happens when a perfect memory has to deal with people who don't have a perfect memory? There's a different maxim for that: "Nobody likes a know-it-all." Ever have a partner who never lets a transgression go, whose memory for your failings is always crystal clear? Multiply that times a billion.

The odd part, logically speaking, is that the person with

HSAM is right. They're likely correct, you're likely wrong. But human relationships don't work like that. Nobody wants to be wrong all the time—especially if they are. We naturally expect reciprocity, shared blame, some balance, even if, strictly speaking, we don't deserve it. "You're right most of the time so now it's my turn" doesn't make rational sense when we have the hard facts. Perfect memories aren't democratic. But relationships are. During a *60 Minutes* interview one HSAM'er said, "To forgive and forget . . . well, one out of two isn't bad."

That episode featured a group of adults with the condition. All were single, and all were childless but one. Yes, Marilu Henner was married. Three times, as a matter of fact. HSAM'er Bill Brown said that out of fifty-five people he knew with the condition, only two had made a marriage work. And every single one of them he's talked to has struggled with depression.

It's safe to say you don't have HSAM. To this day, fewer than one hundred HSAM'ers have been confirmed. (And if you did have it, you'd remember the day you were diagnosed *perfectly*.) But in one small way we all have it. Let's see how the double-edged sword of HSAM is actually the secret to understanding the double-edged sword of first impressions . . .

*

Everybody tells you first impressions are important. Guess what? They're right. Numerous studies show first impressions have a huge impact, not only during that initial encounter, but long after. First impressions are so powerful that snap judgments consistently predict elections. Alex Todorov, a professor at Princeton and an expert on the psychology of faces, says that merely asking people "Which candidate looks more competent?" can tell you who's going to come out on top in political races 70 percent of the time—an effect that has been replicated around the world. And there's a solid correlation between recruiters' pre-interview and post-interview impressions of job applicants, indicating that someone's initial exposure to you may be the most important factor in whether you land that new gig.

The maxim might be "don't judge a book by its cover," and, right or wrong, there's a good reason such advice is given: because we *do* judge a book by its cover. Immediately and instinctively. We can't help it. And that cover is usually someone's face. We make our minds up about someone's assertiveness, beauty, competence, likability, and trustworthiness in less than a second. And, like mind reading, more time doesn't noticeably change our opinions, it just increases our confidence.

More interesting is that not only are these judgments immediate but they're also consistently shared. Faces I see as trustworthy, dominant, or competent are very likely ones you'll see the same way. Fundamentally, these decisions are not rational. There's no time to think them through. They're usually based on shared beliefs and to a lesser extent our personal experiences with others.

The kicker? *Our first impressions are often surprisingly accurate.* Not only do people usually agree on first impressions, but they're also impressively predictive. Just seeing someone smile for the first time was enough for viewers to make accurate predictions two-thirds of the time for nine out of ten fundamental personality traits, from extroversion to self-esteem to political preferences.

You're also good at instinctively determining someone's competence after a brief encounter. When people watch a thirty-second silent video of a teacher in class, they're able to predict student evaluations. Watch someone for five minutes, and accuracy can go as high as 70 percent. Our ability to intuit what someone's like from thin slices of behavior is powerful across a number of domains, providing above-chance levels of accuracy in determining if someone is smart, wealthy, altruistic, or whether they're a psychopath. Again, these impressions aren't rational. That means you're actually *more* accurate when you think *less*.

Some people might be saying, "Thank god. We can just trust our gut. Whew." Hold your horses. We're still talking about human beings here. Nothing is gonna be that simple. Yes, our instincts are good. Good to the 70 percent accuracy level. Would you be happy if your kid brought home all Ds on a report card? I didn't think so.

And, unsurprisingly, a fair amount of this inaccuracy is due to your biased brain. We're not talking about race or gender biases necessarily, but fundamental cognitive biases wired into our gray matter. Often these are shortcuts. Evolution has optimized our brains for speed or fuel efficiency over accuracy.

And that's why baby-faced people get away with murder. I'm not being metaphorical. Studies show baby-faced people are more likely to triumph in legal cases where they're accused of deliberate harm—but more likely to lose when the accusation is negligence. Why? We expect children to make mistakes but have trouble believing they're evil. Our brains extend that to include baby-faced adults in a process known as "overgeneralization." But are baby-faced people actually more innocent? Nope. Baby-faced young men "showed more negativity in childhood and puberty, more quarrelsomeness and lying in puberty, and more assertiveness and hostility in adolescence, all of which contradict impressions of babyfaced individuals."

Now if you think you can overcome these biases with conscious effort, you're probably wrong. Numerous studies have shown we have a bias against noticing our biases. Even if you explain them and point them out (as I'm doing right now), people will see them more often in others but become convinced that they themselves are objective. And it gets even more complicated—some biases *help*. To the extent that a bias is accurate, studies show what you would logically expect: eliminating it makes your predictions less accurate. Yeesh.

We're prone to zillions of cognitive biases, and there's no way to succinctly address them all. But when it comes to first impressions, the main battle is with "confirmation bias." We're prone to searching for and favoring ideas consistent with beliefs we already hold. We don't test theories; we look for information to reinforce the position we've already decided on.

If you look, you can notice others (and yourself) subtly engaging in confirmation bias all the time. Our standards drop for what is necessary to prove our theories, but they go up for the amount of evidence required to disprove them. ("Four hundred studies say I'm wrong? Well, we should keep looking . . . One says I'm correct? Looks like we have our answer.") It's just like what we saw with cold reading: we remember hits, we forget the misses. And we all do this. Yes, even you. No one thinks they're the problem, and that's the problem.

As researcher Nicholas Epley says, "Your sixth sense works quickly and is not prone to second-guessing." Once we get a story in our heads about who someone is, it's very hard for us to update it. And this leads us to our primary insight about the double-edged sword of first impressions. We'll call it **The First Impressions Paradox™**.

First impressions are generally accurate. But once they're set, they're extremely hard to change.

When it comes to first impressions, it's like we have HSAM:

we don't alter our memories. We're all but locked-in to our prior judgments. And it can dramatically affect our relationships. We often think about the perils of stereotyping groups, but we also do the same thing with individuals. Someone has an "untrustworthy" face when you first meet them, so you're less warm than usual. Because you're distant with them, they're distant with you. This reasonable response on their part triggers your confirmation bias. ("See, I knew they weren't a nice person!") Now you're both wary of each other. And that's the most scientific explanation you'll ever get for what it means when two people "don't click."

Some will say that they do update their first impressions, and certainly at times that does happen. But there's another sinister effect hiding beneath the surface. Even when presented with incontrovertible new information about someone, our explicit impressions can change while our implicit impressions don't. In other words, your very rational, evidence-based perspective can change, but your *feelings* about the person stay exactly the same. First impressions are sticky, even when we think they've been overcome.

We'll never totally resist this, but we can improve with effort. First, we need to keep in mind the same principles we learned with reading thoughts and feelings. Motivation is critical, and focusing on making others more readable will deliver bigger improvements than trying to improve your reading skills.

But the critical thing is resisting the dreaded black hole of confirmation bias lock-in. Our brains are going to start generating theories and stories about someone within milliseconds. That's fine (and impossible to stop), but we need to keep an open mind. We want to take a scientific approach of hypothesis testing versus blindly accepting the first impression we get.

So how do we resist confirmation bias? Three key steps:

1. FEEL ACCOUNTABLE

If your opinion of someone could result in them getting the death penalty, you'd slow down and be more thorough. You'd want to double-check your accuracy before the concrete sets for good and there's no changing it. Psychologist Arie Kruglanski's work shows that when we set a high bar for accountability, our opinions don't become inflexible until we've done a thorough review of the evidence. A fun way to do this is to turn it into a game. Push yourself to be more accurate and hold yourself accountable.

2. DISTANCE BEFORE DECISION

In Maria Konnikova's wonderful book *Mastermind* she dives deep into the research of NYU psychologist Yaacov Trope, showing how getting some distance helps us be more rational and objective: "Adults who are told to take a step back and imagine a situation from a more general perspective make better judgments and evaluations, and have better self-assessments and lower emotional reactivity." These are exactly the skills we need to size up new acquaintances more accurately and resist our brain's impulse to immediately go with our first impression.

3. CONSIDER THE OPPOSITE

Since our brains tend to remember hits and forget misses, we must force ourselves to consider those misses if we want to improve. Paul Nurse takes this attitude to the extreme: "If I have an idea and have observations to support it, rather than get that out there, I go around and look at it in different ways and try and destroy it. And only if it survives do I begin to talk about it." And maybe that's why he won the Nobel Prize in medicine.

Over the long haul you can also improve by getting to know your personal biases better. What errors do you make consistently? Too quick to assume people are similar to you or different from you? Trusting too much or too little? Adjusting for your consistent biases is a great way to improve.

Finally, we have two very human takeaways from our little exploration of confirmation bias. First, listen to that advice you've received so many times: *make a good first impression.* You now know just how important it really is. Make sure you show them the side of your personality that you want them to lock onto—because they will. (However, if you really are a jerk and are meeting me for the first time, please be a jerk. It will help me out enormously. Thanks.)

The other thing to remember: *give people a second chance.* Without the above strategies, you're right only 70 percent of the time, max. You're going to be wrong with at least three out of every ten people you meet. But it gets worse than that, as Cornell's Gilovich points out. Say you meet someone who's a good person having a lousy day. They make a bad first impression. What do you do? Avoid them, giving them fewer chances to prove you wrong. But if someone makes a good first impression (whether it's accurate or not), you try to spend more time with them. This gives you a chance to further evaluate them either way. The result is that *your negative judgments about people will be less reliable than your positive judgments.* And research also shows we have a higher bar for rating someone positively than negatively, and our positive impressions are more easily reversed than our negative ones. There's no appeals process when you avoid someone for the rest of your life.

So your first impression intuition just got better. But overall, reading someone like a book is still on shaky ground, and we know that passively reading someone like Sherlock Holmes does is pretty much out. Any other tips from the research we can use to eke out better results? Well, anytime we try to learn about someone, there's a chance that person is going to mislead us. So how do we deal with liars?

4

Despite playing professional soccer for over twenty years, Carlos Kaiser never scored a single goal. In fact, during those two decades he appeared in only thirty games. Carlos Kaiser was not a very good soccer player. But that wasn't a problem. Because Carlos Kaiser was an excellent liar.

He played for some of the best teams in the world, including Botafogo and Fluminense. He made big money, partied with celebrities, and was surrounded by beautiful women. What he didn't do was *actually play soccer*. His nickname among the other players was "171." Why? Because that's the penal number for con artists in Brazilian prisons.

He was born Carlos Henrique Raposo in Brazil on April 2, 1963. He was poor but had big dreams. As he said in an interview, "I knew that the best way to make it happen was through soccer. I wanted to be a soccer player without having to actually play it." Honestly, he wasn't bad at the sport. By age ten he got an agent, and at sixteen he signed with Puebla, a top team in Mexico. There was only one problem: "I didn't want to play." Most young players were eager to get out there and show they had the goods. Kaiser was the exact opposite, doing anything and everything to avoid the ball.

But how do you keep this up for *two decades*? Kaiser developed a system. First, befriend all the top players. Kaiser may not have liked playing soccer, but he loved nightclubs. And he had connections at all the hottest spots in Brazil. Knowing Kaiser meant VIP status, free drinks, and pretty girls for soccer stars.

Next, you get them to vouch for you. His soccer résumé wasn't stellar, but it showed that he had some legitimate talent. So, at his behest, the team stars would nag their coach, and before long, Kaiser would get signed to a short-term "trial" contract. That's all he needed. The Trojan horse was now inside the city walls.

Officially a player, Kaiser would say he needed time to get back into shape. That would get him a few months where he could make money and have fun with no pressure to do that thing he hated, playing soccer. Eventually, he would have to touch a ball. He'd confidently trot out onto the practice field, wind up for a big kick—and immediately collapse, wailing in pain and clutching his thigh. Nobody could fake an injury like Kaiser. He'd give Oscar-worthy performances. And in the era before MRIs, coaches would have to take his word for it, the team's star players all taking his side. And so he'd collect checks for a few more months.

Meanwhile, Kaiser was living the life. Nonstop partying. (Oddly, his injuries never seemed to affect his dancing ability.) The other players knew he was a con man. They knew he couldn't play at their level. But they loved him. He was a charmer. He made sure they always had fun. (And it didn't hurt that he always seemed to be able to introduce them to the prettiest girls in every city they visited.) So when coaches would start to get wise to Kaiser's perpetual injuries, the team stars would rush to his defense.

Of course, he couldn't do this forever. Which was not a problem. He would just move to another team. In the pre-internet era it wasn't easy to get stats on a player. Games from one country were rarely televised in other countries. Much of soccer recruiting worked by word of mouth. And with his teammate-pleasing ways, it wasn't hard to get stars to vouch for him at another club. Soon he had a trial contract, and he'd repeat the whole cycle . . .

Now that's not to say sustaining his scam was easy. Over twenty years there were plenty of close calls. One time he had already worn out the injury scam, and the team was scheduled to do its first public training session. With all the most beloved members of the team singing his praises, fans were eagerly anticipating a glimpse of what he could do on the field. And this was an utter nightmare for Kaiser. So as all eyes fell on him, he suddenly began kicking soccer balls into the stands. Fans went wild, grasping for them. But Kaiser didn't stop. He kicked *all* the team's soccer balls into the stands. They had nothing to practice with. The team just did running drills and calisthenics for the remaining time, nothing that would expose the faker among them.

And he didn't just use his teammates to his advantage: he leveraged anyone he could. He turned on the charm with the journalists and made sure they got the star interviews they so desperately needed. So a player who never played ended up getting a surprising amount of coverage, and it was almost always positive. When the team did publicity matches with youth leagues, he'd slip them cash to be overly aggressive so he could fake another injury. When the owner visited, spectators would be bribed to scream his name. Rinse and repeat until it was time to move on to a new club . . .

He kept this scam up for over twenty years, playing, on average, just over one game a year. The lies never stopped. His grandmother died at least four times. He produced a sick note from a dentist saying his teeth had caused a leg injury. Kaiser joked, "All the teams I joined celebrated twice—when I signed and then when I left."

Until the one day our charlatan faced the greatest challenge of his so-called career. He had signed with the Brazilian soccer club Bangu, and in typical Kaiser style he already had the press raving about his goal scoring despite the fact he had never scored a goal. Anywhere. Ever. Headlines read, "BANGU HAS ITS KING." And

Kaiser being Kaiser, he was showing that newspaper to everyone who would listen. Fans were dying to see him on the field. Unfortunately, so was the team's owner.

Castor de Andrade was not your typical soccer club owner. He was not a titan of business who had purchased a team as a bauble. Castor was a mobster, frequently referred to as "the most dangerous man in Brazil." It's certainly not unheard of for team owners to get into heated disputes with referees—but Castor would do this with a gun visible in his back pocket.

A teammate mentioned to Kaiser that despite being "injured," he was on the roster for the big game tomorrow. This, combined with the fact that it was 4 A.M. and Kaiser was still partying at a nightclub, scared the hell out of him. The next day the coach told him not to worry, they wouldn't make anyone with an injury play. But as the game progressed, it was clear they were in trouble. Down 2–0, Castor himself was insisting that his new star player get out on the field with that magic scoring ability the newspapers wouldn't shut up about.

For the first time in many years, Kaiser was not afraid of being exposed . . . He was afraid of being *murdered*. Kaiser walked out to the field, trembling. It was made worse by opposing fans hurling insults at him from the stands. But then he had an idea . . .

He screamed back at them. Kaiser leapt into the crowd, calling them words my publisher has most likely already edited from this book. In response, the ref threw a red card, ejecting Kaiser from the game. Back in the locker room his teammates laughed that he may not have had to play, but that wasn't going to stop Castor. Kaiser's trickery has finally caught up to him. And as de Andrade entered the room, everything went silent. The club boss was incensed. But before he could even get a word out, Kaiser cut him off. Kaiser said that God took both his parents away when he was a child, but God was kind enough to give him a new father—Castor. The other team's fans had been calling his new father a crook and a thief. Kaiser said he could not stand by and watch that happen, so he let loose on them. He had to defend his new father's honor. And Castor's response to hearing this story was just as swift . . .

He doubled Kaiser's salary and extended his contract for six more months.

I'm telling you this story now, so obviously word got out that Kaiser was a con man. Was he then shamed? Sued? Ostracized? Punished in any way? Nope. He became more famous than ever. Unlike many legitimate soccer stars of that era who are long forgotten, his story of manipulation and deceit still routinely gets told. He's more famous as a liar than he ever was as a player.

Is there *any* way to really get the truth out of some people?

*

When told to rank a list of 555 personality traits, college students put "being a liar" dead last. Which is funny because the average college student lies in about a third of conversations. For adults, it's one in five. Let's not even get into online dating, where 81 percent of profiles deviate from the truth. Most of our fibs are white lies, but Richard Wiseman of the University of Hertfordshire says you tell about two whoppers a day. Whom do you lie to most frequently? Mom. You lie to your spouse the least (one in every ten conversations)—but you tell them the biggest lies. And you're on the receiving end of about two hundred a day. (This is not one of them, I promise.)

And we're *terrible* at detecting lies, averaging a 54 percent success rate. Might as well flip a coin. Police aren't any better, even though they think they are when surveyed. Yes, some folks are good lie detectors, but you wouldn't want to be them; they're people who have had strokes and experienced significant damage to the left lobe of their prefrontal cortex.

Humans have been trying to master lie detection for thousands of years—and failing miserably. In the 1920s the first polygraph was developed by a number of people, including William Moulton Marston, who would go on to create the DC Comics character Wonder Woman. And he probably should have stuck to that character's Lasso of Truth because (at least in the comics) it worked, whereas the polygraph does not. The US National Academy of Sciences has gone on the record, saying that "the Federal government should not rely on polygraph examinations for screening prospective or current employees to identify spies or other national security risks because the test results are too inaccurate." With as little as fifteen minutes of training, people have been able to consistently beat the test, with the funniest effective method being the well-timed clenching of one's anus.

So what about the police interrogations we see on TV? That's the Reid technique, developed in the 1940s and first published as a manual by John Reid and Fred Inbau in 1962. It's an aggressive "third-degree" approach designed to stress a suspect into confessing. Guess what? The Reid technique works. In fact, it works *too* well. Doesn't matter if you're actually guilty or not: it'll get a confession out of most people. Canada and the UK have both dropped Reid-style interrogation, finding it to be coercive and unethical. And yet this is still the dominant method used by law enforcement in the United States today. As if that weren't enough, it's also not scientifically valid. Aldert Vrij, a professor at the University of Portsmouth and a leading expert on lie detection, says the cues it relies on are not predictive.

After Reid training, law enforcement officers' ability to detect deception gets *worse*.

So is there any way to reliably detect lies based on *real* science? Actually, yes. In 2009 the High-Value Detainee Interrogation Group (HIG) was formed to develop new best practices, and by 2016 they had spent more than fifteen million dollars on over one hundred research projects with top psychologists. I've adapted their findings for simplicity's sake (and because I'm assuming you won't be able to handcuff someone to a chair). Also, this system takes some time and patience, so it isn't going to be useful for little lies but can be quite powerful for bigger issues.

No, you won't have to waterboard anyone. The science over-whelmingly recommended a nuanced and sophisticated method humans have never tried in the past five thousand years when attempting to detect lies: *being nice*. We'll call our new system **The Friendly Journalist Method™**.

Never be a "bad cop." Be a "friendly journalist." You have to get them to like you. To open up. To talk a lot. And to make a mistake that reveals their deception. What's the first step? Journalists do their homework before they write a piece, and so will you. The more info you have going into a conversation about a suspected lie, the better calibrated your internal lie detector will be. And even more important, some of the most powerful techniques we'll use later require background info, so we can't skip this step.

And then there's the "friendly" part. The HIG report found that "bad cop" isn't effective and "good cop" is. Everybody wants to be treated with respect. And when people are, they're more likely to talk. Also, never accuse someone of lying. More than one study found that this reduces cooperation. Don't accuse, be curious.

Do lawyers tell their clients to lie? No. Do they tell them to be honest? No. They tell them to *shut up*. Well, Friendly Journalist, you want to get them talking as much as possible. Ask lots of open-ended questions that start with "What" or "How," not things that can be answered with one word. You want to be friendly and say just enough to keep 'em gabbing. Letting them monologue makes them feel in control. They'll relax. You want them to keep talking so you get more info and can evaluate. Everything they say is another fact to be checked, another story that could be contradicted. And this is exactly why lawyers tell clients to just shut up. You want to do the opposite.

If you immediately start challenging what they say, not only might they shut down, but they also might start altering their story. You don't want to help them tell a better lie. You want them to put it all out there and paint themselves into a corner. Herein lies the problem in dealing with slippery people: they get good feedback, you don't. If I lie and don't get caught, I see what works. If I lie and get caught, I see what doesn't work. On the other hand, the vast majority of the time you don't get feedback on whether someone was honest with you. So liars are always improving. You aren't. And that gives them an advantage. Don't help them improve further.

Prior lessons we've learned on reading people also apply here. Again, body language is a false god. Here's our expert Vrij: "No lie-detection tool used to date that is based on analyzing nonverbal and verbal behavior is accurate—far from it." For the record, let me address a common myth directly: "Liars won't look you in the eyes." Wrong-amundo. HIG's review of the research said, "Gaze aversion has never been shown to be a reliable indicator." And if that's not enough to dispel the myth, there's a 1978 study of the interpersonal behavior of incarcerated psychopaths. Guess what? They look people in the eyes *more* often than nonpsychopaths.

Evaluating someone accurately is near impossible if we're misled by what they're telling us. But there is a strategy that can get us the truth. While research shows that there is little variance in lie detection ability, there is a *lot* of variance in the ability to tell lies. So just as with reading people, **The Friendly Journalist Method™** doesn't focus on making your lie detection skills better; it focuses on making their lie-telling skills worse. How do we do that?

The old polygraph model looked for emotional stress as a sign of lying. That doesn't work. What does work is applying "cognitive load"—making liars think hard. As Vrij notes, lying well requires a surprising amount of brainpower. Truth tellers merely have to say what they remember. Liars need to know the truth. They also need to generate a plausible story. They need to make sure those don't contradict. And this model needs to be safely updated in real time as they are asked more questions. Meanwhile, they also need to appear honest, which can require some serious acting. Finally, they must monitor the interviewer's reactions to make sure that the interviewer is not catching on. This is hard. So we want to make it *even harder*. The HIG report found increasing cognitive load can boost our measly 54 percent accuracy to as high as 71 percent.

Now this is unlikely to make liars just directly confess. What it will do is create a stark contrast between how a truth teller would respond and how a liar would respond. Just like when your computer is chewing on a complex problem, a liar's performance will slow down and get wonky. And that's exactly the reaction we'll be looking for as we apply the techniques. Instead of asking yourself, *Is this person lying?*, ask yourself, *Do they have to think hard?* A study by Vrij showed that merely getting police officers to focus on the second question markedly improved their lie detection skills.

Okay, we've got the fundamentals. You did your homework. You're playing Friendly Journalist, and they're gabbing away. You're keeping an eye out for when they have to think hard. Time to (nicely) smoke out a liar with two powerful techniques from the HIG report.

1. ASK UNANTICIPATED QUESTIONS

Ask an underage-looking person at a bar how old they are and you'll hear a crisp, confident "I'm twenty-one." But instead, what if you asked them, "What's your date of birth?" That's an exceedingly easy question for someone telling the truth, but a liar's likely going to have to pause to do some math. *Gotcha.* The HIG report cites a study showing that airport security methods usually catch less than 5 percent of lying passengers. But when screeners used unanticipated questions, that number shot up to 66 percent.

Start off with expected questions. This is unintimidating and gets you info—but more important, it gets you a *baseline*. Then throw them a question that's easy for a truth teller to answer but one that a liar would not be ready for. Gauge the reaction. Did they calmly and quickly answer, or did their lag in answering suddenly increase? Yes, they could just blurt out anything, but that's a minefield of potential contradiction in front of someone who did their homework in advance. Or they'll just shut down, which is very suspicious.

Another angle is to ask for verifiable details. "So if I give your boss a call, she can confirm that you were at that meeting yesterday?" Truth tellers will be able to quickly and easily answer that. Liars will be reluctant to, and it will likely induce cognitive load. "What was Emily wearing at the meeting?" Again, easy for honest people, a nightmare for liars. It's easily verifiable—and they know that.

Okay, time for the killshot. *Mortal Kombat* narrator voice says: FINISH HIM!

2. STRATEGIC USE OF EVIDENCE

You did your homework in advance, right? Good. Build rapport. Get them talking. And lead them to say something that contradicts the info you dug up. Ask for clarification so they commit to it. And then: "Sorry, I'm confused. You said you were with Gary yesterday. But Gary has been in France all week." Ask yourself the magic question: *Do they look like they're thinking hard?* And does their hastily assembled reply contradict anything else, digging their grave deeper?

You want to incrementally reveal evidence. Repeated contradictions may get them to simply confess out of embarrassment. More likely it will make their lying increasingly obvious. A 2006 study of Swedish police showed they typically detected lies 56.1 percent of the time. Those with "strategic use of evidence" training scored an 85.4 percent.

These methods aren't perfect, but they'll get pretty good results if you practice . . . Really. I promise it's true. Look, you gotta believe me. *I swear, I haven't been thinking hard at all while writing this book.*

Will these techniques allow you to read a book by its cover? That would be a stretch. This is no simple process, and it only works when you have time and the other person is willing to be patient with your questioning. Final note: I will not be showing this section to my editor until *after* I've explained why I blew my deadline.

So how is the book-by-its-cover maxim holding up overall? It's almost time for us to render a verdict . . .

5

In 2007 an astronomer at the Parkes radio telescope in Australia was reviewing archival data and noticed something so incredible that people said it might prove the existence of alien life.

It wasn't surprising that it had been overlooked when it originally happened back in 2001. The burst of radio waves had lasted just five milliseconds. (You can't even read the word *milliseconds* in five milliseconds.) The source was unknown, and these radio waves traveled three billion light-years to get here. But NASA would confirm that in those mere five milliseconds it generated *as much energy as five hundred million suns*. (I'd love to use a metaphor to convey the magnitude of that number, but my puny brain can't wrap my head around five hundred million suns, so we're gonna go with "double-extra-super powerful.")

It was dubbed a "fast radio burst." It was, as those of us knowledgeable in the field like to say, double-extra-super powerful. Seems like a stretch that this proves Klingons exist . . . except that when NASA recently discussed what it would take to get to Mars in three days, the scientists suggested it would require a light sail photonic propulsion system that, um, sounds like it would produce a burst just like this. And much later when two scientists ran the numbers on FRBs, they said, "the optimal frequency for powering the light sail is shown to be similar to the detected FRB frequencies." And the two scientists weren't crackpots on YouTube wearing tinfoil hats; they were Avi Loeb and Manasvi Lingam from Harvard's Astrophysics Department.

So "aliens" wasn't as crazy as it might sound. But there was only one of these things, so at first the "Lorimer Burst" was chalked up to an error, some sort of radio telescope hiccup. But soon they found more. A lot more.

In 2010, astrophysicist Sarah Burke-Spolaor uncovered records of sixteen similar bursts that occurred back in 1998. (If this was alien communication, we're that friend who is absolutely horrible about responding to texts.) But even more interesting was that these sixteen signals were *different*. In many ways they seemed like FRBs, but they were actually what would come to be known as "perytons." Perytons are local. They're not from billions of light-years away; they're generated from something right here on Earth.

One could speculate that perytons meant that the aliens had reached Earth. If FRBs were messages from extraterrestrials to our planet, maybe perytons were ET phoning home. But the most popular theory was that perytons just proved this was all bunk. Perytons were probably due to lightning, or even more likely, some sort of human-made interference. And some scientists argued that FRBs were probably just perytons too. The debate raged for years.

But then on May 14, 2014, at the Parkes telescope they detected an FRB *live*, in real time. They confirmed it had originated at least 5.5 billion light-years away. Perytons might be local interference, but this confirmed that FRBs were real. The whole field of astronomy was rocked by the news.

Solving the FRB issue would be near impossible because they originated so far away. But perytons are local. This was potentially solvable. And this could be one of the most momentous discoveries humankind would ever make. And what do we do with intellectually rich, incredibly challenging problems that could change the course of history?

Yup, that's right: we dump them on the intern.

Enter our plucky hero: Emily Petroff. She was twenty-five. Hadn't even completed her astrophysics PhD yet. And she was put in charge of solving one of the biggest mysteries in astronomy. No real help. No big financial grants. Good luck, kid . . . But Emily was fascinated by FRBs and perytons and was prepared to go further than anyone else.

And she quickly realized just how hard finding the cause of the mysterious energy source was going to be. Astrophysicists are not dummies. They don't want interference to cause grief, so telescope sites are in the middle of nowhere in radio quiet zones. Cellphones are banned. Faraday cages are used to shield equipment from electromagnetic waves. What the heck could be causing it?

And there was another, even more curious issue: the perytons detected at Parkes had been at two frequencies, 2.5 ghz and 1.4 ghz. The first was common, but the second was different. Nothing scientists were aware of transmitted at 1.4 ghz. It might *actually* be aliens. And if these were perytons, that meant aliens could be right here among us. Since 1998.

But Emily wasn't buying the aliens story, so she spent months evaluating data from the telescope . . . which turned out to be a dead end. Refusing to give up, Emily installed an interference monitor on the telescope to detect frequencies getting in the way. Again, nothing.

Finally, in January 2015, she caught a break. The telescope detected three new perytons—*in a single week*. This was not random. Could it be an attempt at communication from the extraterrestrial source here on Earth? Every one of the perytons had two signals, one at 2.5 ghz and another at the mysterious 1.4 ghz. Emily was able to compare data from her new interference monitor to results from the ATCA observatory nearby. It didn't pick up the 2.5 ghz, but she did. This clinched it: the perytons were not coming from outer space. Whatever was producing this unknown frequency was close to the telescope. It was here. On Earth.

And the timing of the perytons wasn't random. They all happened during the workday. It finally clicked. They all had something in common. One supremely profound thing that every human alive and every human who has ever lived sees as vital . . .

Lunch. The Parkes perytons were all happening at lunchtime. So what operates at 2.5 ghz? Emily had an idea. She sprinted downstairs. And there was our alien: the microwave in the telescope break room. Most radio telescope sites ban microwaves. The interference monitor data confirmed that the telescope had been pointed toward the break room every time a peryton had been detected.

Yes, the biggest mystery in astronomy wasn't caused by aliens; it was caused by scientists heating up burritos.

But this didn't solve everything. Yes, Hot Pockets were producing the 2.5 ghz signal, not Wookies. But there were *two* frequencies. What about the 1.4 ghz? Nothing the scientists worked with released a 1.4 ghz signal. The alien theory could not be ruled out.

But Emily knew that where there's human error, there's probably *more* human error. True, nothing they knew of *normally* released a 1.4 ghz burst. And microwaves usually operate at 2.5 ghz . . . So our ever-resourceful hero tried a quick experiment: if she turned on the microwave and opened the door before it had finished cooking, guess what happened? The microwave's magnetron released a quick 1.4 ghz emission alongside the 2.5 ghz.

So, correction: *the biggest mystery in astronomy wasn't caused by aliens; it was caused by* impatient *scientists heating up burritos.*

Emily knew it wasn't extraterrestrials. And the majority of reputable scientists never took the alien theory seriously. But it didn't matter. The alien story was irresistible. The media had gone nuts.

People were dying to know more—not about science—but about the possibility of extraterrestrials.

Our brains love simple, sexy stories like aliens. (Our brains are also impatient to reheat pizza.) And whether we're talking about perytons and aliens or trying to read the minds of other Earth dwellers, it's all too easy to misinterpret signals and come up with fantastical interpretations that are clean, simple, sexy . . . and wrong.

Please think of Emily Petroff next time you reheat your leftovers. (And slice them up with Occam's razor while you're at it.) The great peryton mystery was solved . . . however, that doesn't mean everything was answered. FRBs still remain unexplained. Perhaps aliens are out there in a faraway galaxy, impatient to get their own Hot Pockets out of the microwave?

Or maybe that's yet another sexy, inaccurate story I'm telling myself.

*

So can you "judge a book by its cover"? Let's review the big takeaways.

Though we're decent with first impressions, lie detection is a coin toss, and we're horrible at the passive reading of people's thoughts and feelings (I know a horse that's better at it than we are). Even worse, our initial mistakes tend to stick in our minds. We are often our own worst enemy. Confirmation bias causes us to remember hits and forget the misses, blinding us to what might correct our story and make it more accurate.

While passive reading is often inaccurate, we can improve by getting motivated and actively engaging people. But it's a mistake to focus too much on improving your ability. Whether you're trying to decipher their personality or detect lies, the biggest gains in accuracy are achieved by getting them to increase the signals they're sending. You can't make yourself much better at detecting lies, but you can leverage solid methods like cognitive load and strategic use of evidence to make people so bad at telling them that it'll be much easier to notice. (And don't mistake microwaving a Hot Pocket for alien contact.)

All of this naturally leads us to a question: *Why are we bad at reading others?* You'd think this would be a useful skill. Should we launch a class action suit against Mother Nature? Does the human brain need a factory recall? Why is a social species so flawed at something seemingly so valuable?

One reason is our poor accuracy may not be a flaw at all. Being too accurate when reading people can be a nightmare. We all have fleeting negative feelings about our partners, friends, and relationships. That's normal. But if you noticed every negative thought anyone had about you, it would give your anxieties anxieties. The vast majority of the time, being unaware of these momentary issues is preferable. And that's exactly what studies have found. Empathic accuracy isn't a universal good; it's a double-edged sword. A study by Simpson, Ickes, and Ortina found that empathic accuracy is a positive if it doesn't uncover information threatening to the relationship. But if it does, it's a negative. In fact, if there's negative information to be gleaned, *avoiding* accuracy improved relationship stability.

As one team of psychologists put it: "People often want to learn how to improve the accuracy of their social judgments . . . but it is unclear if seeing social reality is a healthy goal." Would you feel comfortable if others could detect every thought *you* had when you're in a foul mood? At times, you second-guess your relationships. It's natural and healthy, but knowing about those moments could hurt others. Let's not forget the curse of HSAM. Too much negative info or too perfect a memory just doesn't make for good relationships. We need to round off the edges, to be able to give the benefit of the doubt, to miss something that's true but unrepresentative. So maybe Mother Nature decided on a healthy compromise: we're pretty good at reading people when sufficiently motivated and engaged—but not *too* good. That would be an exercise in paranoia.

Seeing the world accurately is not our only goal. Yes, you want reliable info to be able to make good decisions. But you also want to stay happy, motivated, and confident, even when things aren't looking so great. (Or *especially* when things aren't looking so great.) This can be a delicate balance because the truth hurts. That's how you know it's the truth. Sherlock Holmes was excellent at always seeing through to the brutal facts. He also became a drug addict. I'm not sure those two things are unrelated.

Along similar lines, it might not be good to be an awesome lie detector either. Do you really want alarm bells going off in your head every time someone who cares about you pays you a well-intentioned but less-than-true compliment? No, you want to enjoy it. And the politeness and diplomacy requirements of most social situations (let alone job interviews and first dates) simply cannot handle utter truth 24/7. You know people who routinely ask questions they absolutely, positively do *not* want honest answers to, and they make you very uncomfortable. The majority of lies are not of the "I did not murder him" variety. They're more like, "Your hair looks fantastic." As T. S. Eliot said, "Humankind cannot bear very much reality."

Assuming people are usually honest is a preferable default. The good news is not only does it make us feel better, but over the long haul it's actually the better bet. One study asked people how much they trust others on a scale of one to ten. Income was highest among those who responded with the number eight. And low-trust people fared far worse than overtrusters. Their losses were the equivalent of not going to college. They missed many opportunities by not trusting. In *The Confidence Game* Maria Konnikova points to an Oxford study showing that "people with higher levels of trust were 7 percent more likely to be in better health," and 6 percent more likely to be "very" happy rather than "pretty" happy or "not happy at all." (Hopefully you trust me, otherwise this book isn't going to be of much use to you.)

So what's the final verdict for the maxim? I'd love to say the "don't judge a book by its cover" was simply true or false, but that wouldn't be very helpful. It's almost true . . . but misleading. The answer is more nuanced.

No, we shouldn't judge others quickly or shallowly. But as the research shows, we always *do*, at least initially, and that's not gonna stop. Utterly suspending judgment isn't possible, and, without practice, more time doesn't make us more accurate, just more confident.

Instead of focusing on not judging a book by its cover, it would be more useful to say we would be better off putting more effort into revising the judgments we will undoubtedly make.

Okay, section 1 complete. We're done evaluating people. Now it's time to look at how we actually deal with them. And that means friends. So we have to ask: What makes a good friend? And how can we be a good friend to others?

The maxim says, "A friend in need is a friend indeed." And that maxim has been around since at least the third century B.C.E. We're going to get to the bottom of whether it's true soon enough, but first things first: *I'm not sure we even know what it means.*

Is it saying, "A friend who is in need is definitely going to act like your friend"? Or, "A friend who is in need is a friend in action"? Maybe, "A friend when you're in need is definitely a friend"? Or perhaps, "A friend when you're in need is a friend in action"?

Which is it? Which do you think it is? Well, when we review the evidence, it turns out it may mean something very different from—or the exact opposite of—what you think it does. Let's look at that next . . .

PART 2

IS "A FRIEND IN NEED A FRIEND INDEED"?

6

Standing in your socks with no coat isn't fun when temperatures drop below zero. But it's even worse when a few hundred soldiers are coming to kill you.

The other members of his squad lay wounded nearby. From the creek bed where he took cover, he could see the enemy closing in. Running was still an option . . . But not for Hector. Hector Cafferata wasn't going anywhere.

Okay, let's rewind a bit. It's November 28, 1950, during the Korean War. Hector's small squad of US Marines was tasked with protecting a three-mile mountain pass, basically an escape route that the eleven-thousand-troop First Marine Division might need in case of trouble. With six inches of snow on the ground, it was so cold that Hector's squad couldn't even dig foxholes, so he and his buddy Kenneth Benson ("Bens") cut down small trees to build shelter and then got in their sleeping bags.

What they didn't know was that a huge unit of Chinese soldiers was advancing on their position. At around 1:30 A.M. Hector was startled awake by gunfire. Explosions. Screams. The bodies of his wounded friends all around. Enemy soldiers literally thirty feet away. There would not be time to put on boots. A grenade exploded nearby. It didn't harm Hector—but Bens was blinded by the flash. For the rest of the night he would be unable to see.

Hector grabbed his rifle and returned fire, but there were simply too many of them, too close, coming too fast. Hector told Bens, "Hang on to my foot. We're going to crawl." They retreated to a trench for cover.

Surveying the scene, Hector realized the rest of his squad was incapacitated. And a regimental-size group of enemy soldiers was closing in. Private First Class Hector Cafferata, who had only two weeks of training before being shipped off to Korea, was the last man standing. He looked around at his wounded pals. And then he got to work.

What did he do? Look, you're gonna need to forgive me here because I'm going to use a total cliché. But I swear to you this may be the only time this cliché was ever 100 percent accurate and not the least bit of an exaggeration at all . . .

Hector Cafferata became a one-man army.

Ankle-deep in snow and wearing socks, Hector transformed into the stuff of summer action movies. As dozens of enemy soldiers attacked with bullets, grenades, and mortars, Hector single-handedly held the line. Heck, he didn't just hold the line: he made them retreat for cover. Racing back and forth through the creek bed as bullets whizzed by and all manner of things exploded left and right, *one freakin' guy* made a regimental-size unit call for reinforcements.

Sound ridiculous? Think I'm making this up? Well, strap in because it gets even crazier: Hector batted away incoming grenades with a shovel. I'm going to repeat that: *he batted away incoming grenades with a shovel.*

Hector fired his M1 rifle so much that it overheated and briefly caught fire. He would plunge it into the snow to cool it down and resume shooting. Bens, still blind, would load bullets into eight-round clips by feel and hand them to Hector when he heard the empty "click" of the rifle.

The enemy tossed a grenade into the gully where Hector's teammates lay bleeding. He dashed toward it and threw it back out. But Hector wasn't quick enough. It detonated before it was clear, shredding one of his fingers and sending shrapnel into his arm. Didn't matter. Hector kept fighting, enemy soldiers just fifteen feet away. And he kept this up for *five hours.*

Then a shot rang out above the others. A sniper's bullet slammed into Hector's chest. He dropped. He struggled to get back up, but his body couldn't obey. On the ground, he looked at his fallen buddies . . . and beyond them, in the distance, Hector saw US Marine reinforcements cresting the hill. It was going to be okay.

Hector would spend over a year recovering. After leaving the hospital, he headed to the White House. President Harry Truman awarded him the Medal of Honor, the highest military decoration a member of the US armed forces can receive. If you check the official records, it says he killed fifteen of the enemy. But that number isn't even remotely accurate. In an interview, his commanding officer, Lieutenant Robert McCarthy, said it was closer to one hundred. Military officials changed the forms because they knew nobody would believe the real number.

"To tell you the truth, I did it. I know I did it. Other people know I did it. But I'll be God damned if I know how I did it. Put it that way." That's Hector, years later. He didn't know *how* he did it, but he knew *why.* And it wasn't because he was a patriot who loved his country. Hector certainly was a patriot who loved his country, but that's not why he did it. In fact, it's not why any Medal of Honor winner has ever done it. Review the stories of the soldiers granted that award, and you'll see the same reason over and over again. Medal of Honor winner Audie Murphy stated it plainly. When asked why he risked his life, taking on a full company of German soldiers during World War II, he replied:

"They were killing my friends."

The same was true for Hector. As he said in an interview, "I don't think I gave any of it conscious thought. You have friends there who are wounded and hurt. You decide you have to stick it out. The thought of leaving never occurred to me."

Hector's friends were definitely friends in need. And Hector was a friend "in deed" *and* "indeed." I'd love a friend like Hector. (Actually, I'd love a Hector Cafferata action figure with removable socks and a spring-loaded shovel arm.)

No one would dispute that friends are one of the most important things in life. But there's a mystery at the heart of friendship that we need to get to the bottom of . . .

*

Old friends in the highlands of Papua New Guinea greet each other by saying "Den neie," which translates to "I should like to eat your intestines." Uh, suffice to say, *some* ideas about friendship vary around the world. But many things are similar globally. On the islands of Micronesia, close friends are called *pwiipwin le sopwone wa*, which means "my sibling from the same canoe"—which is pretty close to "brother from another mother" if you think about it.

One thing is certain: friendship is universal. The Human Relations Area Files (HRAF) at Yale University tracks the 400 most studied cultures around the world, and 395 appear to have a concept of friendship. (The five that don't are communities that explicitly discourage friendship as a threat to the family unit or political structures.) And BFFs aren't limited to humans, or even primates for that matter. Researchers have documented that elephants, dolphins, whales, and other mammals also have buddies.

Reported in 93 percent of societies surveyed, *mutual aid* is the most agreed-on quality of friendship, and nearly every society also has a prohibition on "keeping score" in a friendship. With strangers, it's cash on the barrelhead, right now. But being friends means ignoring the strict accounting of favors. In fact, strict reciprocity is actually a profound *negative* in friendship. Being in a hurry to repay a debt is often seen as an insult. With buddies we act like costs and benefits don't matter (or at least not nearly as much).

A 2009 study found Americans, on average, have four close relationships, two of which are friends. Yale professor Nicholas Christakis notes that those stats haven't changed much in the past few decades, and you get similar numbers when you look around the globe. And while the majority of studies show quality is more important than quantity when it comes to friends, numbers still matter. Which folks are 60 percent more likely to consider themselves "very happy"? Those who have five or more friends they can talk about their troubles with.

Unsurprisingly, we have the most friends when we're young (teens average about nine), and the number generally declines as we age. Which is sad, because friends make us happier than any other relationship. Sorry, spouses. Nobel Prize winner Daniel Kahneman found that when you survey people in the moment, their happiness levels are highest while with friends. Doesn't matter if you survey the young or old, or go anywhere around the world, pals take the title nearly every time. To be fair, research by Beverley Fair shows that we're the absolute happiest when with both friends and spouses. But even *within* a marriage, friendship reigns. Work by Gallup found that 70 percent of marital satisfaction is due to the couple's friendship. Tom Rath says it's five times as critical to a good marriage as physical intimacy.

Amigo impact in the office is no less significant. Less than 20 percent of people see their manager as a "close friend"—but those who do are 2.5 times more likely to enjoy their job. Do you have three pals at work? Then you're 96 percent more likely to feel happy about your life. To be clear, that result was not "happy with your job"; it was happy with *life*. And while we would all love a raise, a 2008 *Journal of Socio-Economics* study found that while changes in income provide only a minor increase in happiness, more time with friends boosts your smiling to the equivalent of an extra ninety-seven thousand dollars a year. (Go ask your boss for a 97K raise and see how well that goes over.) Overall, friendship variables account for about 58 percent of your happiness.

Your friends are also critical in maintaining your not-dead status. Work by Julianne Holt-Lunstad found that loneliness affects your health the same way smoking fifteen cigarettes a day does. And once again, friendship reigns supreme over other connections. A 2006 study compared breast cancer patients who had ten close friends to those who had zero. Being in the first group quadrupled the women's chance of survival—but, more surprisingly, a husband had zero impact. Same thing for men. A long-term study of 736 guys showed friends reduced the likelihood of heart problems. Once again, a romantic partner didn't.

Okay, we get it: friends are a good thing. But we're here to answer a more specific question: *Is a "friend in need a friend indeed"?* Problem is, you and I can't even get started on that issue because we have a much more fundamental problem: *we don't even know what a friend really is.* Go ahead, define it. I'll wait. And no, I'm not going to accept some pyramid scheme of clichés as an answer. We've all heard a million definitions of friendship that sound like a Hallmark Card, but those aren't effective litmus tests.

Are your Facebook "friends" really friends? How about the old friend you have great memories with . . . but never bother to talk to? Or the fun person you always have an absolute blast with but would never trust to watch your kids? That reliable person you can count on for anything but would never call for solace if you received a medical test containing the word *malignant*? Are they a friend? Truly defining that common little word is a lot trickier than you think.

Christakis says, "We can formally define friendship as a typically volitional, long-term relationship, ordinarily between unrelated individuals, that involves mutual affection and support, possibly asymmetric, especially in times of need." A solid, formal definition for research—but I don't think that's going to help you and me day-to-day.

And its nebulous definition is emblematic of a larger problem: friendship gets screwed. Despite the cornucopia of positives mentioned above, including the number one spot for both happiness and health, friendship almost always takes a back seat to spouses, kids, extended family, even co-workers. We'll pay for a child therapist for our kids, a marriage counselor for our union, but nothing for friendship. If it has problems, we often just let it die like a pet goldfish. Daniel Hruschka, a professor and friendship researcher at Arizona State University, points out that *friend* is both spoken and written more than any other relational term in the English language, even *mother* and *father*. And yet this vital, powerful, happiness-inducing, life-saving relationship consistently gets the short end of the stick in everyday life. What's the deal?

Unlike those other relationships, friendship has no formal institution. It doesn't have law, religion, employer, or blood backing it up. And because there's no metaphorical lobbying group pushing friendships' interests, it always ends up second tier. It's 100 percent voluntary with no clear definition and few societally agreed-on expectations. If you go without speaking to your spouse for six weeks, expect divorce papers. If you don't talk to a friend for that long . . . *meh*.

With no formal rules, expectations are blurry. This renders friendships fragile. They wilt without care, but there are no rules for what is required, and negotiating specifics is uncomfortable. Don't show up for work, and you know your boss will fire you. But what calls for the ending of a friendship is often idiosyncratic. And so it's no surprise that when you survey young and old, you consistently find that within seven years, half of current friends are no longer close confidantes anymore. Without institutional obligations, the upkeep friendships require must be very deliberate. And in a busy world, that is beyond what most of us can handle. Often the thirties are the decade where friendships go to die. Around that time is when you gather all your friends for your wedding—and then promptly never see them again. Jobs, marriages, and children demand more and more as we age, and that frequently comes out of the buddy budget. Despite all the joys and benefits of friendship, studies show that the person we are most likely to have a lifelong relationship with turns out to be not a pal but a sibling. It's a tragedy.

However, the weakness of friendship is also the source of its immeasurable strength. Why do true friendships make us happier than spouses or children? Because they're always a deliberate choice, never an obligation. Not supported by any institution, neither is friendship forced on us by any institution. Quite simply: you have to like your friends. Other relationships can exist independent of emotion. Someone does not cease to be your parent, boss, or spouse because you stop liking them. Friendship is more real because either person can walk away at any time. Its fragility proves its purity.

And then there's an exponentially larger institution that

friendship must contend with, and one that provides our biggest challenge to an accurate definition of the word: biology. In a ruthless natural world (somewhere right now a lion is biting into a gazelle) where everything is reduced to the Darwinistic need to spread our genes, why do friends exist? Family, and the need to provide for that family, should be everything, right?

Sure, friends can offer help in achieving those goals and then the math works . . . but then it's all math. Transactional relationships. In that case we'd evaluate friends based solely on what they could do for us and make sure we always profited from the exchange. But that's not the case—an absence of strict reciprocity is one of the few universals about friendship. More important, it doesn't resonate with our emotional idea of friendship at all. It leaves no room for real altruism or kindness in the world. If life is spreading your genes and gaining resources, as biology might seem to say, why did Hector risk his life for his friends? Is that what the "friend in need" maxim means? That friends are only true to us when we or they need something?

Wow, we started out trying to get a simple definition of the word *friend* and somehow ended up in a 3 A.M. dorm room philosophy discussion trying to solve the nature of altruism in the universe. But all this does matter. It's critical to getting a real definition of what a friend is—and is not. In fact, this issue of altruism was Darwin's white whale. He said it was the biggest mystery, and if he couldn't solve it, he feared that his theory of natural selection would prove false.

And that's why we need to look at the tragic story of George Price. Grab the tissues. This is a tough one . . .

7

More than anything else, George Price wanted to make a name for himself. He desperately wanted to be known for having done something world-changing. No one doubted that he was brilliant. Some doubted whether he was mentally well, many doubted whether he was a good husband and father, but nobody doubted his brilliance.

George's math skills and creativity were nearly unparalleled. And driven by that relentless desire to be somebody, he had a work ethic that was even more impressive. He graduated Phi Beta Kappa and then got a PhD, finishing his thesis in a fifty-nine-hour-no-sleep blitz, hopped up on Benzedrine. He corresponded with five different Nobel laureates, seeking the breakthrough that would put him on the map.

Anytime he didn't feel that he could make history where he was, he would move on. And so George became a "Forrest Gump" of scientific advancement, moving six times in ten years. He worked on the Manhattan Project, helping to create the atomic bomb. Then on to Bell Labs, aiding in the development of the transistor. Next was cancer research. Then he moved again, pretty much single-handedly inventing computer-aided design.

He was a man possessed. And that's not much of an exaggeration; George wasn't mentally well. His incredible ambition was born of pathology. And so he went from barely seeing his wife and children to finally abandoning them. His demons would allow nothing to stand between him and greatness.

But it wasn't working. He had made notable achievements in disparate fields but nothing that met his incredible standards.

George spiraled into a crisis. He was unemployed. Alone. At forty-five he hadn't seen his daughters in over a decade. But his tenacity would not subside. He moved again, this time to London. His next area of scientific interest would be beyond ironic . . .

He became interested in families. He wanted to know what makes them stick together. (Feel free to do as much Freudian speculation on this one as you like.) And that led him to the bigger question of altruism: *Why does anyone help anyone?* Darwin's white whale again. But at least as far as families are concerned, George could make sense of it. Why would you risk your life to help your kids? They carry your genes. So George applied his tremendous math skills to the issue and discovered the exact formula by which Darwin's theory of natural selection worked. He had never studied genetics in his life. And the math seemed so simple to him that he was certain someone must have already thought of it before.

University College London had the number one genetics department in the world. George dropped by and showed them his work. Ninety minutes later he was given the keys to an office and an honorary professorship. What he had done was groundbreaking. You can look up the Price equation on Wikipedia. It still stands today as a major achievement in genetics and evolutionary theory. And, as fate would have it, that office is actually the site where Darwin's house used to be.

George had finally done it. Made his name. Achieved his dream. The thing he had sacrificed everything for. But what he thought was a wish come true turned out to be a curse. George pondered the results of his work. If something doesn't promote your survival and reproduction, his math shows that evolution will not select for it. But if you do something because it promotes your survival and reproduction, it's not altruistic. George thought to himself, *Did I just prove there is no such thing as kindness? If my math is right, the world is a terrible place.* He couldn't accept a world like that. But he was a scientist who was supposed to be devoted to being objective. Why could he not accept that the world might be a selfish place? As biographer Oren Harman told *Radiolab*, "Because he had been so selfish for much of his life."

The thing that made his name, that he had sacrificed everything for, he now wanted it to go away. To not be true. He had felt guilt over being so selfish, abandoning his little girls. And now his work showed the whole world was selfish. It was nearly too much for him to bear.

George couldn't change the math. But perhaps he could be the change he wished to see in the world. Maybe he could will the math to be wrong with his choices. And so the man who had tenaciously raced around the world thinking only of success and fame, who had abandoned his wife and daughters when they slowed him down, now began going up to people experiencing homelessness in London's Soho Square, saying, "My name is George. Is there any way I can help you?"

He'd buy them food. He'd give them whatever money he had. He let them stay in his apartment. After a life of thinking only about himself, George was now thinking only about others. He was learning to love. But he was going too far. His friends worried about him. He wasn't well. But his desire to atone, to fight the selfish math of Darwinism he had discovered, took on the same messianic zeal that his quest for fame had. He knew people were taking advantage of him, but he believed that perhaps if he gave away everything he could somehow disprove his theorem.

But one man alone can't save the world. These individuals didn't all get sober and fix their lives because of him. George was like a character in a time-travel film who fights to change the future but realizes he cannot alter destiny. When he ran out of money, he too became homeless. But even squatting in an abandoned house with others, he still devoted himself to helping them. He wrote to his daughters telling them he was sorry. He wished he could start over again.

There's no easy way to say this, dear reader, so I'll be direct: on January 6, 1975, George Price took his own life. Some might say he made himself a martyr to atone. The simple answer is he was not mentally well. George went too far in many areas. Tragically, this was one of them. Many of us would say we don't want to live in a world without love, kindness, and altruism, where unselfishness is just another form of selfishness. George Price was one of those people. But the story doesn't end there . . .

George knew in his heart that people could be good. You and I know it too. And eventually science caught up to you, me, and George. They didn't disprove his math; the Price equation is still rock solid in genetics. But studies have shown that we *are* wired for selfless altruism. Put people in a functional MRI and ask them to think about donating to charity, and the same circuits light up that are triggered by food and sex. Selflessly helping runs as deep in us as survival and procreating. And when researchers Knafo and Ebstein studied how much we were willing to give, they found a strong correlation with the genes that encode for the brain's oxytocin receptors. Translation? In very Darwinian fashion, altruism is in our genetics. No, there's not a contradiction; Darwinism and altruism can both exist in harmony.

Evolution cares only about consequences, not intentions. Evolution doesn't care why you do things, just the end result. Let's say you're a CEO and graciously give all your employees a one-thousand-dollar bonus. This makes them love you, so they work harder. Company profits triple, you're a success, and as a result you have lots of babies that thrive. Does that mean your action wasn't altruistic? Of course not. Your intention was to be nice. Our minds don't need to be thinking "spread genes" all the time. We've talked about how our brains weave stories to make sense of the world. Those stories, our intentions, our choices, are our own.

On January 22, 1975, a diverse group gathered in London's St Pancras Cemetery chapel. University professors with genetics PhDs stood next to junkies. They were there to pay their respects to a man who had influenced their lives. One of those still struggling and homeless was wearing a belt George had given him.

George Price took his own life because he was not well. But his own actions showed that an individual can be selfless, can choose to do things to help others even when it doesn't help the helper. George's intentions were good. He died in a quest to serve others and, in his own way, proved altruism true.

But what is that *story* that our brain tells us about altruism? The one that lets us override our fundamental Darwinian dictates? If we answer that, we'll have our definition of friendship. And we'll solve Darwin's greatest puzzle. And George will be able to rest in peace . . .

*

Okay, this is where I explain the story in our heads that overrides Charlie Darwin's laws. Yup, that's what I'm supposed to do here. No doubt. That's the goal . . . Look, I'll be honest: this had me stumped. Desperate for answers, I started reading a lot of ancient philosophy. Hold on, it gets worse. I looked at Plato's *Lysis*, and even the great Socrates explicitly said that *he* couldn't define friendship. Oof.

Finally, I caught a break. Aristotle, the student of the student of Socrates did have a lot to say about friends. He devoted 20 percent of his *Nicomachean Ethics* to the subject. Transactional relationships based on benefit weren't real friendships to Aristotle. He was a big, big fan of close friends though. And he even had a heartwarming definition of what one was. To Aristotle, friends "are disposed toward each other as they are disposed to themselves: *a friend is another self.*"

Pretty nice, huh? We treat them so kindly because they're part of us. What's interesting is this would also resolve our conundrum. Your brain is like a clever lawyer, twisting the words in Darwin's contract. Selfishness can actually *be* altruism—if I believe that you are me.

And this concept of another self was so damn catchy that it influenced an enormous amount of Western culture for the next two thousand years, to the point where in my review of classic literature I saw it so frequently I created Eric's "Friend-as-Another-Self" drinking game.

Cicero around 50 B.C.? "For a true friend is one who is, as it were, a second self." DRINK.

Edith Wharton in the 1800s? "There is one friend in the life of each of us who seems not a separate person, however dear and beloved, but an expansion, an interpretation, of one's self." DRINK.

And as Mark Vernon notes, in the New Testament it may say "love thy neighbor as thyself," but if you check the Old Testament Levitical code, it translates as "love thy *friend* as thyself." Yes, the concept of another self is even in the Bible. (Forget taking a drink this time; just polish off the whole bottle.)

However, I promised you a book backed by science. Aristotle's concept is brilliant, but Aristotle also wrote about the folly of making all your sacrifices to Zeus, so maybe we should take him with a grain of salt. (I reached out to Aristotle for an interview, but he was unavailable for comment.) "Friends are another self" is perfect for Instagram, but alas, it's not science. So I went back to reading nerdy academic study after nerdy academic study . . .

But then I came across something: "The support for our basic prediction is consistent with the notion that, in a close relationship, other is 'included in the self' in the sense that cognitive representations of self and close others overlap."

Holy crap. Aristotle was right. And he wasn't just a "little" right or "almost" right; not just one but over *sixty-five* studies support Aristotle's idea. In psychology it's called "self-expansion theory"—that we expand our notion of our self to include those we're close to. A series of experiments demonstrated that the closer you are to a friend, the more the boundary between the two of you blurs. We actually confuse elements of who they are with who we are. When you're tight with a friend, your brain actually has to work harder to distinguish the two of you.

The clincher was neuroscience studies that put people into an MRI and then asked them questions about friends. Of course, the areas of the brain for positive emotions lit up. You know what else was activated? *The parts of the brain associated with self-processing.* When women heard the names of their close friends, their gray matter responded the same way it did when they heard their own name.

From this work, the IOS ("inclusion of other in the self") Scale was developed, and it was so powerful that the ranking could be used to robustly determine relationship stability. In other words, tracked over time, lower scores predicted the friendship was more likely to break up, and high scores predicted it was less likely to break up. Beyond that, when friendships with high IOS scores did end, subjects were much more likely to say things like "I don't know who I am anymore." If you've ever had a close friendship end and felt like you lost a part of yourself, well, in a manner of speaking, you were right.

In 1980, Harvard professor Daniel Wegner said that empathy might "stem in part from a basic confusion between ourselves and others." And with that, it seems like we finally have the definitions we've been seeking.

- What is empathy? Empathy is when the line between you and another blurs, when you become confused where you end and another person begins.
- What is closeness? Closeness is when your vision of your "self" scooches over and makes room for someone else to be in there too.
- What is a friend? A friend is another self. A part of you.

I have the urge to say, *In your face, Charlie Darwin!* But the truth is, Darwin was just like us. Remember how he said the problem of altruism was his biggest challenge? How he feared it could disprove his theory? Well, Darwin couldn't reconcile it himself, but his behavior displayed the same distinction. Darwin did great things and had a whopping ten kids. (Nice way to prove your theory, Charlie.) But to do that, his brain didn't need to be thinking "must spread genes" all the time. That wasn't what was important to him as a person. What was?

Believe it or not, friendship. Darwin wrote a memoir and discussed the thing that affected his career more than anything else. His theory of natural selection? Nope: "I have not as yet mentioned a circumstance which influenced my whole career more than any other. This was my friendship with Professor Henslow." Darwin's theory didn't have much to say about friendship, but it played as significant a part in his own life as it does in ours.

Friends expand us. Unite us. And as far as our brains are concerned, the people we care about truly do become a part of us. Yes, Darwin's theory is active in our biology, but our feelings are real. Our intentions can be pure and noble. We can and do make great altruistic sacrifices for friends like Hector Cafferata did.

Now we know what friendship, closeness, and empathy are. Friends are a part of you . . . but how do we make them? There's plenty of work on this topic, most notably Dale Carnegie's classic text. But does *How to Win Friends and Influence People* hold up to scientific scrutiny? We're gonna find out. But before Dale gets the *MythBusters* treatment, we need to learn a lesson or two from a very special group of folks who just happen to be the friendliest people on Earth . . .

8

It can be hard to be a mom. Especially when a tattooed biker size extra-large knocks on your front door looking for your teenage sons. Uh-oh. But, no, he's not here to rumble. As reported in the *New York Times*, the two boys got on a CB radio, made a friend, and invited him over. Just another crazy thing teenagers do? Actually, no. Those twins are part of a special group of people: the friendliest people in the world.

They're a small, little-known group. They absolutely love people, and they're almost infinitely trusting, with zero social anxiety. Meet a member of this clan, and they will immediately shower you with compliments, questions, and kindness. And it's all totally heartfelt and sincere. As Jennifer Latson recounted in *The Boy Who Loved Too Much*, these people make you feel so special it's almost a disappointment when you realize they're like this with everyone. No, they're not part of a cult. No, they're not selling anything. But, of course, there is a twist . . .

Williams syndrome is a genetic disorder. Perhaps the most endearing of disorders. What is fascinating is that while people with this condition are disabled, they are also superhumanly *abled* when it comes to kindness, empathy, and socializing.

Affecting just one in ten thousand people worldwide, Williams syndrome (WS) occurs when roughly twenty-eight genes are missing on chromosome number seven. This causes changes in the fetus, including shorter stature, connective tissue problems, and unique facial features.

Unfortunately, WS also causes intellectual disability. The average IQ is sixty-nine. But from a scientific perspective, the mental challenges are inconsistent. Those with WS possess what the literature calls an "uneven cognitive profile." They have trouble in some areas—but superpowers in others. They have extreme difficulty with math and solving puzzles, but ask them a question and you'll be treated to an amazing storyteller who uses rich, emotional wording. Their performance on abstract and spatial tasks is dismal, yet they excel with things verbal, emotional, or even musical.

When scientists tracked down what was responsible for the asymmetry in deficits, they got a lot more than they bargained for. They realized that they weren't just studying a medical malady but beginning to crack the code of human kindness. MRI scans showed that WS folks have "diminished amygdala reactivity in response to socially frightening stimuli." In English: people with Williams syndrome never see faces as unfriendly. You and I are skeptical, or even fearful, of strangers. For people with Williams, there truly are no strangers: just friends they haven't met yet.

But what caused their brains to develop so differently? Given it's a genetic disorder, the researchers looked hard at the DNA for these "superfriendly" genes. And found them. GTF2I and GTF2IRD1 modulate oxytocin, that bonding hormone you've heard so much about. In WS, these genes basically send oxytocin into overdrive. If you've ever felt that surge of maternal or paternal love, or had an experience with the drug Ecstasy, you've felt something akin to what nearly *every* social encounter is like for someone with WS.

But the insights didn't stop there. Think about the traits we're discussing: always happy to see others, eager to please, infinitely forgiving, and radiating a deep love for others that's unquestionably sincere. Those are all the qualities that make us cherish, well . . . puppies. And if you thought that, you deserve an honorary PhD in genetics. Because the same genes that separate us from those with Williams are the same genes that distinguish wolves from man's best friend. And this might explain why you and I can be afraid of or hostile to strangers outside our "pack," while two twins with WS will talk to a Hells Angel on a CB radio and invite him over.

Alysson Muotri, a professor of pediatrics at UC San Diego School of Medicine, has studied WS: "I was fascinated on how a genetic defect, a tiny deletion in one of our chromosomes, could make us friendlier, more empathetic and more able to embrace our differences." It's not much of a stretch at all to say that people with WS possess the qualities most religions urge us to aspire to: a generous, selfless love for all. Latson writes, "People with Williams don't have to learn the Golden Rule; they don't have to be taught about equality or inclusion. They're born practicing these principles."

A 2010 study examined racism among kids with Williams. The result? They don't show any. Zero, zip, zilch, nada. And this is even more surprising because nearly all children by age three show a preference for their own race. Kids with WS are, in fact, the only children ever found to show zero racial bias.

All of these prosocial, altruistic traits led Karen Levine, a developmental psychologist at Harvard Medical School, to half-jokingly propose *we're* the ones with the disorder. She calls it TROUS: "The Rest of Us Syndrome." Symptoms include hiding our emotions, not treating strangers as friends, and an epic lack of hugging.

If anything, those with WS are *too* trusting. They frequently get taken advantage of. It's like they possess no social immune system to defend them. This presents a problem for parents of WS kids. While such a friendly child is a beautiful thing, having them happily hop into cars with strangers is not. These children must be taught to distrust others—but the lessons rarely stick.

It's not in their nature. And while such threats make mothering a WS child an extreme challenge at times, Latson notes the upside: What mom doesn't want a little boy who sincerely tells her he loves her at least a dozen times a day—no matter what she does?

Maybe WS folks are nature's way of apologizing for sociopaths. That's kinda how Stanford School of Medicine professor Robert Sapolsky sees it: "Williams have great interest but little competence. But what about a person who has competence but no warmth, desire or empathy? That's a sociopath. Sociopaths have great theory of mind. But they couldn't care less."

However, that interest without competence leads to a heartbreaking irony for those with WS: they long for real connection but are often unable to achieve it. What they possess in social desire is not matched in social ability. They fail at processing many basic social cues. They ask repetitive questions and are often too impulsive to wait for answers before asking another one. Fearless about initiating relationships, they lack the ability to deepen and sustain them. Roughly 80 percent of WS kids felt that they lacked friends or had difficulties with their friends. They are the sweet child that everyone is nice to . . . but that no one invites to birthday parties.

And from a happiness perspective, the "uneven cognitive profile" that gives them superpowers can actually be worse than having more severe deficits. It is a cruel tragedy to know you have a problem—but be forever lacking the capacity to solve it. To watch others acquire friends, partners, and eventually children but to experience only frustration and loneliness yourself. As science writer David Dobbs said about those with Williams: "They know no strangers but can claim few friends."

So what happens when your WS twins invite that biker over and he's standing on your doorstep? Dobbs recounted this true story for the *New York Times*. Well, you reluctantly welcome Mr. Hells Angel in for a while. And he's so taken with the two most gregarious, friendly kids he's ever met that he asks if you'll bring them to his biker club to speak to the crew. Which is just about the greatest thing your sons could ever hope for. So you say yes. And you're scared that day because the clubhouse looks like the waiting room for a parole office. But your boys could not be more excited: *Look at all the people, mom!* And they give their little presentation. They talk about how much they love conversations. How badly they get bullied. How confusing the world is to them at times. And how they struggle so very, very hard to just make a real friend. You're scared the bikers will be bored or angry—but that's not what happened at all that day . . .

The mother in question turned to look at the audience and what she saw was a room full of enormous tattooed men wiping tears from their faces.

And no matter what happens today, tomorrow those with Williams will keep loving us all, fearlessly representing the best parts of humanity.

Many of us have had moments in our lives where we could relate to aspects of WS. We struggle to make and sustain deep friendships, despite being kind and friendly. And when it doesn't click, we wonder what we've done wrong. Or if there's something wrong with us.

But the struggles of those with WS actually contain the secret we need to form those true friendships Aristotle wrote about . . .

*

When it comes to making friends, the closest thing we have to the magic powers of Williams syndrome seems to be the work of

Dale Carnegie. Since it was first published in 1936, *How to Win Friends and Influence People* has sold over thirty million copies, and nearly a century later it still sells more than a quarter million copies each year. Carnegie's text intersperses stories with information on how to be better with people and obviously bears no resemblance whatsoever to the book you're reading right now.

So what does Dale recommend? He encourages people to listen, to be interested in others, to speak to them from their point of view, to sincerely flatter others, to seek similarity, to avoid conflict, and many other things that seem obvious—but that we all routinely forget to do. However, Carnegie's book was written before the dawn of most formal research in the area and is largely anecdotal. Does his advice line up with modern social science?

Surprisingly, yes. As ASU's Hruschka notes, the majority of Carnegie's fundamental techniques have been validated by numerous experiments. One of his methods (which has been shown to promote the feeling of "another self") is seeking similarity. Ever watch someone get physically hurt and you flinch sympathetically? MRI studies by neuroscientist David Eagleman show that sympathetic pain is increased when we perceive the victim as being similar to ourselves, even if the grouping is arbitrary. Social scientist Jonathan Haidt comments, "We just don't feel as much empathy for those we see as 'other.'"

That said, good ol' Dale did get one wrong. The eighth principle in his book says "Try honestly to see things from the other person's point of view." Remember back in section 1 when we realized just how terrible we are at reading other people's minds? Yeah, exactly. Nicholas Epley tested Dale's suggestion and doesn't mince words about it: "Never have we found any evidence that perspective taking—putting yourself in another person's shoes and imagining the world through his or her eyes—increased accuracy in these judgments." Not only isn't it effective, but it actually makes you *worse* at relating to them. Sorry, Dale.

But he was only wrong about that one issue. In his defense, millions have used his techniques with great success including famous people like, um . . . Charles Manson. And this leads us to the more relevant problem with Carnegie's techniques: not that they're unscientific, but that they can be manipulative and lead to shallow friendships, the kind Aristotle was none too fond of. (Countdown to lawsuit from the Carnegie estate: five, four, three . . .)

Carnegie's book is great for the early stages of relationships, it's excellent for transactional relationships with business contacts . . . but it's also a wonderful playbook for con men. It's not focused on building "another self" and developing long-term intimacy: it's much more about tactically gaining benefit from people. Carnegie frequently uses phrases like "human engineering" and "making people glad to do what you want." To be fair, Carnegie repeatedly says you should have good intentions, but this rings hollow. Sociologist Robert Bellah wrote, "For Carnegie, friendship was an occupational tool for entrepreneurs, an instrument of the will in an inherently competitive society." If you're looking for a blood brother or sister from another mister, this isn't going to do it. It's the equivalent of using a "How to Pick Up Girls" book to navigate the ups and downs of a multidecade marriage.

So what *does* produce deep, "another self" friendships? This leads us to an area of academic study called "signaling theory." Let's say I tell you I'm a tough guy. Do you believe me? On the other hand, let's say you see the UFC heavyweight championship belt being wrapped around my waist at the end of a televised fight. Which would better convince you I'm not the guy you want to mess with?

A "costly" signal is a more powerful signal. Saying I'm a tough guy is easy. Me faking a live UFC event before a crowd of thousands is far harder. We operate based on signaling theory all the time; we're just rarely aware of it. Carnegie teaches us friendship signals, but they're not costly. That's why as a reader we like them; they're easy to do. That's also why con men like them; they're easy to fake. Saying "I'll be there for you" is one thing. Showing up for a full day of helping you move is a much more costly, and powerful, signal. Which would convince you I'm a real friend?

So which costly signals do we want to display (and look for) when it comes to true friends? The experts firmly agree on two, the first one being *time*. Why is time so powerful? Because it's scarce, and scarce = costly. Want to make someone feel special? Do something for them you simply cannot do for others. If I give you an hour of my time every day, I cannot do that for more than twenty-four people. Cannot. End of discussion. Thank you for calling.

As we discussed, friendship beats other relationships in terms of happiness, but what is it specifically that works that magic? Melikşah Demır of Northern Arizona University says it's companionship—merely spending time together. And, unsurprisingly, what does research say is the most common cause of conflict in friendships? Once again, time. There's no getting around it: time is critical.

So how do we make more time for friends as an adult? The key comes down to rituals. Think about the people you do keep up with, and you'll probably find a ritual, conscious or not, underneath it. "We talk every Sunday," or "we exercise together." Replicate that. It works. Find something to do together consistently. Research from Notre Dame that analyzed over eight million phone calls showed touching base in some form every two weeks is a good target to shoot for. Hit that minimum frequency, and friendships are more likely to persist.

But making new friends can require even *more* time. That process can be slower than inflight internet, which is one reason we're so bad at it as we age. How much time? Are you sitting down? Jeff Hall's research found that it took as many as sixty hours to develop a light friendship, sometimes one hundred hours to get to full-fledged "friend" status, and two hundred or more hours to unlock the vaunted "best friend" achievement. Sometimes more, sometimes less, but either way—yowzers, that's a lot of time.

But that's only part of the equation. Hall also found that *how* people talked mattered. We've all hit that wall with a potential friend where the small talk starts to go in circles. You just can't seem to break through to the next level. And that's one problem with Carnegie's work: the smiling and head bobbing get you only so far. Want to make good friends without dozens of hours? You can do it—but Carnegie won't get you there. Arthur Aron (who developed the IOS Scale) got strangers to feel like lifelong pals in *just forty-five minutes*. How? Well, that leads us to our second costly signal: *vulnerability*.

It's ironic: when we meet new people, we often try to impress them—and this can be a terrible idea. Through a series of six studies, researchers found that signaling high status doesn't help new friendships, it hurts them. Again, might be good for sales calls or conveying leadership, but it makes finding "another self" much more difficult.

There's been a lot of talk about vulnerability lately, but most of us just nod our heads and go right back to trying to seem perfect. Why? *Cause it's really frickin' scary to put yourself out there.* You could be mocked or rejected, or the information could be used against you. Vulnerability gives us flashbacks to worst-case scenarios from high school. (Among the Kunyi tribe of Congo, too much self-disclosure is said to make one more susceptible to witchcraft, so perhaps opening up is even more dangerous than you thought.) We know it's risky. Large-scale studies by Harvard sociologist Mario Luis Small showed that we're often more likely to tell very personal details to strangers than close friends.

We don't want awful people to exploit our weaknesses, but the irony is that our weaknesses are where trust comes from. In a paper titled "Can We Trust Trust?" Diego Gambetta wrote, "The concession of trust . . . can generate the very behavior which might logically seem to be its pre-condition." In other words, trust creates trust. The danger of being exploited creates the value inherent in trust, giving it its power. How do you signal you're trustworthy? By trusting someone else. And then, often, the trust in you creates the trust in them.

Vulnerability tells people they're part of an exclusive club. They're special to you. Aron found that self-disclosure directly aids in producing "another self." And that's how he got people to become best buds in forty-five minutes. (If you want to see the questions that Aron used to produce close friendships that quickly, I've posted them for you here: https://www.bakadesuyo.com/aron.)

Not only is vulnerability effective, it's also not quite as dangerous as you think. Psychology has documented the "beautiful mess effect"—that we consistently overestimate how negatively our errors will be perceived. We think we'll be seen as a moron and exiled to a distant village, but when surveyed, most people see the occasional screw-up as a positive. You make an error and are terrified you'll be seen as inadequate. But when others make the same error, you're rarely as judgmental, and it often warms you to that person.

What's the best way to dip your toe in the pool of vulnerability? Well, here goes: I'm a man in his late forties who coos at puppy pictures on Instagram and occasionally speaks to them in babytalk. *Yes, I write smarty-smart, self-important books about science and I babytalk to pictures of puppies on Instagram.* Do you like me less or more? Trust me less or more?

So next time you're with someone you care about, or someone you want to deepen your friendship with, follow **The Scary Rule™**: *If it scares you, say it.* You don't need to go full bore just yet. Don't confess to any murders at Christmas dinner. Start slow and build. Stretch the bounds of the sensitive things you're willing to admit about yourself, and, by the same token, ask more sensitive questions than you're normally comfortable asking. And when your friend admits vulnerable things, do not recoil and scream, "YOU DID WHAT?!?!" Accept them. Then, Daniel Hruschka says, "raise the stakes." As long as you feel emotionally safe and you're getting a positive reception, share more. That's how you build "another self."

Still hesitant about opening up? Then let me put the metaphorical gun to your head: not being vulnerable kills friendships. That same study on the number of hours required to make a friend showed more small talk in a friendship produced a drop in closeness. Oh, and not being open and vulnerable doesn't just kill friendships: it can also kill *you*. University of Pennsylvania professor Robert Garfield notes that not opening up prolongs minor illnesses, increases the likelihood of a first heart attack, and doubles the chance it will be lethal.

Now, we're not yet 100 percent on how that "friend in need" maxim should be interpreted, but we're a lot closer to seeing how it functions and how it can work in practice. Make the time, vulnerably share your thoughts, and raise the stakes. If all goes well, they do the same. This gets us away from transactional relationships.

With trust established, we can ignore costs to a greater degree, as can they. You don't worry about how big the favor is or what they've done for you lately—you're past that. Now you only have to ask one question: "Are they a friend?" And if they are, you help.

Yes, it can be scary. And plenty of people are using Carnegie's book with manipulative intentions. There are bad people in this world. Like narcissists. But if we're going to arrive at true friendship, we're going to swim in the same waters as bad people.

How do we deal with them safely—and maybe even make them better people? We can learn a powerful lesson about doing that by looking at a story about the group of people who have most come to define "evil" in the modern world . . .

9

His mother had always said that people were complex. But Danny didn't necessarily believe her, and it certainly didn't prepare him for what happened that night in 1941.

The Nazis had occupied France in 1940 and instituted a curfew of 6 P.M. But this night seven-year-old Danny had stayed too late at a friend's house. Briskly walking home, scared, he turned his sweater inside out. He wanted to conceal the yellow Star of David on it that indicated he was Jewish.

Luckily, the streets were empty. It seemed safe. He was almost home. But then he saw a man. A German soldier. And not just any German soldier. This man wore the black uniform of the SS, the type Danny had been told to fear more than any other. And when you're seven, you take that advice to heart.

But he was almost home. Maybe he could hide, maybe he wouldn't be seen . . . Then the two made eye contact. Total "deer in the headlights" moment. It was after curfew. He was Jewish. And he was *hiding it*. This. Was. Not. Good.

The SS officer beckoned him. A lump the size of a planet formed in Danny's throat as he obeyed. He just hoped the soldier would not notice the sweater. Danny closed the distance. And that's when the Nazi moved, sharply, grabbing him . . .

In a hug. A hug so deep and so firm he lifted the seven-year-old off the ground. At first, Danny didn't even react to it, barely noticed it, his brain only thinking, "Don't notice the star, don't notice the star" on repeat.

The Nazi put him down and began speaking emotionally in German. Were those tears in his eyes? From his wallet he took out a picture of a young boy and showed it to Danny. The message was obvious: the epitome of evil had a son Danny's age. And missed him desperately.

The Nazi gave Danny some money and smiled at him. And then they went their separate ways.

This man who was capable of doing the most horrible things, who represents evil better than anything else we know today, still had love compartmentalized inside him. And seeing Danny, to be reminded of his own son, brought that out. Danny's mother had been right: people were endlessly complex.

That brief, terrifying lesson about the complexity of human nature would shape the rest of Danny's life. He would go on to get a PhD in psychology. He would focus on the seeming irrationality of human behavior. He would become a professor at Princeton University. And Daniel Kahneman would tell that story of the night with the Nazi in the statement they have you write when you're awarded a Nobel Prize.

There's a secret hidden in the kindness that happened that night. Something neither of them understood at the time, that science has only recently uncovered: that there may be a way to bring out the good in "bad" people.

*

The data show, on average, for every ten friends you gain, you'll also get a new enemy. Oh, and the old expression "the enemy of my enemy is my friend" isn't true. Nicholas Christakis and James Fowler found that the jerks in your life have their own jerks, and you'd find their jerks to be pretty jerky as well. But unless you're Batman talking about the Joker, an enemy generally isn't the most problematic person in your life. So who is?

"Frenemies" are often worse than enemies. Julianne Holt-Lunstad, a psychology professor at BYU, found that frenemies (the formal designation is "ambivalent relationships") increase anxiety and drive your blood pressure through the roof—even more than true enemies do. Why are frenemies more stressful than enemies? It's the unpredictability. You know what to expect from enemies and supportive friends—but with those ambivalent ones you're always on edge. And that's the reason Holt-Lunstad found that the number of frenemies correlated with depression and heart disease over time. But does that really make frenemies worse than enemies? Yeah, because, believe it or not, ambivalent friends make up *half* our relationships. And studies find that we don't see them any less often than supportive friends.

Now sometimes frenemies are merely people we don't "click" with, but other times it's because they're narcissists. As physicist Bernard Bailey quipped, "When they discover the center of the universe, a lot of people will be disappointed to discover they are not it." What the heck is wrong with these people? Well, it actually fits surprisingly well into our Aristotelian paradigm. Narcissists don't include others in their "self," at least not much or often. Narcissism is when you stop trying to soothe your insecurities by relying on people and instead turn to an imaginary self where you are superior.

We all have fantasy lives where we're rich and awesome and admired. That's human. And we all have dreams of our enemies being crushed beneath our boots, humiliated in the town square, and tortured mercilessly until . . . Okay, maybe that's just me. As Dr. Craig Malkin points out, the distinction is, we *enjoy* our dreams—but narcissists are *addicted* to their dreams. Most of us find strength in others; they find it only in themselves. There isn't "another self." And that lack of empathy is central to the disorder. For narcissists, "getting ahead is more important than getting along." And as for "a friend in need"? To a narcissist, a friend in need is simply a weak person.

So what's the best way to deal with a narcissist? The answer is simple: don't. Say "MEEP-MEEP" and sprint away Road Runner–style as fast as you can. The first-line recommendation of professionals is consistent; we just usually don't want to do it. But what if "no contact" isn't an option? Or you really believe this frenemy can be redeemed?

If they have full-blown NPD (narcissistic personality disorder), forget it. I'd sooner tell you to do your own appendectomy than try and change a clinical narcissist. Guess how well therapy works on them? Often a grand total of not at all. They frequently have "negative treatment outcome"—they get worse. It's well documented that "countertransference" is a big problem in therapy with narcissists. Translation: *they even manipulate the professionals who try to treat them.* And what you'll have to do to contend with them will damage you for other relationships.

But if they're subclinical, there's a shot. We're going to use what are called "empathy prompts." Narcissists have trouble with empathy, but the research shows it's not because they have *zero* empathy; it's more like their empathy muscle is weak. More than a dozen studies show it's possible to activate that weak muscle in lower-level narcissists and, with time, strengthen it. But it's important to remember here that what we're doing is emotional, not cognitive. Wagging a finger at a narcissist, telling them what they did wrong and what you want is just instructing them how to more effectively manipulate you. The goal is to emotionally scooch yourself into their identity as "another self." This involves critical *feeling*, not critical thinking.

What's great is that empathy prompts are both litmus test and treatment. If the narcissist doesn't respond, they're probably past the clinical threshold. (The next step involves garlic and a stake through the heart.) But if they are affected, you can help them improve.

So how do we bring out the best in "bad" people? We'll attack from three angles.

1. EMPHASIZE SIMILARITY

Yup, just like we talked about with Dale Carnegie. The study "Attenuating the Link Between Threatened Egotism and Aggression" found this angle directly increases the feeling of "another self." Emphasizing similarity actually has a *bigger* effect on narcissists than non-narcissists. Why? Because there's some very clever psychological judo built into this angle. The researchers wrote, "This manipulation would also capitalize on narcissists' weakness—self-love. Narcissists love themselves, and if someone else is like them, how can they hurt that other person?" And the result? "Narcissistic aggression was completely attenuated, even under ego threat, when participants believed they shared a key similarity with their partner." And it doesn't take much either. Merely telling a narcissist that they shared a birthday or the same fingerprint type had an effect. *Did you know we're both O+ blood type? Maybe you want to stop stabbing me in the back now.* (No, don't actually say that.)

2. EMPHASIZE VULNERABILITY

Once again, we're returning to our fundamental principles. You have to be careful here because weakness can make a predator pounce. But that's also what makes this a good litmus test: if they move to exploit, they may be too far gone. If they soften, there's hope. Two critical points while executing this: voice the importance of the relationship to you and reveal your feelings. Showing anger will backfire, but disappointment is surprisingly effective. Next time the jerk says something jerky respond: "That hurt my feelings. Is that what you intended?" If they can be saved, they'll backpedal.

3. EMPHASIZE COMMUNITY

Just like similarity, this method is actually more powerful with narcissists than regular people. Researchers analogized it to alcohol: if you're not a regular drinker, booze has a bigger effect. And your narcissist isn't accustomed to empathy, so when it hits, it can hit a lot harder. Remind them about family, friendship, and the connections you have. Their default setting isn't empathy, so you just need to kick that back into gear. And if you get a positive response with any of these, take a lesson from dog training: positive reinforcement. Reward them for it.

They're not going to change in one big moment of Freudian realization. This isn't a Disney film, and giving the Grinch a big hug isn't going to instantly turn him into a sweetheart. This can be a painstaking, thankless process, but for someone you care about, it can be worth it.

It helps to remember they're suffering. Rarely seems like it, but they are. Being an addict to your dreams is a curse. Narcissism is "highly comorbid with other disorders," which is a fancy way of saying these people have more issues than *Vogue*. They suffer from higher rates of depression, anxiety, chronic envy, perfectionism, relationship difficulties, and last, but certainly not least, suicide. When people suffer from depression, anxiety, or borderline personality disorder, we tend to feel sympathy, but with narcissism we often say they're just "bad." That's like feeling sorry for people with tuberculosis but saying those with meningitis are a bunch of jerks. Narcissism shows a heritability of 45–80 percent, with at least two studies pointing to genetic underpinnings. No, your frenemy is not nice. But it's important to remember it may not be their fault.

But what do you do if they *are* clinical level and you can't MEEP-MEEP? The final option is the two Bs: boundaries and bargaining. Basically, you need to aim for the opposite of "another self"—a totally transactional relationship. First, establish boundaries. What will you no longer tolerate? And what will you do if they violate those boundaries? Be firm and consistent but not mean. Next is bargaining. It's *Let's Make a Deal* time. (Ignore that smell of brimstone.) Focus on win-win. Narcissists will often play ball if you have something they want. Make sure they pay in advance and always price above market. Judge actions, not intentions. A final good move that clinical psychologist Albert Bernstein recommends when they're angling for something dishonest is to ask, "What will people think?" They may not feel guilt, but they do feel shame, and narcissists are very concerned about appearances.

The good news is that if you're friends for the long haul, narcissists do tend to soften with age. Over the years, reality hammers at their story, those comorbidities mount, or the abused they have left in their wake realize there's a sale on pitchforks and torches at Wal-Mart. I don't want to invoke the idea of karma here, but very often they get their due. Few can sustain their illusions at the same level forever.

The irony is that narcissists are so full of themselves yet lack self-awareness. Case in point: Tania Singer was a big-deal academic who bullied everyone around her, even the pregnant women in her lab. But eventually her reputation caught up with her. What did Tania Singer study? She was the leading researcher on *empathy*.

Alright, we've covered frenemies. It's almost time to round it all up and get our final verdict on the "friend in need" maxim. But first we need to see just how extreme the power of friendship can be . . .

10

The two men could not have been more different: a pornographer and a preacher.

In the 1970s Larry Flynt built a full-fledged porn empire with *Hustler* magazine as its crown jewel. To be clear, Larry didn't make "erotica"—he made *porn*. The sophistication of *Playboy* magazine was anathema to him. It was phony. He was utterly tasteless—and frequently hysterical. Flynt was a spitfire, satirizing authority with crazy antics, publicity stunts, and chaos. Not without principles, Flynt was ahead of his time in support of abortion, the rights of homosexuals and minorities, and, most of all, free speech. After *Hustler* posted photos of interracial sex, Flynt was shot by a white supremacist and confined to a wheelchair.

And if Flynt was emblematic of the wild 1970s, Jerry Falwell could not have better represented the mainstream 1950s. The televangelist led the surge of the religious right in America as a political force to be reckoned with, helping to elect Ronald Reagan. His outspoken conservative stances espoused traditional values and condemned what he saw as the collapse of morality in the seventies. His lobbying group, the Moral Majority, railed against abortion, homosexuality, the Equal Rights Amendment, and, of course, porn.

Throughout the 1970s and '80s, Falwell publicly bashed Flynt as symbolizing everything that was wrong with the country. And Flynt was growing tired of being smeared by someone he thought of as a hypocritical windbag. *Hustler*'s editorial meetings had always begun by asking "Who haven't we offended this month?"

And for their latest target, Flynt selected none other than Falwell. The magazine published a satirical liquor "advertisement" where Falwell would be talking about losing his virginity. In a Virginia outhouse. To his mother.

Larry just saw it as his turn to hit back in the ongoing debate. He didn't think it was that big a deal. But Falwell sure did. Accusing Flynt of libel and emotional distress, in October 1983 Falwell sued him . . . for forty-five million dollars. The "cold" war had just gone nuclear.

Falwell saw it as nothing less than a battle between good and evil. And he had the high ground. Formal courts of law were the arena of the traditional, the squares. Falwell would use the full power of the mainstream system as a cudgel to bludgeon Flynt, the immoral outsider.

Larry's reaction? A yawn. You have to realize, being sued was not a once-in-a-lifetime problem for him. It was more like an every-Thursday problem. In the film *The People vs. Larry Flynt*, Flynt tells his attorney: "I'm a lawyer's dream client. I'm rich, I'm fun, and I'm always in trouble."

And while it was true that the courtroom played to Falwell's strengths, Flynt was a brilliant tactician with courtroom trolling abilities that tested the bounds of human comprehension. The judge would fine him, and Larry would pay in one-dollar bills, dumped on the courtroom floor by a cavalcade of hookers and porn stars. When the judge fined him again, he did it again . . . this time paying in pennies. If Falwell was a formal military using the courts as a battleground, Flynt was a rebel guerrilla force, well versed in unconventional warfare, and no less well funded. And he impishly printed the offending satirical ad *again* in the February 1984 issue of *Hustler*.

But Larry lost the lawsuit. Yeah, he was making a mockery of the system and stealing the headlines with his antics, but Falwell was winning where it mattered—in the courts. Larry's nemesis had won. But Larry was not about to give in. He appealed . . .

And lost *again*. Flynt had already spent more than two million dollars on the case. His lawyers wanted to quit. The Sun Tzu warrior was now fighting uphill with the sun in his eyes. But he could not stand to give in to his sworn enemy. This was a battle to the death. So the smut peddler played the only card he had left: he appealed to the United States Supreme Court. And on March 20, 1987, they agreed to hear the case.

And Flynt won. Actually, he didn't just win; it was a unanimous decision. If satirists could be sued into silence every time they said something negative about a celebrity, it imperiled the first amendment. *Hustler v. Falwell* is now routinely taught in law schools and regarded as one of the most important free speech cases of the twentieth century. But more important: Flynt defeated his enemy Falwell, and did so spectacularly.

It's an amazing story. So amazing that it was made into a film in 1996, garnering multiple Oscar nominations. And most people think it ended there. It didn't . . .

After the trial Jerry paid a surprise visit to Larry. Falwell walked in holding up his hands and saying, "I surrender!" He had come to bury the hatchet. The two talked for an hour, and Falwell suggested that they do a series of debates together. Flynt accepted.

Held mostly on college campuses, the two sparred over the issue of free speech. And, over time, something started to change between them. They didn't enter auditoriums separately, as prize-fighters might. Falwell would push Larry's wheelchair for him.

Sure, they were always jabbing at each other, but a respect began to grow. Almost a liking. Flynt would joke that Jerry was his pastor. Falwell would fire right back: "And Larry is my most rebellious parishioner!" It got a big laugh from the audience.

On tour, they spent a lot of time together—that "costly signal" we discussed. And both the pornographer and the preacher realized that they were more similar than they had thought. Both were southern boys—one from Kentucky, the other from Virginia. Falwell's father had owned a nightclub and been a bootlegger. Flynt himself had owned a number of nightclubs in Ohio and been a bootlegger as well. They had waged war for over five years. Flynt said, "I disagreed with him on absolutely everything: gay rights, a woman's right to choose, everything. But after getting to know him, I realized he was sincere. He wasn't out to get a buck."

The two opposed everything the other stood for, tore each other apart in the media, and spent millions fighting a lawsuit that dragged on for half a decade. But eventually it came to pass that they had been *not-enemies* longer than they had been enemies. Over the ensuing years they changed each other's minds about, well . . . nothing. But they made time for each other. They went out of their way to see each other. Falwell would drop by whenever he was in California. When one was in need, the other was there. When Falwell struggled with health complications due to his obesity, Flynt recommended a diet that had worked for him. Every year they exchanged Christmas cards and pictures of their grandchildren.

On May 15, 2007, Jerry Falwell was discovered unconscious in his office and was raced to the hospital. Efforts to resuscitate him failed, and he died of cardiac arrythmia at age seventy-three. And on May 20 the *Los Angeles Times* posted an op-ed that was basically an obituary. It was written by none other than Larry Flynt.

He recounted their (literal) trials and tribulations. Their ups and downs. And he concluded it by saying:

> The ultimate result was one I never expected and was just as shocking a turn to me as was winning that famous Supreme Court case: We became friends.

If the pornographer and the preacher could look at each other and find "another self," I'd say there's hope for all of us. Time to round up everything we've learned and find out whether "a friend in need is a friend indeed" is actually true.

*

So what have we learned?

Empathy is when the line between you and another blurs. Closeness is when your vision of your "self" makes room for someone else to be in there too. And a true friend is "another self." A part of you. Aristotle said it first, and after procrastinating for a few millennia, science proved him right.

Friendship may be defined by mutual aid, but it's not transactional. We don't keep score with friends. Our brains tell us the story that friends are a part of us, and this is how we overcome the dictates of ruthless Darwinism and act altruistically, as Hector Cafferata did.

There is no formal institution that regulates friendship. This makes friendship fragile but pure. It's why friends make us happier than any other relationship—they're only there because you truly want them to be. But without a marriage certificate, a blood bond, or a contract to support it, we must be diligent in investing in and protecting our friendships to sustain them.

Dale Carnegie got the initial parts of meeting people right, but we must display the costly signals of time and vulnerability to forge and maintain true friendships that will last. Those with Williams syndrome show us what we must aspire to, a fearless open love that sees in others more good than danger.

And we will meet people who just ain't always so nice. In fact, we already have many of them in our lives. With low-level narcissists we can use the empathy prompts of similarity, vulnerability, and community to remind them of the warmth they lack, and that they so desperately need. Daniel Kahneman's mother knew that people are complex, and sometimes they just need an emotional nudge so that they stop trying to be special and start trying to be better.

And now that we know how friendship works, we're finally ready to address the big question: Is the maxim "a friend in need is a friend indeed" true? Well, as we learned at the end of the last section, there's some debate over what the phrase even means—but in that debate I think we actually learn a lot about friendship.

Two things are unclear in the maxim: (1) Who is the person in need? You or your friend? And (2), is the end of the sentence meant to be "in deed" or "indeed"? That gives us four contenders for the correct interpretation.

1. "A friend when you're in need is definitely a friend."
2. "A friend when you're in need will show it with their actions."
3. "A friend who is in need is definitely going to act like your friend."
4. "A friend who is in need is a friend in action."

And here's where things really get interesting. Scholars are agreed on what they believe the phrase was intended to mean. But when you survey the average Joe and Jane, they prefer a different interpretation. Which one do you think historians believe was the intended meaning and which one do you think the average person preferred? Ponder that for a second; I'll just sit here and hum the *Jeopardy* music.

Now number 4 doesn't even make much sense. That one's out. Number 3 might be true (and, wow, is that cynical), but neither group picked that one. Final answer? Academics believe that number 2 was the intended meaning of the phrase: *A friend when you're in need will show it with their actions.* But the average person preferred number 1: *A friend when you're in need is definitely a friend.*

So everyone's agreed that you're the one in need. But we're still unresolved on the "in deed" versus "indeed" debate. Forgive me if I'm splitting hairs, but we can separate the two by the emphasis between "deeds" versus just "being there." The "correct" one sounds slightly more transactional than the popular one: "What will you do for me?" versus "Be there for me." It's the same Darwin versus Aristotle debate. Number 2 is more rational like George Price's math. Number 1 is more like "another self." I don't think it's any surprise most people preferred the latter. We're just wired to prefer connection over calculating benefit when it comes to friends. We want "another self."

To give the historical version its due, it's warning us about fake friends who promise a lot and deliver little. It's saying "actions speak louder than words" or, in our new knowledge about friendship, "look for costly signals." Good advice, no doubt. We know the importance of time and vulnerability.

But I think we can learn a lot about human nature by the fact that most people didn't read it that way. What was the most common thing people said about friends in surveys? "A friend is there for you." And the popular interpretation of the maxim emphasizes the same. Costly signals are good, but I think people resisted the first notion because we just don't want to keep score. (And maybe the scholarly interpretation feels we need a bit of a reminder there because people do exploit us at times. Fair point.)

Roy Baumeister at Florida State University reports that studies unanimously show we judge the quality of our friendships based on "availability of support": *Are you there for me when I need you?* But as for "deeds," the concrete assistance people can provide, the research is mixed, sometimes even negative. Once someone is a friend, we don't want to think as much about deeds. We don't want to keep score. That gets transactional real fast. It's a slippery slope to ditching those who care but can offer the least and currying favor with those who can give the most but don't care at all.

We're much more focused on feelings and intentions. And those matter. Is there a difference between a fifty-dollar gift and a fifty-dollar bribe? Between murder and self-defense? Of course. But the difference isn't in the deed itself, it's in the intentions.

Now the cynical might wonder what would happen if all we think about is feelings and never get any concrete aid when we need it: we'd be screwed. No need to worry there. Society didn't get this big because people don't default to cooperation. As we saw, we're wired for help. And we're more likely to do it when the stakes are the highest. When friends are in need, we're more likely to help—even when it's not rational and even in the most unlikely of circumstances.

Would you lie for a friend? Let's raise the stakes: Would you lie to the *government* for a friend? Researchers asked thirty thousand people from over thirty countries if they would lie under oath to protect a pal. Was the propensity to help consistent around the world, all of us bound by a single version of human nature? Heck, no. Results varied widely by country. The data were all over the place. But then they found the pattern . . .

Anthropologist Daniel Hruschka, who led the study, sorted the data by whether the countries were fair, whether they were stable, whether they were corrupt. Plain and simple: where life was harder, people were more likely to put themselves at risk to protect their pal. Where friends were most in need, people were friends "indeed" and "in deed."

So what's the final verdict on the maxim? We're gonna go with: true . . . but with an asterisk, because we need to clear up that confusion about the interpretation. We gotta get rid of that clever rhyme and clarify the "in deed" versus "indeed" distinction. In the future, let's say:

"A friend who is there for you when you're in need is definitely a friend."

Far clunkier, I know, but I promised you science, not sound bites. And that does clarify what we all want. Be there for me when I need you. The world may be selfish and competitive, but you and I do not have to be. Maybe you can or can't help with "deeds," but I'm not just looking for transactional gain: most of all I'm looking for "another self" to help me shoulder the burden of life.

There's one key thing the maxim doesn't cover that I think is important to remember: friendship deserves a little more respect even when no one is in need. With no institutional backing, friendship gets no equivalent of a wedding anniversary, a family reunion, or a note of appreciation for ten years with the company. Friendship does the heavy lifting of happiness in our lives, so I'd say it deserves better. Time is critical, vulnerability is essential, but maybe something else we should remember is gratitude. Hug a friend today. We don't celebrate our friendships enough.

While writing this book, I was dealing with some friendship issues myself. Writing this section helped me, and I agree with the conclusions we have come to. (I would be even more vulnerable with my feelings here, but we both know it would make me more susceptible to witchcraft. That said, please rest assured I consider you a friend and would enjoy eating your intestines.) Oh, one more thing before we close out the section:

RIP, George Price. I hope we did you justice.

Okey-dokey. Now that we've plumbed the depths of friendship, it's time to raise the stakes again and dive even deeper into the mysteries of our crazy, crazy relationships. And what is crazier than love? Nothing I can think of. Now romance is a big, big, BIG subject, but we're going to focus on that perennial question about love: Does it conquer all?

Time to find out . . .

PART 3

DOES "LOVE CONQUER ALL"?

11

WARNING

You're going to hate me.

As you're already well aware, this is not your normal *feel-good-happy-happy-ignore-all-the-bad-stuff-tell-you-what-you-wanna-hear* relationship book. In following with that, you are not going to like everything you read in this section, and I just wanna warn you now.

The truth will set you free, but first it will piss you off. As evolutionary psychologist and relationship researcher David Buss said, "Some of what I discovered about human mating is not nice." And in your heart of hearts, you *know* that. The feeling of love is the best . . . but all the actual activities involved in loving, well, nobody denies that they often involve more than their share of unpleasantness.

Most books in this genre just tell you what you want to hear. Then you do what they say, it doesn't work—*and you blame yourself.* After a while you start to feel like maybe you're broken. Like you're the problem. And that's not fair. (And now I'm left to clean up that mess and be the fall guy. That's pretty unfair too.)

The NIH, the FDA, and Eric's mom all want it noted that you may have a truth seizure while reading this. I'm going to give you the best evidence we have. Some of it is gonna be like a whiskey sour, but without the whiskey. The answers may not all be to your liking at first, but we can't fix what we don't accurately understand.

Take pity on me, dear reader. This is a sensitive issue that people have strong feelings about, and delivering the cold facts is undoubtedly an exercise in masochism.

Rest assured, it's not all bad. Far, far from it. And in the end, I do promise you "magic." I promise you love and bliss—or at least the potential for it. But we have a challenging road ahead of us. So please finish the section before posting out-of-context quotes on Twitter, filling my inbox with ALL CAPS hate mail, and calling for this book to be taken out of stores.

There's no Build-A-Bear store for a happy marriage, but I promise you the next closest thing. And the most honest thing. I am the crazy man who is going to attempt to make sense of love in less time than it takes to binge a Netflix show. Wish me luck. Here goes . . .

*

In the mid-1990s, Pfizer was in bad shape. The drugmaker had a storied history as the leading manufacturer of penicillin during World War II, but at the close of the twentieth century it had been eclipsed by competitors and badly needed a hit drug.

Luckily, there was hope on the horizon. Pfizer's UK lab had developed an angina medication, Sildenafil Citrate, which had the curious side effect of giving men erections. Yes, this would become Viagra. And at the time there wasn't a single medication on the market approved to treat impotence. Not one. A drugmaker's dream, right? There was only one problem.

Nobody thought Viagra was a good idea.

As *Esquire* writer David Kushner recounts, "At the time, the idea of selling Viagra was considered crazy at best and immoral at worst." The drug would become a household name and launch the multibillion-dollar erectile dysfunction market, yet from day one, Pfizer's conservative culture resisted moving the project forward. It would be the most uphill battle drug development had ever seen.

The only reason the now-famous tumescent tonic ever made it to market was the strenuous effort of two unlikely heroes: Rooney Nelson, a young marketing guru from Jamaica, and "Dr. Sal," a clinical pharmacist from Queens. They knew that erectile dysfunction hurt marriages, crippled self-esteem, and prevented otherwise healthy couples from having children. These two renegades bucked the system and overcame staggering opposition to bring that little blue pill to the world.

The lab had shown that the drug worked, but would patients be okay with the side effects? Getting corporate approval for focus groups for a drug nobody supported would be difficult enough by itself. But Rooney and Sal needed approval for putting a patient in a room, *literally* showing him *Debbie Does Dallas* and encouraging him to masturbate. Somehow the two managed to get the company to assent. The most common side effect turned out to be four-hour erections . . . which most subjects thought was kinda cool, frankly. The first hurdle had been cleared. They had patients on their side.

But internally Pfizer still saw this as "undignified medicine" and wouldn't budge. The company argued that men would be too embarrassed to ask for it. No man wanted to look weak and say he was "impotent." But Rooney knew this wasn't a real problem, it was just a semantic one. And that's how the term *erectile dysfunction* was born. No, that phrase isn't a medical diagnosis that has been around forever. It's a clinical-sounding euphemism born in the 1990s from marketing, not medicine.

Half of Pfizer still felt the "trivial medication" would never launch. But Rooney and Sal knew if they could just overcome internal Pfizer resistance, people would finally come to their senses and realize this was a license to print money . . . right? Wrong. Dr. Sal discovered they were going to meet at least as much external resistance as internal. Religious leaders of all stripes said they would protest. Conservative legislators did not want insurance companies subsidizing boners. It was a nightmare. The two felt that the world was against them.

But Rooney had a plan. He realized they were going to have to do something stone-cold crazy, the equivalent of marketing heresy, to get this product out the door. He came to the conclusion that the best way to launch Viagra was, unbelievably, to talk about it as little as humanly possible. Yes, zillions had been spent on development and testing, and now they weren't going to do anything in advance of FDA approval to promote it. It was insane, but it was the only way to avoid the resistance. And it worked.

In March 1998 Viagra received FDA approval. And with that, momentum was finally on their side. All they had to do was talk to Pfizer's sales team about how to pitch the drug . . . but the salespeople didn't want to do it. They said they felt awkward talking with doctors about penises. And that's how Rooney ended up at a sales conference, leading groups of people to say "erection" out loud five times to make them comfortable with it: *Erection! Erection! Erection! Erection! Erection!*

As launch day approached, almost everyone thought Pfizer would be a laughingstock. But you already know how this story ends. Viagra was an unprecedented success, a cultural phenomenon, and a comedic gift to late-night talk show hosts everywhere. Soon pharmacists said that they were filling ten thousand prescriptions a day. It outdid the release of Prozac. Within days, Pfizer's share price doubled.

The medication may have been blue, but it ended up being more like Rudolph's red nose: nobody liked it until it saved them all. The drug that no one believed in became the drug everyone wanted.

When it comes to sex, love, and marriage, everything is complicated and nothing is obvious, simple, or easy. The little blue pill certainly conquered all, but can love? On average, Viagra lasts two hours. How long does love last?

*

Around 38 B.C. the Roman poet Virgil wrote, "omnia vincit amor," or "love conquers all." You can find similar wording in the Bible. 1 Corinthians 13:7 reads, "Love bears all things, believes all things, hopes all things, endures all things." And we still hear versions of the maxim to this day in songs and movies and at wedding ceremonies. But is it true? Does love really conquer all?

Of course not. (So far, this is looking to be a very short chapter.) I'm all for poetic license, but have you *seen* any divorce statistics lately? I'll save you the Google search: roughly 40 percent of US marriages end in divorce. The proverbial seven-year-itch is more like four; divorce is most common about four years after the wedding. And that stat is true around the world. (In fact, anthropologist Helen Fisher notes that one in ten US women have been married three or more times by the time they turn forty.)

I'm not trying to be a downer here, but if cars crashed 40 percent of the time you drove them and your marketing slogan was "Honda Conquers All," you'd have a class action lawsuit on your hands. Just like Pfizer initially got it wrong with Viagra, we have a lot of myths and misunderstandings about love. For one thing, it didn't originate with courtly love in the Middle Ages. Romantic love has been around forever. The earliest love poetry dates back over 3,500 years in Egypt. And love is universal. Of 168 cultures studied by anthropologists, 90 percent recognize it, and in the other 10 percent there weren't enough data to confirm it.

The experience of love is largely consistent no matter which country, age, gender, orientation, or ethnic group you study. It's almost certainly innate, and we know this because throughout history many cultures (including the Shakers, Mormons, and East Germans) attempted to suppress romantic love—and all failed spectacularly.

That said, the details can certainly vary. In a Jacksonville, Florida, survey, 60 percent of people said their spouse was their best friend. You know how many said the same thing in Mexico City? Zero. And cultures that romantically kiss are actually in the minority: only 46 percent of the 168 studied smooch. And love is not always associated with the heart. In West Africa the seat of love is the nose, and for Trobriand islanders it's the intestines. (This calls for some serious reinterpretation of sneezing and indigestion metaphors.)

The form that long-term love usually takes for us is marriage, and that leads us to the Big Kahuna of myths we need to contend with. We've all read a thousand articles that say marriage makes you healthier and happier. Umm, no. Many of these studies merely survey married people and single people, compare the happiness levels, find that the married people are doing better, and crow, "See? Marriage makes you healthy and happy." But that's committing an error called "survivor bias." If you want to determine if *getting* married makes you happier, you need to include separated, divorced, and widowed people in with the *currently* married, not with the unmarried. Otherwise, it's equivalent to studying only blockbuster movie stars and saying, "Becoming an actor is obviously an excellent career choice."

When you examine the set of all people who have ever walked down the aisle versus people who never have, the health and happiness results are very different. Simply put: *marriage doesn't make you healthy and happy; a good marriage makes you healthy and happy.* And a bad marriage, even one in the past, can have very (or very very very) negative effects.

What effects does marriage have on health? Well, if you're a winner on the connubial game show, the positives are plentiful. Metrics for heart attacks, cancer, dementia, illness, blood pressure, or even straight-up likelihood of dying all improve. (Today's married men enjoy an average seven-year boost in life expectancy.) But here's where I need to include that nasty word *however.* If you're unhappily married, your health is likely to be notably worse than if you never got hitched at all. A bad marriage makes you 35 percent more likely to fall ill and lops four years off your life. A study of almost nine thousand people found divorced and widowed people had 20 percent more health problems (including heart disease and cancer). And most surprisingly, some of those effects never went away, even if they remarried. Folks on marriage number two had 12 percent more serious health issues than those who never split up, and divorced women were 60 percent more likely to have cardiovascular disease, even if they took another walk down the aisle.

So what about happiness? If you've got a good marriage, getting hitched definitely provides a boost. A 2010 study from Australia even said previous research probably *underestimated* just how happy people in happy marriages are. But the flip side is even more damning than you may have guessed. A study of the medical records of five thousand patients analyzed the most stressful life events people deal with. Divorce came in at #2. (Death of a spouse was number one.) Divorce even beat *going to prison.*

Hold on, it gets worse. Human beings are pretty resilient. With almost all bad things that happen, your happiness levels eventually return to baseline. But not with divorce. An eighteen-year study of thirty thousand people showed that after a marriage goes splitsville, levels of subjective well-being rebound—but not completely. It seems divorce puts a permanent dent in your happiness. And when you look at everyone across the marital spectrum, nobody is more despondent than the unhappily married. If you're going to be lonely, it's better to do it alone.

So marriage is no guarantee of health or happiness; it's more like gambling: big wins or big losses. And, extending the gambling analogy, the odds are not fifty-fifty. As *New York Times* columnist David Brooks wrote, "In the United States, nearly 40 percent of marriages end in divorce. Another 10 or 15 percent of couples separate and do not divorce, and another 7 percent or so stay together but are chronically unhappy." No matter how you slice it, this is no guarantee. It's a minority of people who are happily married and stay that way.

What gives? This is definitely not what society tells us about love and marriage. And how did we get to this place of extremes where marriage either makes you blissfully happy or utterly destroys your life? Was it always like this?

Nope. Marriage *did* once conquer all . . . but back then it had nothing to do with love. In fact, historically speaking, you could say "love ruined marriage." Or "love overcame marriage." As historian Stephanie Coontz notes, for most of recorded history the theme song of marriage could have been Tina Turner's "What's Love Got to Do with It?" (Author's note: I do not recommend playing that song, or U2's "I Still Haven't Found What I'm Looking For," at your wedding.)

For the vast majority of recorded history, marriage had more to do with economics than love. This wasn't part of some evil plan; it was due to the fact that life was really frickin' hard. "Love marriages" were not a realistic option. The model was more like the help-me-not-die marriage. Life was often nasty, brutish, and short. You couldn't make it on your own. Personal fulfillment took a back seat to putting food in your mouth and fighting off brigands. Coontz notes that marriage did what governments and markets do today. It was social security, unemployment insurance, and Medicare before there was such a thing. Just like your career today might be more about paying the bills and have little to do with what you're passionate about, back then who you married was about paying the bills and had little to do with *who* you were passionate about. Marriage was a lot more like workmates than soulmates.

For the rich, the history of marriage is like an MBA class in mergers and acquisitions. It was less about finding the right spouse and more about getting the right in-laws. Yes, today you complain about in-laws, but back then it was actually the reason you married. Think about it: you don't need matrimony to fall in love or make babies, but you *do* need it to forge long-term alliances with powerful families. In fact, in-laws were such a priority that in some countries like China you even saw "ghost marriages." Yes, marrying a dead person. (Upside: fewer arguments.) In the Bella Coola society of the Pacific Northwest, sometimes the competition to get the right in-laws was so intense that people would get married to another family's dog. Yes, really.

Of course, married people back then did fall in love . . . it just wasn't usually with their spouse. After all, that's what affairs were for. As Alexandre Dumas quipped, "The bonds of wedlock are so heavy that it takes two to carry them, sometimes three." Loving your spouse was often regarded as impossible, immoral, or stupid. The great Stoic philosopher Seneca said, "Nothing is more impure than to love one's wife as if she were a mistress." And what did Roman philosophers call someone in the passionate throes of love with his wife? "An adulterer."

More important, Coontz notes that love within marriage was seen as a threat to the social order. Life was too difficult for individual happiness to be very high on the totem pole. You had to put your responsibility to family, state, religion, or community before personal fulfillment. Marriage was too important an economic and political institution to be left up to the whims of love. *Passion? You better keep a lid on that stuff. It gets in the way. We got a good thing here; you wanna turn it into an episode of Jerry Springer?* In polygamous cultures it was acceptable to love your wife—but save it for wife number two or three, okay? We have a society to run here. Thanks.

But then things changed. The 1700s arrived and you had the Enlightenment era. People started talking about these wild new things called "human rights." It wasn't that everybody suddenly wised up or became nice; again, it was economics. Free markets. People were making more coin, and you could survive on your own. Individualism became a realistic option, so by the 1800s many people were marrying for love . . .

And, almost immediately, things kinda went to hell. Yes, individuals gained more choice and the wonderful possibility of love and happiness, but as for conquering all, marriage got a lot less stable. The same thing that increased people's satisfaction with marriage made it fragile. They had to create the word *dating* in the 1890s because the concept didn't even exist before then. The formerly rock-solid institution of marriage was under siege. And by the early twentieth century the wheels were about to pop off. There was a breathtaking level of change going on: electricity, cars, trains, antibiotics. Between 1880 and 1920 the US divorce rate doubled.

But then World War II happened. In its wake, life in the United States got pretty good economically, and so marriage was pretty good. Employment went up and divorce rates dropped. And in the 1950s you had the apex of what many today still consider the "traditional" marriage: the nuclear family. Think *Donna Reed*, *Leave it to Beaver*, and *Father Knows Best*. Mom, Dad, 2.4 kids, and a dog. Everything was swell. But, ironically, this era that many today still consider the platonic form of marriage was actually just a blip. Far from the rule, historians Steven Mintz and Susan Kellogg call it "the great exception." And it sure didn't last long.

By the 1970s that "traditional" marriage was already coming apart. States passed no-fault divorce. For the first time, just being unhappy was a legally acceptable reason to end your marriage. By 1980 the US divorce rate hit 50 percent. The centuries-long shift was nearly complete. The unmarried were no longer seen as broken or immoral. The number of cohabiting couples skyrocketed. Pregnancy no longer meant that you needed to get married. And in 2015 the Supreme Court approved same-sex marriage. Love had triumphed.

Heck, it not only won, but for the first time in history it was *essential*. And we forget just how new a concept that is. Daniel Hruschka notes that in the 1960s, a third of men and three-quarters of women didn't think love was essential before getting married. By the 1990s, 86 percent of men and 91 percent of women said they wouldn't marry unless they were in love. Over the centuries, the song went from Tina Turner's "What's Love Got to Do with It?" to the Beatles' "All You Need Is Love."

But that doesn't mean there's no downside to all this freedom.

Northwestern professor Eli Finkel calls our modern paradigm "the self-expressive marriage." The definition of marriage is up to you . . . which is kinda terrifying. Do you know *exactly* what you want? You better. Marriage is no longer defined by church, government, family, or society. It's a DIY kit. Instruction manual sold separately. Marriages of the past were definitely unfair and unequal in many ways, but the rules were clear. Today we're confused.

And if that wasn't difficult enough, our expectations for marriage have gone through the roof. We still want many things marriage provided in the past, but now we think wedlock should fulfill all our dreams, bring out our best selves, and offer continuous growth. The Rolling Stones' "You Can't Always Get What You Want" is not on the playlist. We don't just divorce because we're unhappy but because we could be *even happier.* Finkel says that before, you had to justify leaving your spouse; now, you have to justify staying. And while our expectations of marriage have gone up, our ability to meet them has gone down. Couples are working longer hours and spending less time together. Between 1975 and 2003 the amount of time spouses spent together on weekdays plunged by 30 percent if they didn't have kids and 40 percent if they did.

And at the same time, marriage has crowded out other relationships that might reduce its burden. Research by Robin Dunbar at Oxford shows that falling in love costs you two close friends. And Finkel points out that in 1975 Americans spent two hours every weekend day with friends or relatives. By 2003 that number had dropped 40 percent. Meanwhile, between 1980 and 2000 the degree to which a happy marriage predicted personal happiness almost doubled. Marriage isn't one of your relationships, it's <u>the</u> relationship. We're experiencing the spousification of life.

With each of the past few decades, marriage stability has been increasing, and divorce rates are down. Problem is, that's mostly because fewer people are getting married at all. Marriage rates are down globally since the 1970s, and they're currently at historic lows for the United States. NYU sociologist Eric Klinenberg writes, "For the first time in history, the typical American now spends more years single than married." Marriage has gone from being a cornerstone to a capstone. It used to be something you did while young and on the path to adulthood. Now its demands seem so onerous that people want to make sure they have all their ducks in a row before attempting it—if they choose to walk down the aisle at all.

No, yelling at me won't make any of this less true. I understand if you're a bit frustrated now that I've spent pages sowing depressing marriage factoids across the land like some sort of statistical Johnny Appleseed. I put that warning at the beginning of the chapter for a reason. If you're about to write a one-star Amazon review, stand down. No need to go to Defcon 1. I do have good news. Very good news, in fact. Yes, the average marriage has been getting worse year after year without much hope, but there's something you should know about the *best* marriages right now . . .

They are better than any in the history of humanity. Period.

Finkel confirms it: "The best marriages today are better than the best marriages of earlier eras; indeed, they are the best marriages that the world has ever known." Divorce may put a permanent dent in your happiness and the average marriage may be pretty disappointing, but if you do this married thing right, your marriage will be happier than anybody's at any time ever. You will rule. So it's not doom and gloom for everyone—it's winner takes all. And that's why Finkel calls wedlock in our era "the all or nothing marriage."

I'm sorry if I demolished your fairy-tale visions. But fairy tales don't help. A 2011 Marist poll concluded 73 percent of Americans believe in soulmates, and a 2000 study found that 78 percent of people's vision of love contain fairy-tale elements. But what researchers also realized was that people who believe in those things actually experience more disillusionment and angst in their marriages than those who were more grounded. Why?

Fairy tales are passive. And these days happy marriages take proactive work. But if you do the work, you can have one of those greatest-marriages-ever. To quote Finkel, "Relative to marriages in earlier eras, marriages today require much greater dedication and nurturance, a change that has placed an ever-larger proportion of marriages at risk of stagnation and dissolution. But spouses who invest the requisite time and energy in the relationship can achieve a level of conjugal fulfillment that would have been out of reach in earlier eras."

So if you're struggling at love these days, you're not crazy and you're not alone and it's not necessarily your fault. We now know love, as a general rule, doesn't conquer all. But *your* love can if you do it right. So we're going to tweak the maxim. Instead of "Does love conquer all?" we're going to solve the mystery of "How can we make sure *your* love conquers all?"

And we'll start down the road to solving that puzzle by looking at the greatest lover who ever lived . . .

12

If you have to read some history and you don't like to read history, read about Casanova. Seriously, this guy's life was more exciting than most summer movies. Espionage, scandals, high-stakes gambling, assassins, duels to the death, secret societies, betrayal, con artistry, exile. He escaped an inescapable prison and did it *by gondola*, no less. Casanova hung out with King George III, Catherine the Great, Goethe, Rousseau, and multiple popes. He toured scientific conferences with Ben Franklin and traded barbs with Voltaire. Oh, and of course, he did that which he is most famous for: seduction after seduction after seduction. In his autobiography he writes, "I can say I have lived." Now there's the understatement of the millennium.

You just cannot imagine how much this guy did, how much trouble he got into, and how many countries he visited, people he scammed, and women he slept with. I'd like to summarize his life for you and do it justice but I can't. Literally *cannot*. His autobiography is twelve volumes totaling 3,700 pages—and he even left out the stuff that he thought was "too scandalous."

He was a scoundrel who existed on wit, fearlessness, and charm. Casanova's life followed a consistent pattern: Befriend powerful people. Start a new career. Get a wealthy patron. Gamble and chase women. Drive everyone crazy, including the authorities. Be thrown in prison or exiled. Move to new city. *Repeat.*

He had a "lust for life." Okay, he lusted for a lot more than life, frankly. And didn't show a whole lot of remorse, either. He callously went from woman to woman, getting involved in sordid tales that make Pornhub seem tame, but we're gonna keep it PG-13 here. Safe to say he was the platonic form of the "bad boy," a patron saint to pickup artists, bouncing from girl to girl to girl . . .

But there was one woman who was special. One who stood out. (There always is, isn't there?)

One woman captured and broke the heart of the great Casanova. We know her only as "Henriette." Her true background is shrouded in mystery. Of course, she was beautiful. But it was how cultured she was that blew him away. She was witty and sophisticated, and it was clear she was slumming by even being with him. A libertine herself, she was so savvy that he assumed she, too, was a grifter. Henriette was every bit his equal in charm and seduction—something Casanova was not accustomed to, to say the least.

His was one of the most epically exciting lives in all of history, yet he would say their time together were his happiest moments and the most obsessive love affair of his life. And, even if only briefly, she changed the callous rogue. This legendary charmer of women, the man whose name would be synonymous with seduction, was transformed into the average Joe head over heels for a girl. He obsessed over her. Dreamt about her at night. He even feared he might just be another one of *her* affairs. And like anyone madly in love, he idealized her.

Being around her softened him. Yeah, he was a rogue, but not a psychopath. It's easy to judge him, but his early life had been far from easy. His father had died when he was just eight. His mother was an actress and prostitute who left him to be raised by his grandmother. Eventually he was abandoned to grow up in a boarding home. "They got rid of me," he would write. You'd be callous too.

Casanova and Henriette's three months together had all the

makings of an epic romance. They were both fugitives on the run. He was fleeing the Venetian authorities, and she was hiding from her controlling family. She was broke, having nothing but the clothes on her back. And they were men's clothes to boot. But Casanova was flush. He impulsively bought her a new wardrobe. And a diamond ring.

Their pursuers were not far behind. It would have been smart to just lie low and hide out. But Casanova was a man in love with a beautiful woman. He wanted them to have fun. He wanted to show her the world and give her everything. And so they threw caution to the wind and lived it up in the city.

But their careless nights on the town would be their downfall. At a lavish party at the Ducal Palace, Henriette was spotted by a relative who confronted her. Casanova blamed himself. Henriette was convinced she would have to return. In their luxurious hotel room in Geneva, she told him they would have to split up. She asked him to never inquire about her and if they saw each other again, he must pretend not to know her. And she left.

Casanova spent the two saddest days of his life in that hotel room alone. When he finally got up and opened the drapes, he saw words scratched into the glass of the window. Words scratched with the diamond ring he had bought her. *Tu oublieras aussi Henriette.*

Translation: "You will forget Henriette too."

A sad message, for sure. But just seeing something from her was, as he would write, "a balm to my soul." And not long after, he did receive a letter from her. Henriette was heartbroken, too, but resigned to her fate. She would never have another love, but she wished for him to find another Henriette. Casanova stayed in bed for days with the letter, unable to eat or sleep.

A dozen years would pass. There were more adventures, but

now an older man, Casanova was getting tired. Arrested for debts in Switzerland, he had to flee yet again. He questioned his life and came to the conclusion that he should become a monk. That he should retire to a monastery and live a life of . . . Then he saw a pretty girl. The monk idea lasted about a day. (Look, he's Casanova. What did you expect?)

But this, too, was another lesson. He was who he was. The rogue. Nothing had changed. Nothing would change. He returned to Geneva. There would always be another city. Another adventure. Another girl. He entered his fancy hotel room, thinking that maybe Henriette, too, was just another tryst. Nothing special. And as he parted the drapes to the window . . .

He realized this was the *same* hotel room from all those years ago. There on the glass, the words were still scratched: *Tu oublieras aussi Henriette.* As he would write in his memoir, "I felt my hair stand on end." The memories flooded back.

"You will forget Henriette too."

No. No, he wouldn't. Yes, there would be more adventures, more women. But for the rest of his life, he would never forget Henriette. To the great Casanova, the seducer of so many, she would always be The One. The only one.

The insanity of romantic love renders us all helpless. But what is this thing? And can it last like it did for Casanova?

*

When a prisoner is on death row, you might expect their last words to be something about God or forgiveness. And a survey shows, 30 percent of the time, that is what they say. But the thing they're most likely to mention, a whopping 63 percent of the time, is romantic love. Family is a distant second.

Romantic love may be the best thing in the world. But you don't need me to tell you that. Its power goes without saying . . . but I'll say it anyway. The world is infused with magic, and your mind is like someone emptied the kitchen junk drawer onto a trampoline. There's a reason so much of art and music is about romance. In Dorothy Tennov's classic study of infatuation, 83 percent of subjects agreed with the statement "anyone who has never been in love is missing one of life's most pleasurable experiences."

But truth be told, we all know it's a mixed bag. We're always up and down. It's both pleasure and pain. Agony and ecstasy. Delight and despair. Dr. Frank Tallis writes, "Love seems to provide a shuttle service that operates between only two destinations: heaven and hell."

And that's the side of love we don't discuss quite as much: *love can be awful*. A massive multidimensional quantum dumpster fire. *Passion* derives from the Latin word meaning "to suffer." While Tennov's subjects almost unanimously agreed about the pleasures of love, over 50 percent also described horrible depression and a quarter mentioned suicidal thoughts. Love can be almost too powerful a force. Like nuclear energy, it can power an entire city but also annihilate one—and leave lasting radiation.

In the 1980s, researcher Shere Hite found that two-thirds of married women and half of unmarried women no longer trusted being in love. This attitude might be unromantic, but it's far from unprecedented. As we discussed above, the ancients didn't trust love at all. It's ironic that when we think of classic love stories, we have positive feelings, considering that most tales of courtly love end in misery and death. (Would you say *Romeo and Juliet* had a happy ending?)

In fact, the ancients didn't see love merely as bad, they saw it as an *illness*. Remember how love was mentioned in old Egyptian poems? Yeah, those verses were describing it as a malady. We still have a fondness for the work of Jane Austen, like *Sense and Sensibility*, but in her time sensibility didn't mean "reasonable." It meant neurotic. Somebody with too much sensibility was prone to mental health issues.

For most of history, from Hippocrates until the 1700s, being "lovesick" was not a metaphor, *it was a legitimate diagnosis*. This dropped off in the eighteenth century and lost all currency in the nineteenth as the father of psychoanalysis and cocaine afficionado Sigmund Freud turned the conversation to sex. But his attitude toward love wasn't much different: "Isn't what we mean by 'falling in love' a kind of sickness and craziness, an illusion, a blindness to what the loved person is really like?" And the idea of love as a malady is still with us. When you're down about love, what do we call it? "Lovesick." What kind of a romantic is someone? "Incurable."

Your mood is elevated. You barely need to sleep. Self-esteem skyrockets. Thoughts are racing. You're talkative. Distracted. Socially and sexually you're more active. You're willing to take big risks, spend more money, and embarrass yourself. Does that sound like love? Well, actually I was giving you the DSM-V criteria for a diagnosis of mania. Yes, modern science basically agrees that love is a mental illness. Psychiatrist Frank Tallis says if you felt all those symptoms above for a week and told a psychiatrist about it (and didn't mention romance), you might very well walk away with a prescription for lithium. In fact, you'd only need four of those symptoms to qualify.

Or are you feeling sad? Lost interest in things you usually enjoy doing? No appetite? Trouble sleeping? Tired? Can't concentrate? Yeah, that's being lovesick. But if you have five of those six, you'd also qualify for "major depressive episode" under DSM criteria. Feeling both sets of symptoms? Sounds like love to me. It's also indistinguishable from bipolar disorder. And Tallis, a psychiatrist, says love actually *is* often misdiagnosed by those in the mental health profession.

Making a case for love as a serious medical illness is far easier than you might guess. Let's not forget how many people kill themselves or others over love. Oddly, though, we don't take love seriously as a malady and generally see it as something not only benign but widely recommended and endorsed.

If we get really scientific, which mental disorder does love best resemble? OCD, actually. You're obsessed. You can't control your attention and turn it toward your responsibilities. Anthropologist Helen Fisher reports people newly in love spend up to 85 percent of their waking hours thinking about that special someone. Not only does love meet the criteria for OCD, but the neuroscience data match. Look at a brain in love or an OCD brain in an MRI, and it's hard to tell the difference. The anterior cingulate cortex, caudate nucleus, putamen, and insula are all working overtime. Psychiatrist Donatella Marazziti took blood from people in love and people with OCD and found both had serotonin levels 40 percent lower than controls. What happens when you test the love group again, months later when the craziness of romance has died down? Serotonin levels are normal again. (Scientist drops mic.)

But why would evolution want to give us OCD over someone? What's the single best framing for the symptoms and behavior of love? Obsession is close, but looking at all the data, the best metaphor is *addiction*. We're not washing our hands until they bleed as a semi-arbitrary ritual; we're in pursuit of something we crave. Ever said, "I can't get enough of you"? Exactly. High highs and very low lows. Get your fix from a text and you're good for a while, but soon your junkie soul will need more texts with even more emojis.

Research shows that the love cocktail of phenylethylamine, dopamine, norepinephrine, and oxytocin flowing through your love-addled brain provides a high similar to that of amphetamines. And MRI data support the addiction paradigm as well. Juxtapose an fMRI brain scan of someone in love with someone injected with cocaine or morphine, and you see the same pattern. Our old friend Arthur Aron says love is a motivation system. Just like addicts will do anything to get their drug, it's that same system that tells us go get that special someone.

Here we are once again. Yes, I just took the thing most people regard to be the most wonderful part of life and said, "No, it's like black tar heroin and we're all just a bunch of mentally ill junkies." I don't blame you if you're thinking, "Barker, I have enjoyed decades of blissful ignorance of these facts and I have no intention of leaving that state today." I get it. So before everyone reading this book has a collective nervous breakdown, let me give you the much-needed good news.

There's an excellent reason for all the crazy. First (but not necessarily foremost), yeah, evolution wants us to make more humans. That's priority number one for our genes. We procrastinate about lots of stuff, but evolution will have no trucking with that nonsense. Reproduction is job one, and it flips the logic override switch, saying, "Let me take the wheel; this stuff is important." As famed playwright W. Somerset Maugham said, "Love is only the dirty trick played on us to achieve continuation of the species."

Evolutionary psychologists are not known to be romantics, but just because love achieves evolution's goals doesn't mean it can't also achieve ours. As with friendship, our brains work with the selfishness of Darwinism to find not only material benefit but also joy and fulfillment. We delude ourselves that friends are part of us and that the crazy makes life worth living. In fact, our heads are rife with positive biases to counter the ever-present difficulties of the world. You know what psychologists call those optimistic delusions? "Healthy." Studies have shown people who lack those biases are definitely better at seeing the world accurately. You know what psychologists call those people? "Depressed."

In the short term, not trusting seems like the smart defensive move. It's often more prudent to do less versus more. We can be lazy and don't always do what's good for us. But just like reproduction being job one for evolution, connection is pretty much job one for us as individuals. And so nature forces our hand by making us, well, a bit nuts. Addicts. A motivational drive to reach for more and do more than makes sense because just as hunger ensures we don't starve from lack of food, the cravings of love make sure we don't starve emotionally in an often harsh world. We need the crazy to push us to live a good life.

Some will counter: "Yeah, we need motivation, but why do we need to go nuts? That doesn't help." Actually, it does. In fact, the science shows that being goo-goo gaga out of your mind with love is nothing less than essential. We've talked about how painful and scary love can be for you but jeez, get over yourself for a second. You're not the only one who is scared here. What about that person you're crushing on? They could get hurt too. What if you're Casanova, but they're not Henriette? You think they want their heart broken? So we have a trust problem. A communication problem. In other words, a *signaling* problem. Remember when we discussed that in the friendship section?

So what's the solution? "Costly signals." And guess what? Running around like a delusional junkie, endlessly professing your love, acting like a maniac, and throwing caution to the wind as you ignore work, forget to pay the bills, and text your obsession three hundred times a day—that's a pretty clear and costly signal. What do people being wooed often say? "Show me you're crazy about me." Bingo. Romantic love not only overrides rationality but also *signals* the overriding of rationality.

As Donald Yates said, "People who are sensible about love are incapable of it." Irrational loyalty is the only kind that matters. If my loyalty stops when the cost-benefit analysis for me goes south, that's not loyalty, it's selfishness. Loyalty is willingness to over-pay. Acting crazy in love is signaling to the other person you're no longer acting out of selfishness; in fact, you're incapable of that: *you can trust me because I'm nuts.*

And at the gut level we know this. We routinely use madness as an indicator of love's depth. We don't want romantic love to be rational, and we're skeptical of rationality in it. Practical and sensible is unromantic. Impractical and wasteful isn't very sensible but makes the heart sing. Paying someone's rent is not romantic. But roses, which die and have no long-term value, are. Diamonds are absurdly expensive rocks and have little resale value—*extremely* romantic. Why pay a lot of good money for flowers or stones that have little practical use and no long-term value? Because it signals you are crazy. The irrationality of love is, ironically, exceedingly rational.

And this isn't just theory. If you lived in a culture that allowed you to easily ditch one person and replace them, would you expect the insanity of love (and its signaling power) to go up or down? Obviously, up. People would be less trusting, and the Cupid parts of your brain would know they'd need to boost the crazy to send a costly signal. And that's what the study "Passion, Relational Mobility, and Proof of Commitment" found. In cultures where it's easier to date and ghost, passionate signals were more intense. The crazy is vital.

And that's not the only upside to love's insanity. Why do we get so crazy jealous when in love? Because, yet again, that crazy is (within reason) a good thing. Research shows the purpose of jealousy is to protect the relationship. Eugene Mathes of Western Illinois University gave unmarried couples a jealousy test and then circled back seven years later. Three-quarters of them had broken up, while the other quarter got married. Guess which group had the higher jealousy score? Exactly. We feel crazy jealous, even when we don't want to, because a touch of jealousy can motivate couples to maintain the relationship.

And then we have the most important, the most vital, and the most wonderful form of crazy that love brings: idealization. As we all know, people in love idealize their partners. It's one of the most recognized hallmarks of love. A 1999 study showed that people in happy relationships spend five times as long talking about their sweetheart's good qualities as bad. As Robert Seidenberg said, "Love is a human religion in which another person is believed in."

You've listened to friends idealize a new partner, and they sound utterly crazy. But guess what? You *better* be crazy. That idealization isn't just sweet: it also predicts the future better than a crystal ball. "Results of concurrent analyses revealed that relationship illusions predicted greater satisfaction, love, and trust, and less conflict and ambivalence in both dating and marital relationships." Realism may be accurate, but it's our illusions that foretell our happiness in love. And the more crazy, the better. People who idealized their partner the most felt no decline in relationship satisfaction over a study of the first three years of marriage.

It may sound like I'm recommending that we just disconnect from reality, but that's not actually how it works. We can see reality *and* be biased at the same time. When researchers ask people in the throes of infatuation about their partner's downsides, they can recognize and identify the bad stuff. They're not crazy *crazy*. But they emotionally discount the negative: it's not a big deal. Or those flaws are even "charming." This attitude helps grease the wheels of a relationship. We're just more accommodating when our lovestruck brains dial down our reactions to our loved one's flaws.

But the benefits of crazy idealization don't stop there. It even prevents cheating at the neuroscience level. If you show photos of good-looking people to men and women in relationships, they'll acknowledge those folks are good-looking. At a later date, you show them the same photos, but now you say the beautiful person is attracted to them. Guess what? Now they're less likely to say the person is beautiful. This effect has been replicated time and time again. It's called "derogation of alternatives." When people are in love, their brain actually dials down how attractive it sees other people who might threaten the relationship. So when the Ghosts of Hotness Past come around, idealization has your back and makes sure those cute exes aren't as cute in the eyes of your partner.

Remember the people with HSAM, the ones who had a perfect memory for personal events? And how it screwed up their romantic relationships? Well, a study validated this. Lovers who misremembered their histories in a positive way were less likely to split up than people with more accurate recollections. The facts don't matter as much as the story we tell ourselves when it comes to happiness. We need the crazy. Love is blind—and should be.

Needless to say, when idealization is not there, bad things happen. If you're about to walk down the aisle, you better be feeling the crazy. Women who have second thoughts before they say "I do" are two and half times more likely to be divorced in four years. For men it's more than a 50 percent increase.

Plain and simple, idealization seems to be the "magic" that's central to sustaining love. A 2010 study found that "positive illusion" was the single best predictor of holding on to those butterflies in our stomach about someone. But can it "conquer all"? Can it last? Yes. And I don't mean people just respond to surveys saying, "Oh yeah, we love each other a whole bunch." You'd expect people to say that, knee-jerk style. But in 2012 social neuroscientist Bianca Acevedo did fMRI brain scans on couples who were married an average of over twenty years. When she showed them pictures of their spouse, some of them did show the same neural responses you see in people who were newly in love. And get this: not only can it last, it can get *even better*. Not only did these couples show the neural signature associated with having the hots for each other, it actually lacked the anxiety we find in new love. All the good crazy without the bad crazy. Yes, it can last . . .

But it usually doesn't. Those couples are the exception. Most of the time romantic love drops off after a year to a year and a half. You see this in the fMRI studies, the serotonin blood tests, and survey data. The addicts become habituated to the drug, and the high wears off. Logically, it's understandable. Everyone can't run around like lovestruck maniacs forever. Your head would explode, and the world would burn down. As Irish playwright George Bernard Shaw said, "When two people are under the influence of the most violent, most insane, most delusive, and most transient of passions, they are required to swear that they will remain in that excited, abnormal, and exhausting condition continuously until death do them part." It's pretty unrealistic that the highest of highs can last forever for everyone.

Much like the physical universe, love is also subject to entropy. Energy dies down. The frenzy regresses to the mean. Romance stories don't discuss this part; comedians do. On the one hand, it's good to know this. You're not necessarily doing anything wrong. A fading of emotions is normal. But it's still distressing. What did a study of almost 1,100 people in long-term relationships show was the biggest threat to the union? "Fading away enthusiasm."

After the first four years of marriage, satisfaction drops an average of 15–20 percent. (Imagine your salary doing that.) How personally happy are most people two years after getting married? Richard Lucas at Michigan State University found that they're about as happy as they were before getting married. Regression to the mean. Entropy. You've probably heard reports of studies showing cohabiting couples are more likely to divorce. One reason for this is believed to be that they burn through the period of crazy love before settling down to get married. By the time they tie the knot, entropy has already kicked in.

This decline doesn't necessarily spell utter doom. Most couples shift from the crazy of romantic passion to what is known as "companionate love"—a more relaxed, durable feeling of comfort without the fireworks. But idealization fades. A 2001 study found that "idealistic distortion" was cut in half as couples transitioned from engagement to marriage. It's the rise of love's mortal enemy: reality.

This is best demonstrated by sociologist Diane Felmlee's research on what she calls "fatal attractions." Those traits that initially attracted us to our partners often shift in our minds to be seen as negatives. Laid-back becomes lazy. Strong becomes stubborn. Caring becomes clingy. Nearly half of couples surveyed experienced this. As idealization drops, it's hardly surprising that after four years of marriage, complaints of selfishness more than double.

And less idealization means less "derogation of alternatives." Your brain stops telling you hot alternative partners aren't hot. Meanwhile, as a marriage continues, sex almost inexorably declines. Again, the love stories don't talk about this; comedians do. Believe the comedians. Most couples have sex roughly two or three times a week. But all around the world, the longer you're married, the less sex you have. In fact, after the first year of marriage, sex declines by half. (If you were expecting wedlock to be a multidecade *Eyes Wide Shut* party, you're going to be very disappointed.) The number one Google search related to married problems? "Sexless marriage." Fifteen percent of married folks haven't had sex in over six months. (And if you're someone who is very distressed about inequality in the world, it's worth noting that 15 percent of people are having 50 percent of the sex.)

Yes, sustaining romantic love during a marriage is tough. Actually, it's even tougher than that: don't forget survivor bias. All the studies above that look at currently married people are doing just that—*only studying the ones that lasted*, not the ones that already threw in the towel.

Sadly, regular romantic love is not as durable as its more pathological variant: erotomania. No, that disorder is not all about sex. Erotomania is the most extreme form of love, and a recognized mental malady. People with erotomania might do some stalking, but they rarely harm anyone or cause too much trouble. The majority of sufferers are women who believe that a famous man is madly in love with them (despite the fact that he has never met her and has no idea who she is). It's classified as a delusional disorder in the DSM; obviously more delusional than everyday love, but not the seeing-aliens-and-fairies level of delusion either. Ironically, they display all the qualities we admire in a lover. It ought to be called "Romantic Comedy Disorder." They never give up, never stop believing, and feel that love will conquer all. They are the ultimate romantics. And their condition is usually chronic, responding poorly to treatment. It's tragic that the form of romantic love that is most durable, most able to last, is the one where you *truly* have a mental disorder. But it's worth noting that it's only erotomania if the other person doesn't reciprocate your feelings. If they do, you're just the most romantic person ever.

We don't want erotomania. If we were going to pick a real mental disorder, it would be "folie à deux" (technically, shared psychotic disorder in the DSM-IV). This is when two people both lose it—together. You have to have achieved an intimate connection with the person to be susceptible, and separating the pair is an essential part of treating it. It's underdiagnosed. Why? Because they rarely seek help. Yeah, they may believe some crazy things together, but the delusions are usually benign. A mild form of folie à deux should be our goal: a unique culture of two, with its own crazy but harmless beliefs and rituals. A silly but fulfilling story of the world and of their union that is special, idealized, and meaningful. One that doesn't make much sense to anyone beyond the pair. But doesn't need to. The most romantic relationships in my life have been like this, and I'm guessing you've experienced the same.

So how do we get something closer to folie à deux? How do we fight the entropy and sustain the idealization? Most love stories are of little help. The trickiness of marriage begins where they end. And, as we saw, the fairy tales lead us astray here. Believing it's supposed to be easy, magical, and passive is a big problem when you know it will take proactive work to resist entropy.

The throes of romantic love are an addiction, but in some ways that's easier. It really is out of your hands. Married love is a choice and one that will require diligent, consistent effort over time.

Love is a verb. If you want to look good and be healthy, you have to consciously work on it. Love is no different.

So what do we need to do? What we're going to find is that entropy isn't the biggest threat we face. A more dangerous enemy looms on the horizon. We can overcome it if we have the right tools. But we get so much lousy advice when it comes to love. Do the answers lie in logical reason or emotional feeling?

Turns out this is a debate that has been going on for a long time, best illustrated, oddly enough, by the work of Edgar Allan Poe . . .

13

Is life all about passion or logic? This reached a fever pitch between the seventeenth and nineteenth centuries. In the 1700s we had the era of the Enlightenment. Rationality. Reason. Cogito, ergo sum. Newton's laws. But that gave way to the Romantic era in the 1800s. It didn't exactly mean "romantic" like hearts and Valentine's Day; it was about the ideas that feelings, inspiration, and the unconscious were more important. The age of Enlightenment was all rules; the Romantic era hated rules and was all emotions.

And no one embodied Romanticism more than Edgar Allan Poe. Poe was like somebody took a list of dark tropes and just checked all the boxes. *Melancholy childhood?* Check. Father abandoned the family before he turned two. Mother died of tuberculosis by the time he was three. *Starving artist?* Check. Poe was the first American author to make a living solely from writing, which was a terrible idea at the time (and, lemme tell you, has not changed much since). *Difficult, misunderstood genius?* Check. His characters were all neurotic, delusional, sad, and vengeful. They were also autobiographical. *Life full of tragedy followed by a mysterious death?* Check. Wife dies of tuberculosis just like his mother. He's later found wandering the streets delirious, dies of an unknown cause, all records including his death certificate unable to be found. Bonus points: he was also an alcoholic with a gambling problem.

But his work left a staggering legacy. Everyone from Mary Shelley to Alfred Hitchcock to Stephen King would say he influenced them. Poe's work is more Goth than black eyeliner. A master of the macabre, Poe wrote fiction and poetry that deal with vengeance, premature burial, and other things that just don't get discussed enough at the family dinner table. We all read him in high school because, frankly, what could be more appropriate for the sullen, attention-poor years of adolescence than morbid stories that are rather short. And nothing would be more emblematic of the Romantic era than his masterwork, "The Raven."

It was published to immediate acclaim in 1845 (even though Poe got only nine bucks for it). Abraham Lincoln reportedly memorized the poem. The Baltimore Ravens football team is named after it. It was even satirized in a Halloween episode of *The Simpsons*. In so many ways it embodies the values of the Romantic era. Tackling love, loss, death and madness, it's a thrilling read, an emotional journey, and a terrible bedtime story for children. Its stylized, musical language weaves a web of grim emotional mystery referencing the occult, the Bible, and even ancient Greek and Roman classics. One can easily imagine it being written in an inspired frenzy or an opium haze like Coleridge's "Kubla Khan."

So we have our winner. Passionate brilliance overcomes cold, clinical logic, right?

Um, actually . . . no. In 1846, Poe published an essay, "The Philosophy of Composition," which describes how he wrote "The Raven," and it's the exact *opposite* of what you probably expected: "It is my design to render it manifest that no one point in its composition is referrible either to accident or intuition—that the work proceeded, step by step, to its completion with the precision and rigid consequence of a mathematical problem."

He explains a process that is as mechanistic and clinical as the assembly diagram that comes with IKEA furniture. Every word, every punctuation mark, was deliberately and rationally chosen, systematically, to achieve an effect in the reader's mind. Far from ineffable inspiration, it's logical problem solving. In discussing the verse's rhyme, it literally sounds like he's describing a math equation: "The former is trochaic—the latter is octametre acatalectic, alternating with heptameter catalectic repeated in the refrain of the fifth verse, and terminating with tetrameter catalectic."

Sounds crazy? Don't forget, Poe was a critic. He analyzed and clinically broke down stories for a living. He also basically invented the detective novel, a rationalist genre if there ever was one. Sir Arthur Conan Doyle credits Poe's work with inspiring the less-than-emotional character of Sherlock Holmes.

So there you have it: underneath Romanticism often lies the logic of Enlightenment thinking. Impulsive emotion must give way to rationality!

Um, actually . . . no. Poe *said* that he used logic and assembled "The Raven" like a fine Swiss watch. But some people—including none other than T. S. Eliot—questioned whether it was true. It's the opinion of many, including some literature experts today, that "The Philosophy of Composition" was written satirically.

And this theory isn't much of a stretch. In his time, Poe was quite the prankster. His first published story was a satire. And he absolutely loved to use pseudonyms to mess with people. He did this not only to dodge creditors but also to accuse people of plagiarism. Whom did he accuse? *Himself.* A writer going by the name "Outis" proposed that "The Raven" had clearly lifted ideas from another poem, "The Bird of the Dream." Many believe Outis was actually Poe. Know what Outis means in Greek? "Nobody." (Poe Troll Level: Expert.)

In our relationships we all struggle with the issue of passion versus logic, especially in the area of communication. When ardor fades, do we focus on reigniting the flame or building a conscientious system that can sustain a busy household and life? It's hard to know the path, to find a balance between scientific skills and feelings of the heart.

So in Poe's case, which was the true answer? Passionate, inspired notions or rigorous logic and systematic practicality? Sadly, we'll never know. But we do know the name of the era that came after the systemization of the Enlightenment and the passions of Romanticism. And what was that period called?

"Realism."

*

Marriage counseling was created by the Nazis. Seriously. It was a eugenics movement initiative created in 1920s Germany. And if it makes you feel any better, it doesn't work. Only 11–18 percent of couples achieve notable improvements. As the *New York Times* reports, two years after therapy, a quarter of marriages that sought help are in rockier shape than ever, and after four years, 38 percent go splitsville.

But why doesn't it work? Most couples wait too long to go. There's an average six-year delay between the first cracks in a marriage and actually getting help. But it should still be able to help somewhat even at that point, right? Nope, and that's because of the greatest enemy a couple can face: NSO.

While entropy decays the happiness of a marriage over time, it's not just a linear downward progression for everyone. Often, there's a phase change. Water gets colder, and then colder and then colder—and then it becomes ice. Something completely different. In marriage this goes by the appropriately intimidating term *negative sentiment override*. NSO is a polyp in the colon of love.

You're no longer "somewhat less happy" with your union, you're as excited about your marriage as Henry VIII's later wives were about theirs. You suspect your partner is secretly a lizard-person wrapped in a human skinsuit. You accumulate grievances the way hoarders keep mementos. Your partner is the source of all your problems, sent here by a malevolent force to ruin your life.

Idealization hasn't faded—it has flipped. If love is positive delusion, NSO is utter disillusionment. You are biased against, not toward, your partner. The facts haven't necessarily changed, just your interpretation of them. Rather than attributing problems to context, attributions now lie in someone's poor character traits. You forgot to take out the trash today, but instead of me assuming it was because you were busy, my go-to assumption will now be it's because you're a horrible person bent on slowly driving me insane.

Famed psychologist Albert Ellis calls it "devilizing." It's a flip from dealing with someone you assume has good intentions but occasionally makes errors, to someone you assume was forged in the darkest pits of Hades but occasionally does something nice. And now that the default has flipped, our old buddy confirmation bias clicks in, and you become a truffle pig for your spouse's mistakes, greasing the skid on an already downward spiral. A study by Robinson and Price showed unhappy couples don't notice half the positivity in their marriage. Your spouse does something nice, trying to dig themselves out of the hole, but now 50 percent of the time you can't even see it.

And this leads to more screaming that ends the marriage, right? Probably not. Escalating shouting matches lead to divorce only 40 percent of the time. More often than not, marriages end with a whimper, not a bang. You scream because you care. And once NSO has seriously set in, you stop caring. People stop negotiating with the demonspawn at all and start living parallel lives. And that's what usually precedes divorce.

How does this spiral start? It begins with a secret. You have an issue with something, but you don't say it. Maybe you think you know what they'd say. An assumption. And as we discussed in section 1, we're terrible at reading minds, even our partner's. As George Bernard Shaw said, "The single biggest problem in communication is the illusion that it has taken place." And with time you talk less and assume more. "He's quiet so he must be angry" or "She said no to sex so she must not love me." Unspoken assumptions start to multiply until you're not having conversations with your partner, you're just having them with yourself because you "know" what they would say. Sometimes we don't ask for clarification or say something because "he/she *should* know." But here on Planet Earth people can't hear what you don't say. The emotional landfill grows. You collect compound interest of marital doom. And your marriage sails toward the future like a bird toward a sliding glass door.

You have to communicate. It's a cliché, but it's true. Communication is so vital that shyness is actually correlated with lower marital satisfaction. Meanwhile, the average dual career couple spends under two hours a week in discussion. You gotta talk.

Yeah, that means you're gonna fight more. But guess what? *Fighting doesn't end marriages; avoiding conflict does.* A study of newlyweds showed that, early on, couples who rarely fought were initially more satisfied with their marriages. But those same couples turned out to be on their way to divorce when researchers checked back in after three years. And a 1994 paper showed after thirty-five years it was actually the passionate bickering couples who were the only ones to still have a happy marriage. Oddly enough, a lower threshold for negativity is good for a marriage.

Something bothers you, you're more likely to bring it up, and then it's more likely to get dealt with. Top relationship researcher John Gottman says: "If they don't or can't or won't argue, that's a major red flag. If you're in a 'committed' relationship and you haven't yet had a big argument, please do that as soon as possible." You. Gotta. Talk.

Sixty-nine percent of ongoing problems never get resolved. No, I'm not saying that to depress you. The point is that it's not what you talk about, it's *how* you talk about it. Everybody thinks the issue is clarity, but studies show that most couples (if they do talk) are actually pretty clear. And it's not about problem solving because more than two-thirds of the time it's not going to get solved. As Gottman notes, it's the affect with which you don't solve the problem that matters.

It's about regulation, not resolution, of the conflict. War is inevitable, but you have to obey Geneva Convention rules. No chemical warfare. No torturing prisoners. Maya Angelou once said, "I've learned that people will forget what you said, people will forget what you did, but people will never forget how you made them feel." And she's right. Survey couples about their most recent disagreements and 25 percent of the time they can't even remember what the argument was about—but they remember how they felt. And that's what affects your marriage. When you ask divorced people what they would change about their previous marriage, the numero uno answer is "communication style."

So we're going to do a crash course in marital communication skills guided by Gottman's work. His research allows him to predict which couples will be divorced three years later with 94 percent accuracy, a number nobody else even comes close to. This guy's face should be on the Mount Rushmore of Marriage. Gottman knows we need Enlightenment era logic to diagnose problems but that Romanticism era feelings are the end goal.

What Gottman realized is that the amount of negativity in a marriage doesn't predict divorce, it's the type of negativity. We're calling this "the Tolstoy effect." In *Anna Karenina* Tolstoy wrote, "All happy families are alike but an unhappy family is unhappy after its own fashion." And lucky for us, he was dead wrong. For marriages, it's the opposite. Happy couples create a unique culture of two, like folie à deux. But, as Gottman found, unhappy couples all make the same four mistakes. And if we learn them, we can avoid them.

He calls these problems the Four Horsemen, and they predict divorce 83.3 percent of the time.

1. CRITICISM

Complaining is actually healthy for a marriage. Again, this prevents those "secrets" that fester, breed assumptions, and lead to NSO. It's criticism that's the deadly problem. Complaining is when I say you did not take the trash out. Criticism is when I say you did not take the trash out because you're a horrible person. The first is about an event, the second is about your fundamental personality. We can fix events. Attacking someone's personality does not tend to go very well. Complaints often begin with "I" and criticisms often begin with "you." If a sentence starts with "you always" and doesn't end with "make me so happy," it's probably a criticism, and you can expect your spouse to respond with both barrels.

So turn your criticisms into complaints. Address the event, not the person. Or better yet, see your complaints as "goals" to be reached or problems to be solved. Criticism is something women do a lot more than men, but don't worry, we'll get to the problems the guys usually cause soon enough.

2. STONEWALLING

And here we have the thing men do in arguments that powerfully predicts divorce. Stonewalling is when you shut down or tune out in response to issues your partner brings up. Yes, there are many times in life when you just don't want to miss a good chance to shut up, but stonewalling conveys "you or your concerns are not important enough for me to deal with." It doesn't reduce conflict: in most cases it dials it up. For many men, Gottman has found the issue actually operates at the physiological level. When guys' adrenaline levels soar, they just don't return to baseline as quickly as women's do. The solution is to take long breaks. If the argument gets too heated, ask to return to the discussion in twenty minutes when fight-or-flight hormones have dropped back down.

3. DEFENSIVENESS

Gottman defines defensiveness as anything that conveys, "No, the problem isn't me, it's you." This, by its very nature, escalates conflict. You're inviting pyromaniacs to put out the fire. Denying responsibility, making excuses, repeating yourself, or using the dreaded "Yes, but . . ." are all examples of defensiveness. Don't counterattack or dodge. Listen, acknowledge your partner's issues (no matter how ridiculous they might seem to you), and wait your turn to prevent escalation.

And then we have number 4, which is in a category all its own . . .

4. CONTEMPT

Contempt is the single biggest predictor of divorce that Gottman found. Contempt is anything that implies your partner is inferior to you. Calling them names, ridiculing or putting them down are all examples. (Yes, eye-rolling is one of the worst things you can do in a marriage, and that's backed by data.) Contempt is almost never seen in happy marriages. Gottman refers to it as "sulfuric acid for love." Simply put, it is the path to NSO. Do not do it.

I'm going to be very realistic here. You're not going to remember everything in this chapter. So if you forget everything else, remember this: *how you start an argument is double-super-extra important.* Just by listening to the first three minutes of an argument, Gottman could predict the result 96 percent of the time. Plain and simple: if it starts harsh, it's going to end harsh. And harsh startup not only predicted the outcome of the conversation, it predicted divorce. If you know you're raising an issue with your partner that might lead to a fight, take a deep breath first. Complain, don't criticize. Describe it neutrally. Start positive. You may be right, but you don't need to make this harder than necessary by starting it as an attack.

This is a lot of stuff to remember, I know. And, in the shrieking confusion of the moment, it will be even harder to do properly. But that's okay. The first three horsemen are present even in happy marriages. Nobody's perfect. Remember how I said the Four Horsemen predict divorce 83.3 percent of the time? Yeah, 83.3 is not 100. And the reason it's not 100 is what Gottman calls "repair": soothing and supporting each other, laughing or showing affection in the midst of an argument. Take their hand. Make a joke. This dials back escalation. Even couples with lots of horsemen riding around can have happy stable marriages if they repair. And one reason NSO is so deadly is that it prevents you from seeing those repair attempts by your partner. That means the conflict car has no brakes.

What's an overall perspective to keep in mind that encapsulates much of this? Well, Gottman emphasizes the importance of friendship in a marriage and that is very true. But I think a more useful idea to keep in mind is writer Alain de Botton's notion of *treating them like a child*. No, don't be condescending like you might with a kid, but we create a lot of problems because we expect our partner to always be a competent, emotionally stable "adult." They're not. I'm not. And you're not. As humorist Kin Hubbard once said, "Boys will be boys, and so will a lot of middle-aged men." Showing the generosity and compassion that you naturally give to a child when they're upset is a simple way to get around many of the problems we create. We're just less likely to think a child is motivated by conscious malice. We think they must be tired, hungry, or moody. This is, frankly, an excellent thing to do with *anyone*.

Don't expect someone to always be rational. When Tom Stoneham, a professor of philosophy at the University of York, is teaching logic, he always says, "Don't use this at home or you'll end up unhappily single." When a five-year-old starts shouting and calling you names, you don't immediately shout back and call them a poopyhead. With kids we usually treat emotions as information, and this is great advice. We suspend judgment, listen, and stick to the real problem at hand. We're just a lot more charitable. And that injection of positive emotion makes all the difference. Adulting is hard, and when someone relieves us of that enormous responsibility and realizes that inside we're always a bit of a moody child, it works wonders. And this isn't just speculation. A 2001 study shows people who are compassionate with their partner during arguments have 34 percent fewer of them, and they last half as long.

Awesome. We're done, right? Nope.

Reducing negativity and fighting isn't enough. That might make a marriage hunky-dory (a technical term for "okey dokey"), but it won't make it great. I currently have a "not negative" relationship with every stranger on this planet. That's not love. Yes, reducing the truly lethal negatives like the Four Horsemen is necessary—but not sufficient. Studies have shown that while negatives hurt, it's actually the loss of the positive that speeds marriages to the grave.

More specifically, Gottman realized that the most important thing is a 5:1 ratio of positive to negative. This is why the raw amount of negative doesn't matter. As long as you have enough good times to offset it, a relationship can thrive. Couples headed for divorce typically have a ratio of 0.8 positives for every negative. But you don't want to have too little negative either. If you hit 13 positives to every negative, you're probably not communicating enough. Gotta talk, gotta fight. It's a balance. (What's fascinating is this applies to all relationships. Friendships need an 8:1 positive to negative ratio. And with your mother-in-law the number is actually 1,000:1.)

So we know our next goal: increase the positive. Time to put the funk in functional relationship. We want the "all" version of Eli Finkel's all-or-nothing marriage.

But we don't merely want the incremental increase of more positive. We want a phase change like NSO—but in the other direction. We want a return to the magic, the idealization. We want confirmation bias back on our side. A brand-spanking-new pair of rose-colored glasses.

This puts me in an interesting spot, actually. I'm the science guy always saying we need to look at the facts and the data and be rational. In the introduction to this book I swore a blood oath to destroy unscientific myths with Occam's chainsaw. Very Enlightenment era. But now we need some Romanticism. The delusion. The idealization that is the magic of love. The world is harsh, and we need our illusions to forge a greater truth together.

This is new territory for me. I have to go from killer of bias to protector of bias. I can see the summer movie tagline: *What it was designed to destroy, it must now defend.* (Why is the theme from *Terminator 2* playing in my head right now?)

So how do we increase the positive and renew the magic of love? Let's look at someone who has to do just that. On a daily basis, actually . . .

14

Imagine you wake up tomorrow thinking it's 1994. In that year you were thirty-one years old, with a partner. You expect *Friends* to be a brand-new show on TV and *The Lion King* to be number one at the box office. But, of course, once you get up, the calendar most certainly does not say 1994. You look in the mirror and you're clearly decades older than thirty-one. Oh, and no more "partner"—now you're married. (Congrats, by the way.) But you remember nothing that occurred between 1994 and right now. Pretty disorienting, huh?

Now imagine this happens *every single day*. Every morning you start off thinking it's 1994, remembering nothing that has occurred since then. You have what's called "anteretrograde amnesia." No, not what Jason Bourne had. He forgot his past. That's "retrograde amnesia." Anteretrograde is when you cannot make new memories, at least none that last for very long. For you, they persist for roughly a day. You move through the world just fine, but nothing sticks until tomorrow. People will say you did this or that, and you'll have to take their word for it. If you're reminded of the movie *Memento*, you're spot on. And that film has actually been praised by neuroscientists at Caltech for being extremely accurate.

Please excuse all the movie references, but although various forms of amnesia are common in fiction, they're actually rare in real life and usually brief. The closest most of us get to any of this is a temporary version brought on by one too many cocktails. But not for you and your 1994 issue. This is chronic. And as we saw with HSAM, memory is poorly understood, even by experts. Doctors can't fix this.

So reading this book is kind of a lost cause for you. Tomorrow you won't remember what you read today. Upside is you can enjoy your favorite TV episodes again and again like it's the first time you watched them. Dealing with people is harder. Unless you met them in 1994, they'll always be strangers to you, even if you see them every day. You'll register the awkwardness, their expectations, but you won't know why they think they know you. Every day.

Thank god you trust your own handwriting. You've left a lot of notes for yourself. A system that helps you get by. But going out is still always a risk. Sometimes the memories don't last a day; sometimes it's just minutes and you're full-on Dory from *Finding Nemo*. And it'll be like this again tomorrow. And every day. You will awaken with your mind in 1994, but the world will have moved forward.

Luckily, this is not your life. But it is the real life of Michelle Philpots. After two vehicle accidents in the mid-90s, she had seizures and her memory began deteriorating. And then one day it just stopped making new memories that lasted more than a day.

Yes, it's tragic, but it's not all bad. She's not alone. She has her husband, Ian. Um, actually, it's more nuanced than that. In 1994, Ian was her boyfriend. So every morning, to her, he's still her boyfriend (and a boyfriend that has aged dramatically overnight). But to Ian, and to the rest of the world, he is her husband and has been for over two decades.

So Ian must remind her. Every day. Well, actually, not "remind" her, because the memories aren't there. He doesn't say "we're married" and then she replies "Oh yeah!" He says "we're married" and she says "Really?!?" And Ian breaks out the wedding album, just like he did yesterday. (And in our continuing discussion of amnesia-related cinema, if you're thinking of the Adam Sandler–Drew Barrymore movie *Fifty First Dates*, you get a gold star.)

And he must be pretty convincing, because he gets her to believe it every day. Imagine having to gaslight your spouse every morning—but with the truth. It must seem like an elaborate prank to her at first. Sure, she can see in the mirror that she's no longer thirty-one, but emotionally it must be difficult to accept this thing everyone else keeps calling "reality."

Can love really survive when the memories are gone? I'm pleased to be able to answer that with a confident yes. The science here is fascinating. As we saw with HSAM, all memories are not the same. With that condition, memory for abstract facts ("semantic memory") is normal. But HSAM'ers had perfect recollection of personal events ("episodic memory"). Those are distinct and separate in the brain. Jason Bourne didn't forget his martial arts skills, and that's accurate. In retrograde amnesia people forget their past, but they don't lose "procedural memory"—how to walk, how to drive a car, or, in Bourne's case, how to kick ass. Michelle has lost the ability to make new semantic and episodic memories, but her procedural memory is okay. She may not remember the password to her smartphone, but she can remember the pattern of digits she punches in with her fingers.

But those aren't the only types of memory we have. Wonderfully, we also have "emotional memory." In anteretrograde amnesia those feelings of love remain and can still grow, even if the facts and events don't stick. Luckily, Michelle remembers the love she and Ian had back in the nineties. And those emotional memories can compound. Only the facts of their story must be refreshed every day. So tomorrow morning, Ian will take out their wedding album yet again to patiently remind her of the story of their love.

Maybe he tweaks the story some days. Not maliciously, of course. He certainly edits and condenses it, so it definitely changes. He must rewrite it to some degree simply because his own brain does that.

What would you give to be able to rewrite the past a bit? A second chance. To live a fresh, new story of love? The feelings are always there, but imagine a new and improved story to bolster them. To rekindle it daily. A ritual of reminding and rewriting love. A small ember can become a roaring fire yet again when tended to. A phoenix reborn.

You may not have anteretrograde amnesia, but that doesn't mean this is less true for you. You can not only remind yourself of your love story, but you can rewrite it as well. The hope and power of a rewritten story is no less true for you.

To stay the same, it must change. This is how you fall in love with someone over and over again.

*

Romantic love requires a defibrillator. Something that keeps the heart going when it stops or gets wonky. We want the magic back. That story, that idealization from early love. And we can get it. We saw in the MRI data some couples do maintain it for decades. But how?

I am happy to report there is some balance in the universe. Yes, NSO is scary, but there's also PSO: positive sentiment override. That's the fancy term for the magic, the idealization, the not-exactly-true but oh-so-wonderful story. If those caught in the Hades of NSO are biased negatively, constantly scanning for their partner's errors, those with PSO wake up seeking to confirm all that is good and wonderful about their partner and their relationship. The positive things are lasting; the negative stuff, well, my wonderful spouse must be having a tough day.

The idealization of early romantic love is not under our control. That's why it feels like a fairy tale. But we've seen it often fades, and entropy can be equally inexorable. To renew love, we must be proactive and deliberate. We can't wait for the magic; we must make magic. Lucky for us, PSO can be built and sustained.

I dumped a lot of sad stats on you at the beginning of this chapter, but a lot of good stuff is coming—or at least it can be good if we roll up our sleeves. We're going to cover a lot of techniques speed-round-style to not only build that 5:1 ratio but to shift things closer to that wonderful state of biased PSO. Paralleling Gottman's Four Horsemen, we're going to take four steps to get there. We'll call them the Four Rs.

FOUR Rs TO MAGIC
- *Rekindle* feelings through self-expansion.
- *Remind* yourself of intimacy through "love maps."
- *Renew* your intimacy with "the Michelangelo effect."
- *Rewrite* your shared story. Again and again.

Love is a verb, so let's start verbing:

1. REKINDLE

In a 2002 study, Karney and Frye found that overall relationship satisfaction has more to do with recent feelings. Unsurprising, but just how important are those recent emotions? Eight times as important. Ian renews those feelings with Michelle every morning. We want to bootstrap a feedback loop for those emotional memories.

But how? You don't just "choose" to feel warm and fuzzy about your partner. Here's where the concept of self-expansion comes in. Because of entropy, you're either growing together or drifting apart. The most commonly cited reason for divorce isn't fighting or affairs; 80 percent of couples said it was losing closeness. We often talk about feeling like we're growing, learning, and expanding ourselves as a result of love, but it turns out this is actually one of the creators of love. Arthur Aron and Gary Lewandowski found that when couples do stuff that makes them feel they are learning and becoming better, it increases love. Just like boredom kills love, when we feel our partner is helping us become a better, more interesting person, we love them all the more.

Doing things together that are stimulating and challenging stretches our self-concept wider and provides a buzz. The angle of attack is simple: never stop dating. You did all kinds of cool stuff together when you first fell in love. You probably saw that as a result, not the cause of romance, but it's both. "Quality time" together won't do diddly if you're merely making more time to be bored together. The research is clear here: you need to do exciting things. It's the antiboredom EpiPen. Researchers did a ten-week study comparing couples who engaged in "pleasant" activities versus those who pursued "exciting" activities. Pleasant lost. Couples who went out to dinner or a movie didn't get nearly the marital satisfaction boost that those who danced, skied, or went to concerts did. Another study Velcro-strapped partners together and had them complete an obstacle course. Huge increase in relationship satisfaction. We need interaction, challenges, movement, and fun.

Psychologist Elaine Hatfield said it best: "Adrenaline makes the heart grow fonder."

But how does this increase love? It's due to the criminally underrated concept of emotional contagion. When we feel excited, we associate it with what's around us, even if that thing is not directly responsible. When we feel partner = fun, we enjoy their presence more. And that lets us be somewhat lazy by letting environments do the work for us. Go to a concert. Get on a roller coaster. You want a fairy tale? Great. Go fight a dragon together.

In fact, any strong emotion can increase love. People often reference Stockholm syndrome, the phenomenon of hostages coming to sympathize with their captors. It's real. And what many people forget is that after the actual 1973 event in Stockholm, two of the hostages actually got *engaged* to the criminals. This is why some people stay in toxic relationships. Though they may not realize it, to them, the drama and fighting are preferable to another night watching TV. (Obviously I'm not recommending this, and, for the record, there is research on make-up sex, and it doesn't live up to the hype.)

Not only do "self-expansion" activities improve relationship satisfaction, but studies show that they also increase sexual desire. Couples who did exciting stuff were 12 percent more likely to have sex that weekend than those who did typical stuff. And speaking of sex: have it. Only 58 percent of women and 46 percent of men are happy with the current amount of sex they're getting. (Yes, they're getting an F in sex this semester.) Denise Donnelly of Georgia State reports that sex less than once a month is a harbinger of misery and separation. And a low-sex relationship isn't just a result of unhappiness, it's also a cause. Let those hormones do the happiness work for you. It's fun.

(I do *not* need data to prove that.) And don't be afraid to get kinky. A 2009 study found S-M activities can boost intimacy. Definitely qualifies as novel, stimulating self-expansion . . . Just sayin'.

Excitement, learning, experiencing, growing. This allows you not only to feel better in the moment but to collect emotional memories. Scenes for your story of love. Gottman says those feelings are the antidote to contempt. When fondness and admiration leave a relationship, you're on your way to NSO. And when those feelings are gone, he advises therapists to terminate treatment. The patient cannot be saved.

Want a concrete way to get started? *Go out with your spouse and pretend it's your first date.* This isn't just some cheesy advice from Aunt Barb: it's been tested. To fall in love again, redo the things you did falling in love the first time.

2. REMIND

Okay, I cheated. This is not really "reminding." I needed an R word. What we're really doing here is going deeper and learning more about your partner to build intimacy. A 2001 study found couples who really open up to each other are nearly two-thirds more likely to say they have a happy union. Our buddy Casanova once said, "Love is three-quarters curiosity." And Gottman's research backs him up. The happiest couples understand a lot about their partners. He calls this deep knowledge a "love map." Knowing how they like their coffee, the little worries that bother them, what their biggest hopes and dreams are. This info not only increases intimacy but also reduces conflict by what Gottman calls "preemptive repair." We all have concerns and sensitivities, rational or not, and when you're aware of those, you can avoid them before they become an issue.

So look up from your smartphone and get to know your partner better. Use those questions Arthur Aron created that I mentioned in chapter 2. (You can download a PDF of the questions here: https://www.bakadesuyo.com/aron.) Not only did answering those questions build friendship, but the very first pair of research assistants who answered them together ended up getting married.

Knowing how they like their coffee is good, but the real value here is in understanding the personal, idiosyncratic meanings they have of things. What does love mean to them? Marriage? Happiness? Dig for their unique perspective on things like what "being fulfilled" entails. When you know that your partner sees the completion of household chores as an important expression of caring, then it's not a mystery why they're getting upset—and you can do something about it.

Dan Wile once wrote, "Choosing a partner is choosing a set of problems." But when you take the time to get to know somebody, you can see the emotional reasons why things don't mean to them what they might mean to you. That understanding can change "difficult problems" into "lovable quirks." When you know they leave the lights on in the bathroom sometimes because of a childhood fear of the dark, the lazy idiot becomes a sympathetic human with acceptable foibles.

And, more important, Gottman says that understanding people's idiosyncratic meanings is how you overcome those perpetual problems—the intractable 69 percent. What does gridlock on an issue mean? It means this is tied to something important to them. Values. The same thing causing you all that grief can be a door to a deep insight into your partner. If you know what something really means to them, maybe you can find something that honors both of your visions of life.

Or maybe you can at least respect each other's position instead of the NSO path to thinking they're trying to sabotage your happiness. Like Gottman said, dealing with those perpetual problems is about regulation, not resolution. And that works a lot better when you're honestly able to tell them "I don't agree, but I see why you feel that way."

Expanding on meaning, talking about dreams and values may sound saccharine, but it's crucial. You're on a journey together, so it's kinda important that you both wanna head in the same direction, eh? What's their ideal life? Their ideal self? These are big questions, but if you start answering them, the smaller stuff starts falling into place and that crazy person you live with can start to make sense. All couples argue about money. Why? Because money is all about values. It's a quantification of what's important to you. Get closer to an understanding of their values, and the money problem magically gets easier to deal with.

You don't want to just "get along." God, how low a standard is that? Do all the above right and you get on the path to shared meaning. That's the first step toward the good side of "the Tolstoy principle": your unique culture of two. Folie à deux. To have your own secret language. An emotional shorthand. Silly stuff infused with rich personal meaning. Those inside jokes, things you say that are crazy to everyone else but mean so much to the two of you. Building your own little religion. This is when couples truly can't bear to be apart, because they have a shared identity, a shared story, because the other person is inextricably a part of their future progress, future goals, and how they will become their ideal self.

And that unique culture should be supported by unique rituals. A big part of making this special culture of two and cementing a shared identity is infusing the day-to-day with that special meaning. These aren't the big, exciting moments of expansion; they're the little things. Mealtimes, bedtime, vacations, date night, partings, reunitings, scheduled snuggling appointments, and celebrations are all perfect moments for having a special, weird something that sets your love apart.

A good concrete one to start with? At the end of the workday when you reunite, you each take a turn sharing the good news of the day. And both of you support and celebrate what the other says. Repeated studies have shown this can boost happiness and relationship satisfaction. UCSB professor Shelly Gable has found that how couples celebrate can actually be more important than how you fight. Again, like Gottman said, in many cases, if you increase the positive, the negative doesn't matter quite as much.

But what about when change is necessary?

3. RENEW

Okay, so you know your partner better. It's a natural response to want to change them a bit. No, this is not good, at least not the way it's usually done. A study of 160 people found that this usually doesn't work and decreases marital satisfaction. Why? Because you're not objective. You're saying you know better than they do who they should be. There's always a bit of selfishness in there. The enormous irony here is that you have to accept someone fully before they can change. As John Gottman notes, our instinct for autonomy is wired deep, so, ironically, people change only when they feel they don't have to.

There's a healthy (and effective) way to help your partner move in the direction of positive change. But it starts with who they want to be, not who you want them to be. You have to help them become their own ideal self. That's one reason why the love maps process above is so important, for you to ask and know, rather than guess, what this ideal self is.

We got some help from Aristotle on building friendships; for improving partners, we'll receive assistance from another master: Michelangelo. Speaking about his artistic process, he once said, "The sculpture is already complete within the marble block, before I start my work." He didn't feel that sculpting was creating; it was revealing. The sculpture just has to be freed from the stone around it. And psychologists found the same idea applies to improving your partner.

Just as in romantic love we're able to see our "real" partner but discount the negatives and idealize them, we can benefit from that here. With the knowledge of the current block of marble and what it has the potential to be, we can better see how the idealized version parallels it.

So how do we actually do this? Think back to when we talked about narcissists and "empathy prompts." (No, I'm not saying your partner is a narcissist; I'm saying humans are more alike than they are different.) The best way to help them improve was by encouraging instead of shaming. Same applies here. In accepting them as they are, you can still focus on and encourage those aspects aligned with their ideal self, who they most want to be. See the "idealized" sculpture in their realistic marble and encourage that. Nurture the ideal them through support and affirmation. Work on that raw diamond to reveal the beauty within; don't try to turn it into an emerald because you like the color green.

Simply put, this is a more proactive effort to "bring out the best in someone." And, given it originated with their own goals, it meets far less resistance. You're not encouraging them to become what you want them to be, you're encouraging them to be more them. Speak to their best self, encourage their ideal self, and treat them like they already are that person. In a 1996 study, researchers Sandra Murray, John Holmes, and Dale Griffin found that, much like children, adults often come to perceive themselves the way we perceive them. This is why supporting the ideal works and shaming them as bad fails. The delusion of love is necessary because it is a North Star. The lie becomes the truth.

Again, this promotes self-expansion, so guess what? It has some of the same results as self-expansion: "movement toward the ideal self showed positive associations with life and relationship satisfaction." But not only that, it does help people change, improve, and meet their goals. They do get closer to their ideal self: "Analyses revealed that when partners were more affirming during goal-relevant conversations, targets were more likely to achieve their ideal self goals." And you can encourage an old dog to learn new tricks. The Michelangelo effect has been shown to work at any age.

It's idealization all over again, but the deliberate "enlightenment era" version. If we know the "negatives" of a partner but learn the meaning beneath them, we see who they really are and who they can really be. We can then encourage that ideal in a partner and help them actually become that ideal. They become the idealized self, and so the idealization can last. This is a path to a continued romantic love that defies entropy. The Michelangelo effect allows us to fall in love over and over again with same person (without amnesia). Somerset Maugham wrote, "We are not the same persons this year as last, nor are those we love. It is a happy chance if we, changing, continue to love a changed person." But we don't have to leave it to chance.

Okay, we boosted the feelings and intimacy with self-expansion, created a unique culture of two supported by rituals with love maps, and increased positive growth and improvement with the Michelangelo effect. What encapsulates all this? What ties it all together? It's the same thing we've seen to be central throughout the book thus far. The same thing Michelle Philpots needs daily, and Ian provides. A story . . .

4. REWRITE

In the end, love is a shared story. (My deep and insightful realization that lasting love is inextricably part of a shared story is due to congenital brilliance on my part and has nothing whatsoever to do with the fact that leading love researcher Robert Sternberg wrote a book titled *Love Is a Story*.)

Remember how John Gottman could predict divorce with 94 percent accuracy? Know how he does it? It's simple: he asks the couple to tell their story. That, and that alone, is his crystal ball to the future of any romance.

So what's your story? Every relationship has one. Sorry, did I put you on the spot? Don't worry, I didn't expect you to be able to answer. The stories we have about our relationships are usually intuitive and unconscious. But they're there. Some people have a "business" story where they're all about making sure things in the relationship run smoothly. Others do have a "fairy tale" story of wanting to save or be saved. And there are those who have a "home" story where everything is centered on building a lovely environment. There are an infinite number of stories. None guarantee happiness, but Sternberg found some make it pretty hard. (I recommend avoiding a "war" story.)

And people can repeat their problematic stories, which is why some friends of yours might complain, "Why do I always attract jerks?" They're casting an actor for the "role" in their story, and decent people might not fit the part. Sternberg's research has shown that we end up with people who have similar ideas about what the story of a relationship will be. And if they don't, we're far more likely to be dissatisfied with the partnership.

First, you need to know what your "ideal" relationship story is so that you can align with it, tweak it, or change it. It can be a great way to diagnose what's wrong with a relationship, but that's hard to do if you don't know what your story is. If you secretly love "drama" but won't admit it to yourself, you can say you're seeking a "fairy tale" but keep ending up in a "war" story, saying "Jeez, why does this keep happening to me?" Often people have confusion between the story they're seeking and the story they think they "should" have.

Our stories are influenced by upbringing and experiences, and the environment we live in. Stories are now far less culturally scripted than in the past, which is a good thing if you craft one deliberately, but if you're not as proactive about this, it can end up more hellish than being on a group text.

Look at your past behavior to find your "ideal" story, the one you've been unconsciously seeking. What kinds of people did you get involved with? Reject? How has that changed? Ask friends for insight because you're probably not going to be objective. And then you want to think about what your "actual" story currently is with your partner. Has an "adventure" story become a "running a small business" story since the kids arrived?

Talk to your partner and find out their "ideal" and "actual" story. Again, this is why you discussed dreams and values with them and tried to understand their ideal self. Failing to get on the same page about this is why when talking to couples who split, you often hear a *Rashomon* of two tales that sound completely different. Sternberg's research found that couples with similar stories are more satisfied.

A critical element is understanding the issue of roles and power in the shared story. Today many couples have a knee-jerk desire to say they're equals, but that may not reflect their true ideal. Do you feel uncomfortable when you're leading or uncomfortable when not leading? Roles can be asymmetric, and that's okay. One can be the race car driver and the other the mechanic.

Remember, there's no "right" answer, just something both of you are comfortable with that's in line with your needs. Yes, this is the choose-your-own-adventure marriage. Objectivity and facts aren't central here: it's the framing, the perspective, and the mutual buy-in. There is no objective truth here, just two subjective truths.

And that lines up with what Gottman has found about story: the facts don't matter. It's all about the spin. Getting his 94 percent prediction accuracy didn't come from what the couple said but how they presented it. The single most important thing? The theme of "glorifying the struggle." That means everything. A story of problems that has a positive spin ("We had troubles but we overcame them") bodes well, but a story of good things with disappointment ("We're doing fine, I guess; this isn't what I wanted but whatever") means problems.

The goal here is to create what journalist Daniel Jones calls "retroactive destiny." The story isn't the events: it's the lens you see them through. We tend to assume that the way we see things now is the only way, but a triumph can be a tragedy when you shift the perspective. The meaning can't happen until after. You don't find the fairy tale ready-made, and events unfold according to it. The events happen, and you weave the positive fairy tale and interpret everything through that. A cynic would say this is rationalization, but we've already accepted that romantic love is a type of delusion—a good kind.

NSO is a negative rewriting of the story. PSO is the positive version. The facts didn't change, the lens did. And the story is forever being rewritten, tweaked here and there, as it certainly has in Ian's daily telling to Michelle. Why are kids such a challenge to happy marriages? You just added a whole new primary character and didn't update your story. Without a conscious rewriting of the storyline, you shouldn't be surprised that a "whirlwind romance" became a "sitcom."

As the research shows, the perfect memory of HSAM'ers harms relationships. We need to be able to rewrite and reframe. To emphasize or de-emphasize parts of the story, as we do with our partners in idealization. Luckily, we do not have HSAM, so we can rewrite the story. Instead of a new story of love through a new relationship, you can forge a new story with the same person. Think of it like recycling. Your shared story of love is quite green. As Mignon McLaughlin said, "A successful marriage requires falling in love many times, always with the same person."

It's not going to happen overnight. But the goal of your "glorifying the struggle" story comes down to a single word: *we*. Professor James Pennebaker found that the use of we-words predicts a happy relationship. We already saw the other side of this. What did Gottman say often defines criticism, one of the four horsemen? Using the word *you* in an argument. UC Riverside professor Megan Robbins reviewed studies of 5,300 subjects and found that *we* use correlated with success in all metrics evaluated, from relationship duration to satisfaction to mental health. And it doesn't just boost happiness. In a survey of people with heart problems, it was the ones who used *we* most often that were in better shape after six months.

But is the word *we* chicken or egg? Does it just signal a good relationship or does using it more improve a relationship? Robbins says it's likely both. So use more *we*.

It's almost time to round everything up. Yes, "we" are almost done. (No, you and I are not in love. You're wonderful, but I really just think of us as friends.) We're going to get the final verdict on love's conquering ability. But first, you might be curious to see what love looks like when it does manage to conquer all . . .

15

John Quinn loved his wife. And on the night of Wednesday, September 21, 1960, the twenty-three-year-old English literature major at Humboldt State College brought his sweetheart to Trinity Hospital in Arcata, California, to give birth to their first child.

As she went into labor, the doctor told him he'd have to leave. Many of us know that fathers didn't used to be present in the delivery room during a birth, but what many of us don't know was that it was actually discouraged—if not outright illegal. (And if a man wasn't married to the mother, it remained against the law right up until the 1980s in some jurisdictions.)

But John Quinn wasn't having it. He told the obstetrician, "I love my wife. I feel it's my moral right as a husband and father to be there." But the doctor was just as stubborn as John.

This was getting heated. Hospital management came and backed the obstetrician. It wasn't safe. Having John there would be "impossible."

John Quinn loved his wife. He was a solid dude. He wasn't going *anywhere*. And that's when they threatened to call the cops.

But John had expected it to come to this. In fact, he'd prepared for it. So that's when he took out the chain . . .

And in a courageous deed that would make national news, he took his wife's hand, wound the chain around their arms, and padlocked the two of them together. Obviously, I wasn't there at the time, but I see a *How ya like them apples, Doc?* look on his face.

Hospital staff called the police. But the doctor wasn't going to wheel them both out of the delivery room, and with no acetylene torch nearby, he proceeded with the delivery.

And John Quinn watched his little boy enter the world. When the delivery was over, mother and son both fine, John unlocked himself and walked out, passing right by Officer Don Mann, who was noted to be scratching his head at the whole incident.

Sometimes love requires more of us than we expect. But if you're devoted, if you're prepared—and maybe if you've got a chain and padlock—sometimes love can conquer all.

*

Everyone asks how you got together; nobody asks how you stayed together. And it's the latter that is often the real achievement to be proud of. Let's round up what we've learned.

The long era of the "help-me-not-die" marriage is over. Love won, and the self-expressive marriage reigns. But this is also the "all-or-nothing" marriage. These days more than ever, marital happiness = life happiness. We're all-in. Doing love right is very, very good. Doing it wrong can be very, very bad.

Love is a mental illness. It's a crazy addiction that even clouded the mind of the callous Casanova. But it turns out we need the crazy. That wild-eyed idealization, that positive bias, is the magic of love. Life is hard, so we need its drive not only to fulfill our genes' goals to make more genes but to fulfill our hopes, dreams, and hearts.

We need the rational thought of the Enlightenment era to help us understand the process just like the science of medicine can heal the body. But in the end, our goal isn't to be not-sick, it's to be happy. So, in the end, we must jump headlong into the bias and madness of Romanticism.

There's a bit of an emotional bait-and-switch involved when

the force of early romantic love fades. We have an inaccurate paradigm of assuming the initial high of romantic love will continue indefinitely on its own, while it's much more likely entropy will cause that force to wane. Fairy tales are passive and won't help over the long haul. It will take work. As poet Carroll Bryant said, "Love is a two-way street constantly under construction."

To prevent NSO from transforming your beloved into your personal piñata, we must talk, we must fight. To deal with the 69 percent of ongoing relationship problems that will never be solved, we must reduce the deadly negatives in communication, Gottman's Four Horsemen of criticism, defensiveness, stonewalling, and contempt. Avoiding a harsh startup and showing our partner the compassion and generosity we would give a child are key.

But, in the end, reducing the negative is not enough. We must increase the positive and achieve PSO, the angel to NSO's devil. To be positively biased as we were in the early days of romantic love, we need the four Rs. To rekindle feelings with self-expansion (and have more sex!). To remind ourselves and go deeper into intimacy toward a unique culture of two. To renew and make each other better with the Michelangelo effect. And, finally, to continually rewrite a shared story of love that glorifies its inevitable struggles.

As Milan Kundera wrote, "A single metaphor can give birth to love." Love is a story. And stories are never perfect renditions of the facts. But we don't want realism. We want an always renewing idealization. And with time, that lie can become greater than the truth. When people buy into benevolent stories, humans form nations, religions, and communities that allow us to survive and thrive. Just as the falsehood that a friend is "another self" binds us together and improves the world, so does the mutually agreed-on delusion of love. The fake becomes real if we both believe. It's the wonderful insanity of folie à deux. And that shared story can be summed up in a single, deceptively powerful word: *we*.

It's a lot. It will be a challenge. (Did you really think it was going to be easy?) But with effort, today we have the ability to build the best marriages that have ever existed. It's a tall order, but you have a partner to help.

And the verdict on this maxim? No, love doesn't conquer all. But *your* love can. And it can be among the greatest humanity has known if you have the right story. And that story will continually be rewritten. This draft might not "conquer all," but the next draft could.

With the responsibilities of adulthood there's a desire to turn everything into a stable routine, but this turns love a shade of stultifying monochrome. In the end, we don't want to conquer love's challenges and mystery. In being vague, there is uncertainty and in uncertainty tension, serendipity, and surprise. Just enough harsh Enlightenment science to keep the fragile Romantic era fire burning. Irrational, yes. But so is life. And, as we saw with signaling, sometimes irrationality is the highest form of rationality.

Whew, time to take a deep breath. So what's next in our "Consumer Reports" for social maxims?

Now we need to broaden it a bit and look at community. Lots going on lately in that department. The world is more connected than ever, yet we're all more individualistic than we've ever been. Makes you wonder how much we actually need others. And in what ways.

This is the part where I'm supposed to say other people are essential and wonderful and the death of community is horrible, blah blah blah . . . But then why do we all keep choosing this increasingly individualistic path, huh? So rather than flood you with platitudes, let's start with the question you're not supposed to ask, the complete opposite of what you're supposed to say in a book about relationships: *Do you even need other people at all?*

Is "No Man an Island"? Or could you be really happy as an awesome island like, say, Maui?

Time for you and me to find out . . .

PART 4

IS "NO MAN AN ISLAND"?

16

Chris didn't like stealing from people's homes, but winter was coming. He had no choice.

Once inside he went straight for what he needed. Steaks, batteries, peanut butter, and books, books, books. If anything looked truly expensive, he ignored it. Chris was a thief, but he had a Code. Occasionally he'd steal a handheld video game, but never one that looked new. He wasn't going to deprive a child of a favorite toy.

He'd been at this for so long the people of central Maine had almost gotten used to it. Many knew he was harmless, but others were still irked. Law enforcement of all stripes had tried to arrest him and failed. Nobody could catch "the North Pond Hermit." But that was about to change.

As Chris exited the building, a flashlight blinded him. "GET ON THE GROUND!" If Chris could see anything, it would have been the barrel of Sergeant Terry Hughes's .357 magnum. Chris got on the ground. Soon backup arrived to arrest the man responsible for over one thousand burglaries. It was a record for the state. Heck, probably for the world.

They asked Chris questions, but he didn't respond at first. Frankly, it seemed like he had trouble speaking. When asked how long he'd been living in the woods, he replied, "When was Chernobyl?"

Chris had been a hermit for twenty-seven years. The original *Ghostbusters* was the most recent film he'd seen on the big screen. He had never used the internet. In the past quarter century, he had only encountered other people twice—accidentally. Even then he had spoken a grand total of only one word: "Hi." This interview with the police was more conversation than he had had in almost three decades.

But how? How had he managed to go this long with almost no human contact? How had he managed to survive the wilderness? Winters in Maine are no freakin' joke.

Chris took them to his campsite. Despite living in the woods, his home is probably cleaner than yours. The police were shocked. Yeah, he lived in a tent, but it had a metal bed frame and a mattress. Food was stocked in rodent-proof plastic containers. Chris even had a Purell dispenser. He clearly had no intention of returning to civilization. Diane Perkins-Vance of the Maine State Police asked him why he had left. Why did he flee society to live here alone in the woods? He didn't answer. But, with time, details about how he ended up there emerged.

Christopher Thomas Knight had excellent grades in high school, but he had always felt like a weirdo. Dealing with people was frustrating for him. After graduating early, he took a job working for an alarm company. And then one day, inexplicably, he decided to drive away as far as he could. When the car was out of gas, he put the keys on the dashboard and just walked into the woods. There was no plan. He told no one. Frankly, he had no one to tell.

It was harder than he thought. He'd never even gone camping before. At first, he ate from gardens but eventually turned to stealing to survive. His work for the alarm company helped him break into homes, but he took no pleasure in it. After two years of being a nomad, he found the spot that would be his home for the next quarter century.

This was not *Walden* and Chris was not Thoreau. For all Thoreau's talk of solitary living in the wilderness, Thoreau was only two miles from Concord, Massachusetts. He had friends over for dinner parties, and his mother even did his laundry. Chris would later say, "Thoreau was a dilettante."

For Chris, every winter was an existential threat. He'd begin preparations at the end of summer. That meant a lot more stealing to make sure he had supplies. And it meant getting as fat as possible. He'd pig out on liquor and sugar to pack on the pounds like a bear preparing for hibernation. And he would shift his schedule, going to bed at 7:30 and waking at 2 A.M. You need to be conscious when the Maine nights reached their coldest point. "If you try and sleep through that kind of cold, you might never wake up," he remarked.

But all this suffering only makes one more curious: Why? Why do this? He didn't have a traumatic childhood. Why flee the world? Why give up so much that others consider essential to a good life? He sacrificed the possibility of a career, spouse, and children. He'd never even been on a date.

And now Chris found himself in the complete opposite circumstances. He was a resident of the Kennebec County Correctional Facility. It was the first time in decades he had slept inside four walls, and, of course, he could not leave. The hermit even had a cellmate. Food was plentiful, but he found himself too anxious to eat.

He gave no interviews, made no statements, and refused all the numerous offers of help he received after the story hit the papers. But after a while he did talk to one journalist, Michael Finkel. First it was by letter, but eventually Finkel visited the prison. They sat across from each other, separated by plexiglass, talking via phone. Finkel could barely hear a word Chris said. But that was because Chris wasn't holding the phone properly. He'd forgotten how. It had been almost thirty years since he'd used one.

Prison was beyond hard, and the hermit was coming apart at the seams. He was surrounded by people. All the time. So much interaction was overwhelming. He could barely sleep. After six months awaiting trial, he had broken out in hives. His hands shook. Chris told Finkel, "I suspect more damage has been done to my sanity in jail, in months, than years, decades, in the woods."

The good news was he would be getting out soon. The prosecutors took pity on him. He was going to be sentenced to seven months, and he'd already been in jail nearly that long. But would life outside prison be any better? It would be a condition of his parole that he couldn't go back to the woods. He said, "I don't know your world. Only my world, and memories of the world before I went into the woods . . . I have to figure out how to live."

Finkel tried to get the answer everyone wanted: Why? Why did he leave? Chris had dodged the question many times before. Finkel asked again. And Chris gave the closest thing to an answer anyone would get: he had never been happy in our world. He had never fit in with other people. But then he ventured into the woods and for once in his life that changed. "I found a place where I was content . . . To put it romantically: I was completely free."

We all occasionally dream of running away. Of tossing our smartphone. Of escaping the pointlessness of so many trivial daily struggles that weigh us down. We go on vacation and see a place filled with natural beauty, and we fantasize about never returning to our lives. But we do. Chris didn't.

Finkel would go on to write a bestseller about Chris, *The*

Stranger in the Woods. And he would stop wondering why Chris left the world. He would now wonder why more of us don't.

*

In his 1624 book, *Devotions upon Emergent Occasions*, John Donne wrote, "No man is an island." But Donne was a poet, so he didn't back up his statement with any proof. In other words, he wrote a five-word maxim that made him famous for centuries and left me to do all the heavy lifting. Jerk.

Anyway, plenty of classical thinkers have agreed with Donne. Aristotle wrote, "Man is by nature a social animal," and felt that anyone who could exist alone was "either a beast or a god." In chapter 2 of Genesis you'll find, "And the Lord God said, it is not good that the man should be alone." Throughout much of history, exile was one of the most terrible sentences, sometimes regarded as worse than death. Being Aloofus Maximus was not a good thing in the ancient world. And not all that much has changed. Know what the United Nations calls solitary confinement in excess of fifteen days? "Torture."

I'm not here to make the case for being a hermit. (If we were really better off completely without other people, this would be a very, very short book.) The irony is, increasingly, we're all acting like hermits. Social scientist Bella DePaulo writes, "Never before in history have so many people lived alone."

In 1920, 1 percent of the US population lived alone. Now one in seven adult Americans do, meaning more than a quarter of US households are just one person. The percentage of solo households has gone up in every census since 1940, when the question was first asked. And America is not alone in its alone-ness; it's not even in first place. The UK, Germany, France, Australia, and Canada have rates even higher. Scandinavian nations have solo living numbers approaching 45 percent. And the rest of the world is following. Between 1996 and 2006, the number of people living alone increased by a third, globally.

But unlike solitary confinement, we've been deliberately choosing this. Before World War II, it wasn't all that economically feasible. As we've gotten richer, understandably, we wanted more freedom and control. (I can relate. I live alone and I'm cooped up writing a book, a process I describe as "how to develop agoraphobia in one easy step.") We love autonomy, but some suggest this is what's making us lonely.

And we *are* lonely. Even before the 2020 pandemic, 75 percent of UK doctors said they saw patients every day whose main complaint was loneliness. In 2017 the problem got so bad—with more than nine million lonely Britons—that the country appointed a minister of loneliness. And the number of people in the United States who report being lonely stands, according to one study, at around sixty-two million. That's the entire population of the United Kingdom. Studies vary, but it looks like just over a quarter of Americans report regularly feeling lonely. Leading expert John Cacioppo has said that number increased by 3–7 percent just over the past two decades.

The health and happiness effects of sustained loneliness on your body is, to use a technical term, poop-your-pants scary. It makes me want to run outside, hug the first stranger I see, and maybe reconsider my career choice. Cacioppo's research has shown that loneliness is the emotional equivalent of a physical assault. The elevation in stress hormones is comparable to what you would experience by someone beating you up. Loneliness sends your brain into perpetual high-alert mode. In the lab, lonely people notice risks twice as fast as nonlonely people, 150 milliseconds versus 300 milliseconds. We don't usually think of loneliness increasing reaction time, but the evolutionary theory behind it makes sense. *You better have eyes in the back of your head, pal. Because if things go sideways, nobody is coming to help.* An attitude like that may have been quite useful in our ancestral environment, but it certainly isn't conducive to happiness.

Repeated studies have shown that what the happiest people have in common is good relationships, hands down. An economics study titled "Putting a Price Tag on Friends, Relatives, and Neighbours" put the happiness value of a better social life at an additional $131,232 per year. Meanwhile, loneliness leads to depression far more often than depression leads to loneliness. Johann Hari notes that a shift from the fiftieth percentile of loneliness to the sixty-fifth percentile doesn't increase your chance of depression a little—it boosts it by a factor of eight.

But it's not just happiness at stake here. Loneliness is so bad for your health, I'm surprised insurance companies don't mandate you put this book down and go see friends. Studies connect it with an increased rate of heart disease, stroke, dementia, and pretty much every other awful thing you can think of. A UC Berkeley study of nine thousand people found good relationships add another *decade* to your life span, and a 2003 review of the research said this: "Positive social relationships are second only to genetics in predicting health and longevity in humans." I could fill a book just with the results of studies on relationships and health. What predicts whether you'll be alive one year after a heart attack? Pretty much two things: how many friends you have and whether you smoke. Oxford professor Robin Dunbar says, "You can eat as much as you like, you can slob about, you can drink as much alcohol as you like—the effect is very modest compared with these other two factors."

Seems like a slam dunk for John Donne and his maxim. If I was trying to convince you to be a hermit, it'd already be game over. Being alone is bad. But here's where things get weird. *Really weird* . . .

What if I told you that before the 1800s, loneliness didn't exist. Not that it was uncommon: it *did not exist*. Okay, I'm exaggerating. But not by much. Fay Bound Alberti, a historian at the University of York, says, "Loneliness is a relatively modern phenomenon, both as a word, and perhaps more controversially, as an experience."

Yup. Before 1800, you can barely find the word in a book. And when you do, it's used to mean "being alone" without any negative connotation. In Luke 5:16 it says that Jesus "withdrew to lonely places and prayed," but it just means he went off to be by himself, not that he was all bent out of shape about it. Samuel Johnson's 1755 *A Dictionary of the English Language* uses the adjective similarly. When Johnson writes "lonely rocks," he doesn't mean that they were geologically all sad and emo but that they were in the middle of nowhere.

But then in the nineteenth century there was a shift. The Romantics, like Lord Byron, started using the word more often, and it was a clear negative. The best example? Good ol' Frankenstein. Yup, Mary Shelley's 1818 monster can teach us a lot about an enormous change in Western culture. The monster says, "Believe me, Frankenstein, I was benevolent; my soul glowed with love and humanity; but am I not alone, miserably alone?" Then he heads north to kill himself. And, arguably for the first time in history, alone is portrayed as a very bad thing.

So how the heck was loneliness not an issue until a couple of centuries ago? Well, we did feel something while alone, but usually it wasn't bad. You know the word: *solitude*. That word did appear before the 1800s, and it was almost always a good thing. And you know that today. If I say the word *wisdom*, you probably think of guys with long beards comfortably alone on mountaintops. Solitude played a critical part in the spiritual paths of Jesus, Buddha, and Muhammad. Nobody thinks you find deep spiritual insight at a house party.

Solitude is what you mean when you say "I need time to myself" or to "get away from it all." We need alone time to recharge and reflect. And we rightfully associate solitude with creative breakthroughs. Isaac Newton discovered the law of gravity when he was isolated in Woolsthorpe during 1665. Albert Einstein swore by daily nature walks. Pablo Picasso said, "Without great solitude, no serious work is possible." Ludwig von Beethoven, Franz Kafka, Fyodor Dostoyevsky, and countless others did their best work while alone and wouldn't have it any other way.

Historically, people generally had a good balance of socializing and alone time in their lives. Your house usually had a dozen people running around, so you got your face-to-face time, but you also did plenty of roaming outdoors, so you got your solitude. (At the beginning of the twentieth century, 90 percent of traveling was on foot if you were going under six miles.)

But these days we're a bit mistrustful of solitude. Use that word today and you sound like a weirdo. *Loner* conjures up images of the Unabomber. In the modern world, "quiet guy who keeps to himself" sounds less like a Zen master and more like an active shooter incident waiting to happen. But who would you think was more mature: someone who can spend a lot of time comfortably alone, or someone who can't stand to ever be alone? In many ways, we've pathologized being by yourself. It's obvious from the statistics I've cited above: we have a bazillion metrics for loneliness but nobody measures solitude. Oh, and then there's this: "Solitude, paradoxically, protects against loneliness." You know who said that? Vivek Murthy, surgeon general of the United States.

Okay, this is confusing. What the heck is the answer here? Is being alone good or bad?

And that's the error we make. It's the wrong question. *Loneliness doesn't care if you're actually alone.* Loneliness is a subjective feeling. It's not necessarily about physical isolation. We've all felt it: lonely in a crowd. And a 2003 study by Cacioppo showed, on average, *lonely people actually spend as much time with others as nonlonely people do.* So living alone is not the real culprit here. It's a symptom, not a cause. While a lack of face-to-face contact can certainly create problems, it's a red herring in terms of big-picture loneliness. Cacioppo writes: "The amount of time spent with others and the frequency of interaction did not add much to the prediction of loneliness. What did predict loneliness was, again, an issue of quality: the individuals' ratings of the meaningfulness, or the meaninglessness, of their encounters with other people." Loneliness isn't about being alone: it's about not having a feeling of meaningful connection.

But what caused the shift? Where did the meaning go? More specifically: *What the heck happened in the 1800s?* Don't blame it all on Frankenstein's monster. He's a victim too. In the nineteenth century, our collective cultural story changed. Paralleling the shift in marriage over the same period, a monsoon of new ideas overhauled our societal narrative. It can be summed up in one word: *individualism.* Alberti writes, "It is no coincidence that the term 'individualism' was first used (and was a pejorative term) in the 1830s, at the same time that loneliness was in the ascendant." We went from seeing life as ensemble drama to a one-man show. We went from a default "someone cares" to "no one cares."

It's hard to understate just how many profound ideas and cultural shifts—political, philosophical, religious, and economic—came about in the nineteenth century, moving the individual to the forefront and sticking community in the back seat. Secularism. Utilitarianism. Darwinism. Freudianism. Capitalism. And consumerism. The social contract gave way to autonomy, and we went from communal to competitive. And this only accelerated in the twentieth century with even more isms like existentialism and postmodernism.

We so take these ideas for granted that it's hard to see past them. We've internalized these concepts as the way the world *is*. I'm not saying those ideas are necessarily bad, but the shift was profound and we may have lost something in the deal. Before, the default was to see yourself as part of a community. You are a child of god. A member of Clan Barker. Warrior in the Tribe of Los Angeles, California. But the focus shifted to the individual as the primary unit. The very positive upside of that is you are free, like our hermit Chris Knight.

But what your brain hears is you are also now, fundamentally, alone. And that's why you can be lonely in a crowd. We think a lot about the great things we gained from this story shift but have trouble pinning down what we lost. There's just a vague feeling of unease and an ever-present hum of anxiety. It's awesome to feel in control and free, not bound by social obligations, but your brain knows that also means *others* are also free and not obligated to look out for you. And millions of years of evolution taught our physiology that that means one thing. *Help is not coming. You're on your own.*

Obviously, I like science and modern ideas. The changes of the nineteenth century produced a world that gives us great freedom and control but isn't very emotionally fulfilling or meaningful. The ancients were clearly wrong about a lot of stuff, but many of their ideas, though not factually correct, did serve an essential purpose, like binding us together. We haven't filled that gap. Actually, we've dramatically expanded it with our hyperindividualism. But our physiology can't keep up. Biological wiring that is millions of years old still needs meaningful connection, which is why this new story affects our health and happiness so drastically. Loneliness is less a personal affliction than a cultural pathology.

No need to cock that eyebrow at me. This chapter isn't some Luddite call to arms or an anticapitalist screed. The modern world and a greater emphasis on individual freedom and control have given us benefits that are almost incalculable. We cannot and should not go back. But that doesn't mean we didn't lose something in the shift, something we desperately need. These new ideas are rational, but human needs are not always so rational. Millennia of material deprivation produced a burning desire to escape dependence, but we may have overshot the mark and gone to utter independence when what we really needed was communal interdependence. To feel that we're free, but still in it together.

Outside the Western world, many people are still connected to everyone around them by communal story and meaning. But our new story, with all its objective benefits, is imposing heavy costs on us. As Sebastian Junger writes, "Numerous cross-cultural studies have shown that modern society—despite its nearly miraculous advances in medicine, science, and technology—is afflicted with some of the highest rates of depression, schizophrenia, poor health, anxiety, and chronic loneliness in human history. As affluence and urbanization rise in a society, rates of depression and suicide tend to go up rather than down." It's ironic that modern advances gave us vaccines that addressed the medical challenges of COVID-19, but changes in our culture made social distancing so much more painful than it would have been centuries ago.

We used to be forced to be together by necessity, but we got rich and didn't have to be connected to one another anymore for survival. Understandably, we wanted more freedom and control. Like a nuclear reaction, we broke bonds and released tremendous, useful energy into the world. But a nuclear reaction can go Chernobyl if we're not careful. We need some of those bonds. According to Robert Putnam of Harvard, 77 percent of Americans agreed with the statement "most people can be trusted" in 1964. By 2012, only 24 percent of people did.

The important question is how are we all addressing this problem right now?

I'll give you a little hint: it's not a very good solution . . .

17

It had been nothing less than a whirlwind romance. Nisan first locked eyes with Nemutan at a comic-book convention in Tokyo. It wasn't long before they were taking trips to the beach together. And then it was weekend getaways to Kyoto or Osaka, smiling and giggling as they took pictures of themselves as a couple. In the blink of an eye, they'd been together three years. As Nisan would tell the *New York Times*, "I've experienced so many amazing things because of her. She has really changed my life."

By the way, Nemutan is a pillow. More accurately, a 2-D animated character printed on a pillow case. (Yeah, I know, things just got real weird real fast.) Nemutan is a sexy, bikini-clad anime character from *Da Capo*, a video game. Nisan actually has seven pillowcases of her. He keeps one at the office for nights when he has to work late. "She's great for falling asleep with on an office chair."

Sorry, ladies, he's taken . . .

Okay, that was mean. And it's really, really easy to be mean here. Thing is, he's not the only one. Falling in love with 2-D characters is becoming somewhat of a trend. And it's not just pillowcases. *Love Plus* is a popular video game in Japan where men can interact with virtual girlfriends. Flirting and kissing with digital beauties that, uh . . . don't really exist. Romantic video games are becoming a big business in Japan, with the market leader bringing in over one hundred million dollars in 2016.

And it's not all 2-D either. Sex robots are already here and quickly going full *Westworld*. Abyss Creations is adding voices, AI software, and animatronic faces to their silicone sex dolls. Of course, you have control over what they look like. Choose the hair color, bust size, and body shape you prefer.

Yes, the needle on the creepy meter has just gone into the red—but don't get the impression that this is all about sex. As for Nisan, he might be a better boyfriend than I am. He escorts Nemutan out for karaoke on Friday nights, and they even take adorable photo-booth pictures together. And Konami, the behemoth company that makes a number of dating sim games, even organizes a summer beach convention where players can unite for a weekend getaway with their digital sweethearts. Sociologist Masahrio Yamada reports 12 percent of young adults surveyed said they had experienced serious romantic feelings for video game or other fictional characters.

And the virtual love market isn't limited to socially awkward dudes; it's gone equal opportunity with the equivalent of Stepford husbands. Otome games for women are basically interactive romance novels. Far from dating Mario, they're a digital world of hot, dominant hunks; think Jane Austen meets *Fifty Shades of Grey*. And, again, this is no quirky fad. In 2014 romantic games by Voltage Inc. were played by over twenty-two million women. Nor is this just a "Japan thing." In November 2015 two games by Voltage broke into the top thirty highest-grossing apps in the United States. Which leads us to the biggest question that is on your mind right now:

JUST WHAT THE HELL IS GOING ON?

A 2020 academic study appropriately titled "What Factors Attract People to Play Romantic Video Games?" found that there was only one trait associated with wanting to play: loneliness. In interview after interview, when asked about their digital loves, the gamers don't talk about beauty or sexy bodies, just themes of a desire for companionship and acceptance.

Between 2002 and 2015 the percentage of unmarried and unpartnered Japanese women ages twenty to twenty-four went from 38.7 percent to 55.3 percent. For men the same age it grew from 48.8 percent to 67.5 percent. And the percentage of that age group who have *never* had a sexual experience hit roughly 47 percent for both men and women in 2015.

Okay, so they need to get out and date more? But here's the thing—that doesn't seem to be the problem. A Japanese government survey found 37.6 percent of young people don't *want* a romantic partner. Why? Most said it was "bothersome." Real relationships seem too difficult, too much of a risk. Japanese men say they don't want the *mendokusai* ("too much trouble") of human relationships. And their female counterparts agree. When talking about the upside of Otome games, one woman said, "It's an ideal love story—there are no female rivals and no sad endings."

They want the frictionless control and convenience that comes only from technology, with someone who isn't human. Virtual partners don't have unreasonable expectations. They don't reject you, ghost you, or cause you anxiety. And if there are problems, you can restart the game with no awkward breakup conversations. It's none of the grief with, well, *some* of the upside.

No, I don't think most of us will be finding our future soulmate in the Bed Bath & Beyond pillow aisle, but this is a long way from the harmless distraction of Tamagotchi games. We're dealing with an epidemic of loneliness, but what's even more concerning is the new ways we're trying to address it, ways that don't seem headed for long-term fulfillment and happiness.

Why do we keep reaching for technology instead of each other?

*

Being lonely sucks. Meanwhile, being popular is good. Like *really* good. Being popular as a kid made a huge difference in people's lives decades later—and in some very surprising ways. Research by Mitch Prinstein, a professor of psychology and neuroscience at UNC Chapel Hill, shows popular kids do better in school and go on to have stronger marriages and better relationships, and make more money as adults. They're happier and they live longer. Popularity was more predictive of these positive results than IQ, family background, or psychological issues. And what about the unpopular? You guessed it: a greater risk of illness, depression, substance abuse, and suicide. Yeesh.

Now before I trigger a class war between the jocks and the nerds, it's important to note something else: there are *two* kinds of popularity. The first is status. Status is about power and influence. Think of the cool kids in high school. And you can achieve status by some very unsavory means like bullying. "Proactive aggression" doesn't make you well liked, but, sadly, it does increase status.

Like it or not, we all naturally have some desire for status. We would all like to be more successful in achieving what psychologists call "extrinsic goals": power, influence, and control. This is wired deep. The reward centers of our brains light up in fMRI studies when we just *think* about high-status people. And those reward centers glow even brighter when we think people see us as high status. And it makes sense. Status gives us that control over the world that we crave so much. Survey people, and you'll see that more than half the time they'll choose status over money. They'd rather have two dollars when everyone else has one than have three dollars when everyone else has four.

The problem with status is that it isn't fulfilling over the long term. (Ah, the revenge of the nerds.) Joe Allen at the University of Virginia followed the "cool kids" for a decade after middle school and found that they had more substance abuse problems, lousy relationships, and criminal behavior. And this effect has been replicated around the world. Focusing on status, power, and "extrinsic goals" didn't lead to good things.

This isn't just true for thirteen-year-olds. What's it like to have ultimate status? To be famous? The academic research confirms another maxim: it really *is* lonely at the top. One study titled "Being a Celebrity: A Phenomenology of Fame" showed that while most of us want to be famous to be more loved, ironically, being famous leads to more loneliness. Celebrities have to put up walls to deal with the flood of attention. Other people always wanting something from you makes it difficult to trust anyone. Friends become envious. And so being loved by everyone often ends up producing what the authors call "emotional isolation." And that has similar effects to what we saw with the middle school cool kids. Celebrities have nearly twice the rate of alcohol problems that the average person does and more than a quadrupling of the suicide rate. Pray that you never get your Warholian fifteen minutes.

Why does a focus on status and extrinsic goals so often lead to problems? Because it's usually a trade-off. Only 35 percent of high-status people are also very "likable." When we devote our time to acquiring power and control, what we're not doing is focusing on "intrinsic" goals like love and connection. And maintaining status can require behaviors that are downright antithetical to good relationships, like bullying. Being liked often means ceding power.

And that leads us to the other type of popularity: being likable. A focus on intrinsic goals. Likable people may not have the same sway that high-status folks do, but they're the ones we trust and feel warm around. They're cooperative and kind. And this type of popularity does lead to happiness. Edward Deci, a professor at the University of Rochester, summarizes the research: "Even though our culture puts a strong emphasis on attaining wealth and fame, pursuing these goals does not contribute to having a satisfying life. The things that make your life happy are growing as an individual, having loving relationships, and contributing to your community." Those stats I mentioned about all the benefits of popularity? Those come from the likable-popular, not the status-popular. A multidecade study of over ten thousand kids in Sweden showed that more often it was likability that led to long-term happiness and success.

This parallels what we were discussing earlier at the cultural level. Our desire for individualistic control gave us a lot of power, like status does. But it also bred disconnection and isn't as fulfilling as being likable and having a community of people who love you. So we're dealing with the status versus likable death match at the societal level. Guess what? Likability and intrinsic goals aren't winning.

What do you want your daughter to be when she grows up? A CEO? A senator? President of Yale? Those were all options on a survey given to 653 middle school students. And they all lost to "personal assistant to a very famous singer or movie star," which garnered 43.4 percent of the vote.

Today's young people want to be famous more than anything else. A 2007 Pew Research study of young Americans found "their generation's top goals are fortune and fame." We can see it in the media. Between 1983 and 2005 there were no TV shows about kids becoming famous. After 2006, nearly 50 percent of shows on the Disney Channel are about that subject.

In our individualistic culture today, status is on its way to becoming synonymous with self-worth, and as Prinstein points out, this isn't a great recipe for happiness. It is, however, a great recipe for narcissism. A 2010 study of over fourteen thousand college students noted a *40* percent decline in empathy over the past few decades, while a separate study ("Egos Inflating over Time") found scores on the Narcissism Personality Index increased by almost 50 percent between 1990 and 2006 among a similar cohort. In the twenty-first century, narcissism has been increasing as quickly as obesity.

When we feel connected to others, control is less important because we feel help is there. But when we're lonely, our brain scans for threats twice as fast. We need control over the environment to feel safe. And that desperate need for control in an ever more individualistic world is affecting our relationships. Not only how we handle them but the kind we choose and the form they take. We want ones where we have control. We don't want social relationships; now we want what psychologists call *parasocial* relationships.

The concept was created in 1956 to describe the pseudo-relationships people would develop with television characters. Researchers Cohen and Metzger wrote that "television represents the perfect guest—one who comes and leaves at our whim." Relationships on our terms. Laughs and warmth without all the grief of dealing with other people who have their own needs. They don't let you down, they don't ask to borrow money, and you can turn them off when you've had enough. MIT professor Sherry Turkle says that they "offer the illusion of companionship without the demands of friendship."

And it's shocking how powerful these parasocial relationships can be. In 2007 there was a television writers' strike, and a lot of shows temporarily stopped releasing new episodes. What was the emotional effect on viewers who had developed strong parasocial bonds with their favorite fictional characters? A 2011 study put it bluntly: it was like a *breakup*. If you're starting to think "real relationships are to parasocial relationships what sex is to porn," you have the right idea. Emotional porn.

And just like time spent trying to acquire status steals time away from being likable, guess where the time for TV comes from? Exactly: from time spent with real people. But TV isn't as fulfilling as social time. Heavy TV viewers are less happy and have higher anxiety. It's trading a sumptuous dinner for the empty calories and low nutritional value of junk food. But this isn't just a problem for individuals; throughout the twentieth century it became a problem for society.

Harvard professor Robert Putnam's book *Bowling Alone* is the best dystopian science fiction novel you'll ever read—except that it's not fiction. He meticulously details the decline of American community involvement over the final quarter of the twentieth century. Between 1985 and 1994 there was a 45 percent drop in involvement in community organizations. No time for bowling leagues and Boy Scouts anymore. The time spent on family dinner dropped by 43 percent. Inviting friends over dropped by 35 percent. Putnam writes, "Virtually all forms of family togetherness became less common over the last quarter of the twentieth century." And the primary culprit he identified? Television.

But now it's the twenty-first century. Our parasocial desires haven't changed but the technology has. Those studies where the loss of TV characters was like a breakup? Well, guess what happens when you put people in an MRI and play the sounds and vibrations of a smartphone? No, it doesn't show all those awful signs of addiction. It's not a brain screaming with drug-addled craving—it's love. You react to your smartphone as if it's a family member or a significant other.

Technology isn't as inherently evil as some have made it out to be. The real problem is, just like television, we often use tech time to replace face-to-face interaction and community activities. Norman Nie of Stanford says, "For every personal e-mail message sent or received there is almost a 1-minute drop in the amount of time spent with family. With a mean of 13 personal emails sent and received, that amounts to about 13 minutes less of family time a day, or about 1.5 hours a week." Chocolate cake is not evil, but if 50 percent of your meals were chocolate cake, um, that's not a good idea. Use tech to arrange live meetings and it's an unadulterated good. But when it replaces face-to-face, we're not getting more connected, we're growing further apart. And we now spend more time on digital devices than we do sleeping.

And all this time focused on screens has created a flywheel effect for our problem with status and extrinsic values. People's focus on fame, money, and achievement grew significantly between 1967 and 1997, but it positively exploded after 1997. What happened in 1997? The rise of the internet. And just like Putnam noted the decline in community attributable to television, Jake Halpern says those trends have only increased with the rise of digital technologies. Between 1980 and 2005, the number of times that Americans invited friends over to their house declined by half. Club participation dropped by two-thirds in the three decades after 1975. And we are experiencing severe picnic deprivation. Yeah, picnics are down 60 percent over the same period.

Famed biologist E. O. Wilson once said, "People must belong to a tribe." But where are many finding their tribes these days? Video games. Which ones are preferred by people suffering from internet addiction? Psychotherapist Hilarie Cash told Johann Hari: "The highly popular games are the multiplayer games, where you get to be part of a guild—which is a team—and you get to earn your status in that guild . . . It's tribalism at its core." But online communities and live ones are not interchangeable. When Paula Klemm and Thomas Hardie studied online cancer support groups, they found 92 percent of participants were depressed. How many people in live groups were? Zero. They report: "Traditional cancer support groups can help people cope with their cancer, but the efficacy of Internet cancer support groups . . . remains to be proven." It's exceedingly easy to replace face-to-face contact with online interaction, but it doesn't build the same connections. Psychologist Thomas Pollet found that "spending more time on IM or [social networking sites] did not increase the emotional closeness of relationships."

And it's a double whammy. As we shift more of our time and energy to less fulfilling digital connections, we degrade our ability to connect with others. Remember that 40 percent reduction in empathy among the young? What was it due to? Edward O'Brien, who was part of the research team, said, "The ease of having 'friends' online might make people more likely to just tune out when they don't feel like responding to others' problems, a behavior that could carry over offline . . . Add in the hypercompetitive atmosphere and inflated expectations of success, borne of celebrity 'reality shows,' and you have a social environment that works against slowing down and listening to someone who needs a bit of sympathy."

You're probably thinking we're all broken forever and the only thing any of us will be able to connect with at this point is a phone charger. Nope. Turkle points to another study of youth:

"In only five days in a sleepaway camp without their phones, empathy levels come back up. How does this happen? The campers talk to each other."

I don't know about you, but I can't afford to have my ability to connect degrade even further. My social skills peaked in preschool. This morning I failed at captcha three times, and all day I've been convinced I'm a robot. Technology has brought us tremendous positives, but it also cannibalizes time we could be spending with others as a community. Konrad Zuse, who is considered the father of the modern computer, said, "The danger that computers will become like humans is not as great as the danger that humans will become like computers."

We end up in a place where we have neither community nor solitude, always connected but never fulfilled. Technology and social media aren't evil, but when they replace real community, we have a problem because we don't get the meaningful bonds we need. We don't truly feel "in it together" or "a part of something." We have too much control and autonomy to have any kind of collective identity.

If we got hit with an EMP blast tomorrow, it would destroy our smartphones but it wouldn't fix our cultural problem. We're filling the gap with tech and status and control because we're lacking something better. Psychologist Scott Barry Kaufman said, "The thirst for power is an attempt to escape from loneliness. However, power is never as satisfying as love."

Deep down, we're still those Homo sapiens on the savannah, and what did they need? Well, there's an answer. And we'll get to it by exploring something that will sound totally crazy coming from me, the-science-writer-guy.

We need to look at healing crystals and auras, and all the

things I roll my eyes at. (Good grief, I just said something positive about pseudoscience. If you listen closely, you can hear me dying inside.) No, they don't work. They're all bunk. But in all that bunk we'll find the secret to why our modern world has become so problematic, and where we'll find the much-needed hope for the future we need right now . . .

18

It all started with a Persian rug. The patient brought it as a gift for Ted Kaptchuk because he had "cured" her. Ted accepted it gracefully . . . despite not believing a word she said. He wasn't a surgeon or an oncologist, he wasn't even an MD. Ted dispensed herbs and acupuncture.

Ted's a sincere and reasonable guy. He believed his work had *some* ability to make his patients feel better; that's why he did it. But this woman was saying he had cured a problem with her ovaries that required surgery. As he told the *New Yorker*, "There was no fucking way needles or herbs did anything for that woman's ovaries. It had to be some kind of placebo, but I had never given the idea of a placebo effect much attention."

Years later he was invited to visit Harvard Medical School. Researchers were exploring potential new therapies based on alternative medicine and wanted his insight. And this is where he first got some formal exposure to the placebo effect. Often, the effect was so strong that it was more powerful than the drug being tested. This made doctors angry because it got in the way. Ted was confused. *We're trying to relieve pain and this relieves pain. Why would you hate it?*

And that's when Ted knew what he would spend the rest of his career doing. He wanted to help patients by understanding this "nuisance" that brought so many people relief. Ted would remark, "We were struggling to increase drug effects while no one was trying to increase the placebo effect." He thought we were ignoring one of the most powerful tools in medicine. So Ted devoted himself to showing doctors the error they had been making.

And that was not going to be easy. He was going to have to prove this scientifically, or no one would listen to him. He didn't have an MD or a PhD. He knew nothing about conducting clinical studies or the statistical methods necessary for research. So he would have to learn . . .

CUE THE ROCKY THEME.

Ted asked the top medical statisticians at Harvard to take him under their wing and teach him. It was absurdly difficult to go from herbs and acupuncture needles to rigorous math, but he was dedicated. Ted worked hard. And that hard work paid off when he was able to start leading studies—and especially once he started seeing the results. He wasn't crazy. The placebo effect couldn't kill viruses or excise tumors, but it had incredible power to make "real" medicine even better.

He split migraine patients into three groups. The first received a placebo in an envelope labeled "Maxalt" (an FDA-approved migraine drug). The second got real Maxalt in an envelope labeled "placebo." The third got Maxalt in an envelope labeled "Maxalt." What was the result? Thirty percent of those receiving the placebo labeled "Maxalt" felt better. And 38 percent of the ones who got the real drug labeled "placebo" got relief. Statistically, the results were indistinguishable. The placebo was as powerful as the drug in relieving pain. But that wasn't the most important insight. The ones who got Maxalt labeled "Maxalt" felt better 62 percent of the time. *That's 24 percent better than the same exact medication when it's labeled differently.* To get maximum effectiveness, you needed to maximize the placebo effect.

And he even learned how his previous work had helped people. Ted took two groups of patients and gave one real acupuncture and the second "sham" acupuncture (seems the same to subjects but the needles don't penetrate the body). Both reported similar improvements. So Ted's acupuncture didn't "really" provide any relief—but the placebo effect did.

Of course, Ted's research met with resistance. But now he could hit back with rigorous research. He made it very clear he wasn't saying the placebo effect was going to cure cancer or fix broken bones. But Ted could now prove placebos had legit physiological effects on patients when it came to pain and anxiety, and boosting the results of "real" treatments.

Ted showed it wasn't magic and it wasn't fake. Naloxone is a drug that blocks opiate receptors, usually used to counteract heroin overdoses. But Naloxone also blocks the body's natural opiates, endorphins. Guess what else happens when you give Naloxone to people? *The placebo effect stops working.* So placebos aren't multidimensional-quantum-crystal-healing-magic: they're a normal process that leverages the body's natural painkillers in some way that modern medicine did not yet understand. And that effect could be profound. Eight milligrams of morphine is a lot. But patients who receive it and patients who are merely told they received it experience the same amount of relief. You have to up the dosage by 50 percent to get the drug's effect to surpass that of a placebo.

It wasn't long before the no-MD guy with a degree from a Macao Chinese medicine program was receiving grants from the NIH to further his research. But what was troubling Ted now was though he knew the placebo effect was real and useful, he wasn't sure just how and why it worked. And he was finding some strange results in the data that told him the rabbit hole went even deeper than he thought . . .

Four placebo pills a day work better than two. Blue placebo pills are superior at improving sleep; you'll want green placebo pills for reducing anxiety. But placebo capsules beat placebo pills—and placebo injections were even better. Oh, and expensive, brand-name placebos beat cheap generic ones. *Huh?* Why would the method of administration make such a difference when the (inactive) substance delivered was always the same? And the craziest result of all? Placebos even worked when they were "open label" placebos—yes, you could tell people that the fake medication was fake and they'd *still* feel better.

And that's when he realized why he had been such a good healer even when dispensing alternative medicine treatments. The placebo effect was about the ritual. It was about the patient's belief that they would get better. Injections look more serious than pills, so they increase the placebo effect. Brand-names and big price tags scream legitimacy, ergo, more placebo effect. But it wasn't all about deception. More empathy, more attention, and more concern from a doctor conveyed the same power. One of his studies showed that 28 percent of patients given no treatment had symptomatic relief after three weeks. They got better on their own. But 44 percent of patients given sham acupuncture with a doctor who was "business-like" improved. The ritual and attention had a positive effect. But what happened when the sham acupuncture was combined with a doctor who really showed concern? When the physicians were instructed to have a forty-five-minute conversation with the patient? Sixty-two percent of the patients felt better. Caring had a dose-dependent effect.

Again, this isn't going to kill the Ebola virus or replace bypass surgery. But then again, how often are we going to the doctor for those serious things versus little stuff where we just want less discomfort? And "real" medicine works even better with the placebo effect. But what that means is "real" medicine works better when someone shows us they care.

Ted Kaptchuk proved that while we have certainly gained

enormously from improvements in technology, we also lost something along the way by ignoring the power of compassion. Rushed doctor visits reduce the placebo effect and reduce patient recovery. We pay lip service to bedside manner, but it has real effects on patients. Of course, we want real drugs and real surgery with "real" effects. But they work so much better—scientifically better—*with* the human element that delivers those "fake" placebo effects.

Ted Kaptchuk hasn't practiced acupuncture in over twenty years. But he has been applying the lessons he learned back in those days in his new role. In 2013 Ted was appointed to full professor of medicine at Harvard Medical School. He still doesn't have an MD or PhD. He leads the Program in Placebo Studies and the Therapeutic Encounter at Harvard. It's the only program in existence dedicated to the placebo effect, the human side of medical science.

So that's Ted's story . . .

But we're not done yet. We still haven't explained <u>why</u> the placebo effect works. Yeah, yeah, doctor-relationship-heals-you-blah-blah is nice and poetic and pretty perfect for my book, but we're not here just for feel-good stories. If our body can just turn off the pain, why doesn't it? What's the evolutionary logic behind why those warm feelings can sometimes matter as much as "real" treatment?

Think of pain not as a direct effect of injury but more like the "NEEDS SERVICE" light on your car dashboard. It tells you something is wrong and needs addressing. Your body is saying: *You need to stop what you're doing and take care of this.* Care. As we saw, it's central to the placebo effect. It's why placebos work even when we know they're placebos. When someone cares for us, the more attention they give us, the more competent they seem, the better tools they use, the more time they spend with us, the more our bodies notice. And then your body can tell you a new story: *Someone is caring for us. I don't need to shout at you with pain anymore. We're safe now.* And it turns the "NEEDS SERVICE" light off.

Loneliness heightens our attention to negative emotions because you're not safe, you have no one looking out for you, and your body knows that historically this has been mucho bad for Homo sapiens. The placebo effect is the reverse. It says, *Someone is looking out for us. Backup has arrived. We are safe now.* Up to 66 percent of therapy clients say they felt better before they even had their first appointment, just as a result of an intake interview. *Help is on the way. I can turn the light off.* Caring can heal you. Usually when I hear fluffy sentences like that, my eyes start to uncontrollably roll upward, but it's true, scientifically.

It turns out placebos do have an active ingredient: human beings caring for one another.

*

So what happens in a world so focused on status and the extrinsic and so little on care and the intrinsic? We become depressed. Happiness levels have declined in the Western world over the past fifty years and the incidence of major depression is up, despite our enormous material success. In 2011 the National Center for Health Statistics announced that nearly a quarter of middle-aged women in the US are currently on antidepressants.

But today we get the causes of depression all wrong. We're quick to think it's due to a chemical imbalance or some other endogenous reason. That's definitely part of it but far from the biggest cause. Psychologists George Brown and Tirril Harris did a series of studies showing that 20 percent of women who did *not* experience depression had major problems in their lives. For women who did become depressed, the number was 68 percent. Yeah, I know, the only surprise about that stat is nothing. Life problems make you sad. But here's the twist: it wasn't just the amount of bad stuff that led to depression; it was the ratio of problems to stabilizers in your life—how much support you received from those around you. Big problems and no support? The chance of depression hit 75 percent. Johann Hari covered the results of the research in his book *Lost Connections*: "[Depression] wasn't just a problem caused by the brain going wrong. It was caused by life going wrong." And these effects have been replicated around the world.

A 2012 study on depression concluded, "General and specific characteristics of modernization correlate with higher risk." Another study, "Depression and Modernization: A Cross-Cultural Study of Women," found that rural Nigerian women, who materially have it the worst, were the least likely to be depressed, while US women in cities were the most likely to be. The Western world is richer than ever but more depressed than ever. Since problems in life are inevitable, it's clearly an issue of support. We're not getting it the way we're living.

So what did we do about it? Oh, we gave them a placebo. Yes, I'm talking about antidepressants like Prozac. A 2014 paper concluded: "Analyses of the published data and the unpublished data that were hidden by drug companies reveals that most (if not all) of the benefits are due to the placebo effect." And another study, titled "Listening to Prozac but Hearing Placebo," looked at over 2,300 subjects and found "approximately one quarter of the drug response is due to the administration of an active medication, one half is a placebo effect, and the remaining quarter is due to other nonspecific factors." Did these papers result in a torrent of pushback from the scientific community at large? Nope.

I'm not saying everyone should toss their meds in the trash. They do help people. But for many, it's not because of the reasons we thought. The biggest explanation for their effects is that they simulate care. Care we're lacking in the modern world. But what happens when someone doesn't get the placebo? Or when the placebo effect isn't enough? Well, they address the lack of a feeling of care more directly. With illegal drugs.

We all know the story of the lab rat feverishly pressing the lever to get more drugs. Bruce Alexander, professor of psychology at Simon Fraser University, wondered if addiction was the only cause. He realized that in all those experiments, the rodent junkie was *alone*. What happens when you put rats in a cage with friends and toys and create a rat-topia? They don't want the drug. When alone, rats used 25 mg of morphine. In rat-topia, the animals used under 5 mg. Of course the original rats used drugs, they were in solitary confinement.

In the paper "Is Social Attachment an Addictive Disorder?", neuroscientist Thomas Insel's conclusion was: yup, our brains are addicted to other people. And substance abuse mimics the results in our gray matter, leveraging the same dopaminergic pathways. Remember how Naloxone, the opiate blocker, killed the placebo effect? It also knocks out the bonding effects of religious rituals. When we're in a community, we get high on our own supply, but when there is no community, we must get our supply elsewhere.

Between 1980 and 2011, morphine usage increased by a factor of thirty. But it didn't increase everywhere. Sam Quinones notes, "Use didn't rise in the developing world, which might reasonably be viewed as the region in most acute pain. Instead, the wealthiest countries, with 20 percent of the world's population, came to consume almost all—more than 90 percent—of the world's morphine." In a land of individualism, focused on status and control but with little care, we see an explosion of mental health problems and addiction.

So let's consider the opposite. What happens in a world where individualism is not at the forefront? Where status and extrinsic values aren't just secondary, they're temporarily gone? Heck, I'll up the ante. What happens when we experience war and disaster? When things are about as objectively awful as they can be?

The answer is, we revert to human nature. Maybe you think that's a bad thing, especially after all the awfulness I've described about our current situation. Maybe you think human nature is all Darwinian cruelty. To be fair, thus far I've sometimes given Darwin a bad rap. Survival of the fittest, ruthless competition, modern individualism, and the story of poor George Price. But that's not the full story of our evolution.

Why do you think we're the Big Kahuna of species on this planet? Because we were the smartest? We weren't. Neanderthals were. Your brain is 15 percent smaller than theirs. Recent discoveries show they had fire and music and culture and cave paintings. Heck, it's looking like we Homo sapiens learned a few things from them, like using tools. So why did we win?

We became the Grand Poobah of life on Earth because we were the most cooperative. That's the story of our species' success. Rutger Bregman says, "If Neanderthals were a super-fast computer, we were an old-fashioned PC—with wi-fi. We were slower, but better connected."

As I discussed in the first section, we're terrible at detecting lies. But our lie detection weakness is our collective strength. Our default is to trust one another. To work together. When individual Neanderthals said, "Screw this, I'm outta here," we stuck together. Our ability to collaborate, to help, even when things were at their worst, meant, over time, we won and they lost. Despite their bigger brains, Neanderthals could work together only in tribes of ten to fifteen, but our collaborative superpowers allowed us to scale to bands of over a hundred. You can imagine how those battles went. And a closer reading of Darwin shows he wasn't ignorant of this: "Those communities, which included the greatest number of the most sympathetic members, would flourish best and rear the greatest number of offspring."

We tend to believe that when things are at their objective worst, like during war and disaster, humans go all "every man for himself"—but that's just not the case. Sociologist Charles Fritz did a study in 1959 interviewing over nine thousand survivors of disaster, and he found that when modern society goes to hell, we return to our natural state of cooperation. Status is temporarily put aside. We ignore squabbles over politics, class, and religion. No time for that stuff right now, grab a bucket. We gain clarity over what is truly important, a clarity that seems impossible during day-to-day life. When the stakes are life and death, what's meaningful is stark.

When you have a problem, it's your problem. But when we all have a problem, like tsunami devastation or enemy invasion, it's *our* problem. We're in it together. Fritz wrote: "The widespread sharing of danger, loss, and deprivation produces an intimate, primarily group solidarity among the survivors . . . This merging of individual and societal needs provides a feeling of belonging and a sense of unity rarely achieved under normal circumstances." And so we revert to our nature. The need for connection is wired deeper than the desire for comfort. And when things are at their objective worst, humans are at their best.

In 2005, Hurricane Katrina hit New Orleans. Eighty percent of the city was flooded, over 1,800 people died. How did humans respond? Well, the news was filled with reports of lawlessness.

Murder, rapes, looting, and gang dominance filled the head-lines. But it just wasn't true. The next month a deeper analysis revealed that "the vast majority of reported atrocities committed by evacuees—mass murders, rapes, and beatings—have turned out to be false, or at least unsupported by any evidence, accord-ing to key military, law-enforcement, medical, and civilian of-ficials in positions to know." Rebecca Solnit spoke with Denise Moore, who was there in the midst of it all, and she said, "We were trapped like animals, but I saw the greatest humanity I'd ever seen from the most unlikely places."

The Disaster Research Center at the University of Delaware re-viewed over seven hundred studies on similar incidents and found this type of response is true in general. We don't exploit, we unite. Bregman quotes one researcher as saying, "Whatever the extent of the looting, it always pales in significance to the widespread altru-ism that leads to free and massive giving and sharing of goods and services."

When the group is threatened, we sacrifice willingly because it's not sacrifice. We are happy to be needed and to contribute. When disaster strikes, more people head toward the scene than away. Fritz wrote: "Movement toward the disaster area usually is both quantitatively and qualitatively more significant than flight or evacuation from the scene of destruction." And this is the norm. Adam Mayblum recounted his experience at 9/11 to Re-becca Solnit: "They failed in terrorizing us. We were calm. If you want to kill us, leave us alone because we will do it by ourselves. If you want to make us stronger, attack and we unite."

When we are one, we don't need placebos. We give care and are provided with care. During war, psychiatric admissions de-cline. This phenomenon has been documented time and time again. When Belfast experienced riots in the 1960s, depression plummeted in the districts with the most violence and went up where there was none. Psychologist H. A. Lyons wrote, "It would be irresponsible to suggest violence as a means of improving mental health, but the Belfast findings suggest that people will feel better psychologically if they have more involvement with their community."

And, perhaps most shockingly, we are often happy. Famed humanitarian Dorothy Day wrote about San Francisco's 1906 earthquake saying, "What I remember most plainly about the earthquake was the human warmth and kindliness of everyone afterward . . . While the crisis lasted, people loved each other."

And when the threat is quelled, ironically, we miss it. Not the pain or the misery, but the community. Sebastian Junger spoke to journalist Nidzara Ahmetasevic, twenty years after Sarajevo's war, asking her if they were happier then. She replied, "We were the *happiest*. And we laughed more." She went on to add, "I do miss something about the war. But I also believe that the world we are living in—and the peace we have—is very fucked up if somebody is missing war. And many people do."

No, I'm not suggesting we go to war or all live in grass huts with no electricity. Obviously, there are many, many, *many* great things about the modern world, and I don't mean to come off as some alchemist of melancholy making modernity seem like an air-conditioned nightmare. But James Branch Cabell wrote, "An optimist believes we live in the best possible of worlds. A pessimist fears that this is true." There is little doubt that when it comes to community and happiness, we are, in some ways, victims of our own success. It's easy to notice the benefits of modern life, but so much harder to calculate the loss of meaning and community.

Early human life was routinely a disaster, and we could not survive without help. Individualism was not even on the menu. There are a near-infinite number of reasons to want to put that behind us. We no longer have to depend on each other, but we are still wired to. We need each other, even when we don't *need* each other. If all of your child's needs were provided for, you would still want to do things for them, to protect them despite the fact that they're safe, to feed them though food is plentiful. If your kid had everything they could ever want, you would still desire to perform the process of caretaking. As a culture, we seem to believe we can "solve" all the needs and get to zero, but we still need to be needed. Junger wrote, "Humans don't mind hardship, in fact they thrive on it; what they mind is not feeling necessary. Modern society has perfected the art of making people not feel necessary." It took a global pandemic for many of us to be reminded how important our relationships are.

We have grown smarter, but less wise. And that's not just a warm platitude, it's science. Wisdom isn't just raw IQ; it involves understanding others. And when researchers surveyed two thousand Americans from different income levels, they found wealthier meant less wise. No, money's not bad. But the poor have to depend on one another more, like we did in the past, like we do during disaster. And that's what the scientists found: "The effect of social class on wise reasoning was at least in part accounted for by a greater sense of interdependence expressed by participants with lower [socioeconomic status]."

Remember how friends were "another self"? Communities are the same. The self-expansion research found the same effect for groups. We include them as part of ourselves when we belong. Communities are another self, another friend. In fact, the effect is stronger in some ways: a 2020 study found that we feel the most support from friends when they're connected to one another. Feeling loved by five separate pals is less loving than five mutual pals. Friends are great. Communities can be even better.

We may giggle at the Amish, but they know this better than we do. They don't eschew technology because they're Luddites. They do adopt some of it, like tractors. How do they decide what gets approved and what doesn't? By the effect it has on the closeness of the community. Tractors help you grow crops. Sounds good. But cars let people live farther apart. No bueno.

When Amish youth come of age, they participate in what is called "Rumspringa." They don't have to follow the rules and can live in the modern world for a while. They get a chance to see the other side. After a couple of years of this, they have to choose: modern world or Amish world? More than 80 percent choose to return and become Amish. And since the 1950s, the percentage that chooses Amish life has only been increasing.

It's not enough to merely have face-to-face contact. We need a community. Remember those health benefits of human contact? Psychologist Julianne Holt-Lunstad reviewed 148 longitudinal studies and found that people who were enmeshed in a community had a 50 percent lower chance of death over a seven-year stretch. But that community aspect is paramount. Employees and digital connections had no effect. You lived longer only by spending time with those you really knew and felt close to.

With community comes obligation. But we need the burden, as we need the responsibilities of parenthood. We have gone a little too far in the way of freedom. We want a two-way street because too much control is unfulfilling. We need to share and be cared for, just as we need to care for others. Look at a list of the happiest careers and it's dominated by helping: clergy, firefighters, physical therapists, teachers. (Authors are up there as well, much to the surprise of yours truly.)

I don't raise all these depressing points about modern life to make you sad. I want you to be happier. But Johann Hari points to research showing if you try to be happier, you will likely fail. Why? Because the Western definition of happiness is individualistic. And, as Brett Ford of UC Berkeley found, that doesn't work. Your efforts will be all me-me-me, and we saw that doesn't jive with millions of years of human nature. You'll be going at it all wrong because you're aiming for the wrong target. More status, more money, more control, fewer obligations won't do it . . . Oh, by the way, if you live in Asia, ignore what I just said. There, the definition of happiness is more collectivist. To be happier, you'll try to help others and your efforts will be more successful. As Ford told Hari, "The more you think happiness is a social thing, the better off you are." You can get happier. But to rise, you must first think of how to lift others.

Hopefully, it's all starting to come together like Voltron. It's almost time to wrap this up. We need to get the final word on whether we're islands or not. But before we do that, maybe we should look at a real island and see what it can tell us about the story of our species . . .

Legally, they were already dead. Everything they owned was taken from them. Their marriages had been annulled. But they had become accustomed to horrible treatment. They were lepers. Literally.

It was 1866, and the territory of Hawaii was "fixing" its leprosy dilemma. Frightened of the disease, the authorities decided to exile lepers to the island of Molokai. There were sixteen; only four were relatively healthy. Two were very sick. Soon three more would be gravely ill as well.

There would be no hospital, no staff to care for them on Molokai. They were provided with almost nothing. Some blankets and some farming tools they didn't even know how to use. Enough food to last only a few days. The huts on the island were in disrepair. To say they were left to survive on their own would be too generous; they were abandoned to die.

And they were strangers, not a family or a group of friends. There was simply no reason for the healthy to help the sick. In fact, quite the opposite. If the fit kept all the food for themselves and didn't waste time tending to the weak, they would greatly increase their chances of survival. The salt pork and sea biscuits would last weeks if split among the four who were healthiest.

Only triage would allow them to create a livable existence. It was time to ditch the weak. They were burdensome strangers who would cause them all to die. It was the only rational thing to do . . .

The ship returned two weeks later, not to bring aid, but to drop off more lepers. And the crew was stunned by what they saw.

The huts were fixed. Crops had been sown. Fires burned 24/7 to keep the sick warm. Fresh water had been found. The healthiest had not taken the food for themselves; they spent all their time caring for the weak. The others cooked and tended to the sustainable life they had started to build. And every single one of the initial group was alive.

The strong didn't do the "rational" thing and choose selfish survival. They operated on instinct. Human nature. They made the seemingly irrational choice to care.

A "just-so" story? Hardly. As detailed in *Pirates, Prisoners, and Lepers: Lessons from Life Outside the Law*, University of Pennsylvania professor Paul Robinson and Sarah Robinson explain that this response has been seen over and over in groups that find themselves in the most dire of situations, all around the world, all throughout history. Not always, but very often. Because "irrational" cooperation is what led to our success as a species.

We forget that our supremacy on this planet was far from fated. We lived on the edge of extinction for most of the 125,000 generations of Homo sapiens. The ultimate proof is that if we didn't cooperate more often than not, if we didn't take the gamble and choose to help when it didn't make sense, quite simply: *you would not be here reading this.*

The Molokai leper colony actually was an island. But what it proves is that you and I are not.

*

So what have we learned?

Loneliness sucks and we're lonelier than ever, but it's less about a lack of people and more about lack of community. And loneliness is new, born of our relatively recent story of individualism.

We could also use a little more deliberate solitude to be more creative, to find wisdom, and to get in touch with ourselves. But, no, we don't need as much as our hermit Chris Knight got. (Harvard psychologist Jill Hooley actually believes he has schizoid personality disorder. If you don't, you're gonna require more people time than he did.) We need a balance between community and solitude, like we had pre-nineteenth century, but right now we're not getting enough of either.

Popularity is a good thing, but as a culture we're choosing the wrong kind, opting for status, power, and fame over being likable. This generally doesn't lead to good things, and that's why your daughter wants to be a celebrity assistant instead of a CEO. The lack of community makes our gray matter feel unsafe, pushing us toward a greater need for control in our lives and relationships. This has led to choosing parasocial relationships with technology, which are unfulfilling. Social media isn't evil, but since we often use it to replace real relationships and community, its harms frequently outweigh its positives. Machiavelli said if you have to choose between being loved or feared, choose feared. But you're not a prince, so sorry, we all need a bit more love. As Pepperdine psychology professor Louis Cozolino puts it, "The problem is, when you depend on a substitute for love, you can never get enough." And please do not fall in love with a pillow.

Happiness is down and depression is up as a result of our hyperindividualistic society. We've tried to cope via the placebo effects of antidepressants and the pseudo-cuddles of opiates, but that's not going to do it. What we need is more community. It's our natural state, and when disaster briefly peels back modernity, we can see how naturally good and cooperative we are. When life is at its worst, we're at our best, as we've shown time and time again from Katrina to Molokai. When the need for status is cast aside, when we're "in it together," facing our collective problems, we find that personal comfort matters little, we don't need the obsessive control, we sacrifice for one another, and, shockingly, we feel better. Let's not wait for catastrophe or war. We can take a lesson from the Amish and better prioritize community. As the placebo research shows us, we all need to know that someone is looking out for us. That we're not alone. That despite whatever ails us, help is on the way.

What's the final verdict on this section's maxim? Do I even need to say it? Okay, for the record:

"No man is an island" = True.

The 1800s brought revolutionary new ideas that led to a lot of good things but also to some not-so-good-things. Individualism went a little too far, and we ended up nutritionally deficient on community, resulting in emotional scurvy. And that's where our lovely theme of "story" comes back. How do stories play into community? Lee Marvin once said, "Death is only the end if you assume the story is about you."

You're not the only character in the story.

The story is not a "one-man show." Maybe it's an hour drama (or on bad days, a sitcom), but if this thing doesn't have a full cast of characters, it's going to be a tragedy. Heck, if you have kids you might not even be the main character in the story anymore, but instead the wise mentor who aids the protagonist in the journey ahead. (Me? I'm just the comic relief.)

Consciously, we always strive for more autonomy and control, but deep down a "one-man show" is not what we're wired for. If we were, the placebo effect wouldn't work. You need someone to tell you "it's going to be okay." The hero needs to save others and occasionally be saved themselves.

Whoa. We made it through the final chapter. You and me. *We* did it.

Now it's time to solve the biggest mystery of them all: the meaning of life. We've got a handful of pages left. Shouldn't be that hard, right?

Let's begin our ending with one final story . . .

SOMETHING VAGUELY
RESEMBLING A CONCLUSION

Dr. Giovanni Borromeo just wanted the deaths to stop. In 1943 a lethal new disease swept through his district in Rome. The doctors called it "Syndrome K" because they had no idea what it was. Contagious in the extreme, the infected had to be kept in a separate, locked ward.

The initial stages of the disease resembled tuberculosis, but its progression was far more diabolical, causing neurological symptoms like paralysis and dementia. Finally, patients would die from being unable to breathe. The children suffered the worst. You always knew when you were close to the Syndrome K ward because the harsh, relentless coughing of the little ones pierced the air and echoed through the halls.

No one had ever seen anything like it before. The underlying pathogen had not been identified, and there was no treatment. Epidemiology was still in its infancy and the war was still raging in Europe, so there was no help. Giovanni's greatest fear was that it would spread, not merely inside the confines of his beloved hospital, but to the rest of Rome. Only twenty-five years prior, the 1918 flu had infected five hundred million people and eliminated nearly 5 percent of the world's population.

The situation was bad and quickly getting worse, but at least he was at the perfect place. Fatebenefratelli Hospital sits on a small island in the Tiber River and had a tradition of waging war against burgeoning epidemics. In 1656 it battled plague; in 1832 its enemy was cholera. It was a sanctuary, and its doctors would do what they had always done: fight to save lives, no matter the cost.

But disease was not the only threat. If Syndrome K didn't kill Giovanni, the Nazis might. They did inspections of the hospital, and they didn't appreciate his interference. Some of the staff would mumble that he should let them check the Syndrome K ward as they wished. But Giovanni was committed to saving lives. He hated the Nazis, but he was not going to let them die. He repeatedly refused them entrance to the Syndrome K wing.

One time it became heated. Giovanni wondered if they would drag him away for his impudence. But when the Nazis heard the savage coughing of the children, they changed their minds and left.

It was a terrible time. He did what he could. Giovanni just wanted the deaths to stop. Eventually, the war ended. The Nazis never did kill him. And as a good doctor, he never did let them risk their lives entering the Syndrome K ward. Another miracle was that he never became infected himself . . .

But, then again, Judaism isn't contagious.

You see, my dear reader, Syndrome K didn't exist. It was a story. A lie. Like I said, Giovanni Borromeo *just wanted the deaths to stop.* The deaths of innocent Jews, that is. Fatebenefratelli was a haven.

Back in October, the Nazis rounded up ten thousand of Rome's Jews and shipped them to the camps. The Jewish ghetto was across from Fatebenefratelli. The few who evaded capture sought refuge in the hospital. Giovanni and his fellow doctors took them in. But there were too many to conceal. And they kept coming. Without a plan, the Nazis would notice and everyone would die. And so they created a story: "Syndrome K."

As Adriano Ossicini, another doctor at the hospital, later said in an interview, "We created those papers for Jewish people as if they were ordinary patients, and in the moment when we had to say what disease they suffered? It was Syndrome K, meaning 'I am admitting a Jew,' as if he or she were ill, but they were all healthy."

The doctors were terrified, but that didn't stop them from having a little fun to relieve the tension. The K in Syndrome K? They named their fictional disease after the local Nazi commander, Kesselring. And by making the disease seem so horrible and locking the "victims" in a private ward, they scared the Nazis away from further investigations.

Yeah, that one time it reached a scary point. It seemed like the Nazis were going to arrest Giovanni, march into the Syndrome K wing, and discover the ruse. Luckily, one of the staff was in the ward and playfully encouraged the children to cough as loudly and horribly as they could. That did the trick. The Nazis didn't want to catch whatever was causing those terrible sounds.

In 1961, Giovanni died in the same hospital he saved lives in. He didn't die from the terribly virulent Syndrome K. No one ever had. But over one hundred people lived because of it. And in 2004, Yad Vashem, the Israeli Holocaust remembrance organization, declared Borromeo "righteous among the nations." A hero.

The story was a lie. Syndrome K was not real. But, far more important, the lives it saved were.

*

In the introduction to this book, I promised you the answer to the meaning of life. And now we're almost at the end. So, uh, time to deliver, I guess. (Note to self: gotta handle this tactfully. People have been burned at the stake for getting this wrong.)

Almost by definition, meaning is something that must connect *everything* in life. The meaning of life must be something that, beneath the surface, motivates the majority of what we do, makes us happy when we are in line with it and unhappy when we are not.

So, enough throat clearing: What is the one true meaning of life?

Heck if I know. Look, I understand you were expecting some real Morgan-Freemanesque wisdom here, but I'm not licensed to practice metaphysics in the state of California. Sure, I have a metric ton of research studies, but I don't have a hotline to eternal truth. Ask me about something as deep as the one true meaning of life, and I'm looking around like the kid at the mall who can't find his mom.

I know, I know, that's not a very satisfying answer. But, really, you can't blame me. I looked it up, and the question of "What is the meaning of life?" is actually pretty new. Believe it or not, it first appeared in English in 1843 . . .

Hey, hold on a second. Nineteenth century. Just like loneliness. Before then, meaning came prepackaged and ready-made. We had stories that satisfied the need for meaning, so we didn't bother to ask. Then all those new individualistic ideas started taking over. Science bloomed. It gave us better answers about the material world and more control over it, which was quite welcome. But it didn't fill the emotional void it created when we lost our stories of meaning . . .

Hmm. Maybe there is an answer. Let's come at this from another angle. Let's ask: *What predicts how meaningful we perceive life to be?* And a 2013 study found a very robust and clear answer to that question: a sense of belonging.

In fact, that paper, "To Belong Is to Matter: Sense of Belonging

Enhances Meaning in Life," didn't just find a correlation. Belonging *caused* a feeling of meaning in life. And this wasn't some scientific one-off. Another paper by the same author, Roy Baumeister, a professor at Florida State University, posited a need to belong as the "master motive" of our species. And far from being met with resistance, that study has been cited more than twenty-four thousand times.

Belonging. It's why our species' superpower is cooperation. It's what we saw with drug addiction hijacking the social reward pathways of the human brain. It's what we saw with the placebo effect curing ills by telling your body someone cares.

Alright, I'm not looking for mom anymore. Morgan-Freemanesque wisdom coming up. I humbly submit to you: *belonging is the meaning of life*.

Before the nineteenth century and individualism, all our ideologies were stories of belonging and connection, reminding us that we're not alone and that you're not the only character in the story. Meaning and belonging have always come wrapped in stories and helped form the ideologies we live by.

Now some are gonna say, "Most of those stories weren't true." And I don't deny that. As Neal Gaiman said, "Stories may well be lies, but they are good lies that say true things." The stories aren't always true, but, like Syndrome K, the people around us *are*. Science builds models to try and understand the world, and they're never perfect, but they do give us insights. That's why the old saying is "all models are wrong but some models are useful." That phrase is true for our stories as well. Their primary purpose, whether we knew it or not, wasn't truth but unity. They don't always get the facts right, but they do get the meaning of life right: belonging. Just like your body accepts a fake story in the placebo effect. The acupuncture doesn't help, but the care it delivers is a clear signal of belonging, and that's what's important.

The inaccuracy of our stories hasn't been the biggest problem for humans. Oh, no. What's really screwed things up for us is when the story of Group A didn't match the story of Group B. The power of belonging is so strong that we put the brass knuckles on when our stories are challenged. You don't need a history PhD to see that fighting over stories has caused a lot of problems for humankind. I talked a lot about the bonding that occurs within a group during war, but I conveniently didn't mention what caused the war in the first place. Our species superpower may be cooperation inside a group that shares a story, but we've been all too willing to kill members of a group who have a different story.

So what's the answer? How do we maintain belonging when our stories are mutually exclusive? The solution is simple: *more stories*. We can always create another story to unite us in a new way. We do it now. You may not be my family, but you are my friend. You may not be my religion, but we are part of the same nation. We may not have any of these in common, but we may both be Star Wars fans. New stories can unite us when the old ones fail to. We can always be a part of the same tribe and share a story of belonging. We have an infinite number of ways to connect if we try. We don't need war or disaster to refresh our factory setting of cooperation. In the nineteenth century our dominant meta-story changed. But we can change it again if we want to.

Maybe it's time for a little less science and a few more stories. Yeah, that's ironic coming from me. I'm the guy who's been pushing scientific studies into your eyeballs for a few hundred pages. But I also included stories in this book, didn't I? And a 2020 study said: "We find anecdotal evidence to be more persuasive than statistical evidence when emotional engagement is high, as when issues involve a severe threat, health, or oneself." Yes, I am a sneaky bastard. But it's all the more proof that we *need* stories.

I still like facts and statistics. They're incredibly valuable and have dramatically improved our lives. That said, we won't find the meaning of life through scientific theories. We need a uniting story that goes beyond the individual and makes us feel we belong. Mark Twain wrote, "Don't part with your illusions. When they are gone you may still exist, but you have ceased to live."

You need to belong. And we all need a story to unite us. This book isn't "choose your own adventure"—but your life is. So this is not an ending. It's a beginning.

We've looked at alien microwaves, genius horses, thieving hermits, the perils of perfect memories, Casanova, leper colonies, super soldiers, soccer liars, pillow girlfriends and placebos, friendships between preachers and pornographers, Mrs. Sherlock Holmes, the trolling of Edgar Allan Poe, hostage negotiators, handcuffs in the delivery room, the friendliest people in the world, vetoing Viagra, and fooling Nazis with fake diseases. I want to thank you for coming on this crazy journey with me.

I hope you learned something. I sure did. I have experienced deep regret in learning some of these lessons too late. I hope to have spared you some of that. I'm the guy who scored a four out of one hundred on Agreeableness, but the most memorable moments of my life, the ones that moved me the most, are not the ones where I was alone. They're always the ones when I was with a group where I felt accepted. Where I felt I belonged.

And if you're not feeling you belong right now, don't forget the magic placebo healing powers of this book. Seriously, they're as pain relieving as acupuncture. Just by holding it in your hands right now the midi-chlorians embedded in the cover are healing your pain. Science says so. Here's my email if you want to write to me: eb@bakadesuyo.com.

I now realize I needed this book more than you do. All my life, my story has been a solitary one. Not a buddy comedy or a romance or an ensemble drama. A one-man show. But I've learned a lesson from the loneliness of Frankenstein's monster. A book like this doesn't come together by spending a lot of time with friends. It comes from time spent alone. Perhaps too much time alone.

So I have to go now. I have to see my friends. I need to hug them and tell them I love them. Maybe say to them, "I'd like to eat your intestines." I have a lot to fix and make up for. But now, I have a better idea how to start.

There's an old African proverb that says, "If you want to go fast, go alone. If you want to go far, go together." I have gone fast for many, many years. But the road is much longer than I thought. Fast isn't going to cut it anymore. I need to go far.

Can we go together?

RESOURCES

As we discussed, loneliness is serious. If you're struggling, help is available. I've assembled a page of top-notch resources on my website. You can find it here:

https://www.bakadesuyo.com/resources

Getting assistance is nothing to feel ashamed about. After the science fiction novel that was 2020, all too many of us have felt cut off—including me. Under lockdown my mood ring exploded, and it felt like my soul had been deep fried.

If you're having a tough time, please visit that page. The problem of loneliness gets ignored so much you'd think it was a "terms and conditions" page. Letting yourself suffer constitutes existential malpractice. More important, please remember:

You are not alone.

BEFORE WE SAY GOODBYE

No matter how isolated you are and how lonely you feel,
if you do your work truly and conscientiously, unknown
friends will come and seek you.

—CARL JUNG

As I said in the book: this is not an ending, it's a beginning. A beginning of a better understanding of ourselves, understanding others, and learning more ways to just "human better."

This is an ongoing journey. Over 500,000 people have subscribed to my free newsletter. Join us:

https://www.bakadesuyo.com/newsletter

Let's go far. Let's go together.

ACKNOWLEDGMENTS

> Writing a book is like telling a joke and having to wait
> two years to know whether or not it was funny.
>
> —ALAIN DE BOTTON

Almost nobody reads the acknowledgments section. Frankly, that's a shame, because "No book is an island." Many people helped get this collection of words into your hands, and they deserve some praise.

Even though few people will read this, I'm thrilled to write it because I get to show some much-deserved gratitude—and it's as close as I'll ever come to being able to knight people.

- Jason Hallock. My Aristotelian true friend. He is definitely Another Self—and a much more agreeable one at that. All too often he has been the single Jenga piece preventing my collapse.
- Nick Krasney, Josh Kaufman, and David Epstein. They are mighty heroes in the BCU (Barker Cinematic Universe). They kept me going during pandemic lockdown when I was very much alone. Whatever my bank balance says, I am wealthy for having you guys in my life.
- My parents, who clearly had no idea what they were in for.
- My agent, Jim Levine, and my editors, Gideon Weil and

Hilary Swanson, all of whom tolerate my smorgasbord of eccentricities with fewer audible sighs than one would expect.

- Tyler Cowen, who put my blog on the map and helped me prove F. Scott Fitzgerald wrong: American lives can have second acts.

- I would also like to eat the intestines of Gautam Mukunda, Don Elmore, Mike Goode, Steve Kamb, and Tim Urban.

- And to all the people who read my blog, you are amazing. Simply amazing. You are my community, my tribe. You have changed my life in ways you will never know, all of them for the good. I cannot tell you how much you mean to me.

Okay, back to my rant. Like I said, it's not fair that acknowledgments sections never get read . . .

Wait. Hold on a second . . . That's not true anymore, is it? *You* read this. That's mighty awesome of you. Thank you for recognizing the contribution of my friends. You deserve something special. Perhaps a Wonka "Golden Ticket" of sorts? Go here to claim your prize, Charlie:

https://www.bakadesuyo.com/goldenticket

Aren't Easter eggs fun? I think there aren't enough of them in books. Then again, maybe there are more of them in this book somewhere. Who knows?

REFERENCES

Science is magic that works.

—KURT VONNEGUT

INTRODUCTION

Gottman, John M. *The Marriage Clinic: A Scientifically Based Marital Therapy.* New York: W. W. Norton, 1999.

Hahlweg, K., et al. "The Munich Marital Therapy Study." In *Marital Interaction: Analysis and Modification*, edited by K. Hahlweg and N. S. Jacobson. New York: Guilford, 1984.

Lieberman, Matthew D., et al. "Putting Feelings into Words: Affect Labeling Disrupts Amygdala Activity in Response to Affective Stimuli." *Psychological Sciences* 18, no. 5 (2007): 421–28. https://pubmed.ncbi.nlm.nih.gov/17576282/.

Shenk, Joshua Wolf. "What Makes Us Happy?" *Atlantic*, June 2009. https://www.theatlantic.com/magazine/archive/2009/06/what-makes-us-happy/307439/.

CHAPTER 1

Alison, Laurence, ed. *The Forensic Psychologist's Casebook: Psychological Profiling and Criminal Investigation.* Milton Park, UK: Taylor and Francis, 2005.

Case Western Reserve University. "The Lost Life of a Woman Who Searched for the Missing." The Daily, January 26, 2017. https://thedaily.case.edu/lost-life-woman-searched-missing/.

Douglas, John E., et al. *Crime Classification Manual: A Standard System for Investigating and Classifying Violent Crime*, third edition. Hoboken, NJ: Wiley, 2013.

Dutton, Denis. "The Cold Reading Technique." *Experientia* 44 (1988): 326–32. http://www.denisdutton.com/cold_reading.htm.

Forer, Bertram. "The Fallacy of Personal Validation: A Classroom Demonstration of Gullibility." *Journal of Abnormal Psychology* 44, no. 1 (1949): 118–23.

Gilovich, Thomas. *How We Know What Isn't So: The Fallibility of Human Reason in Everyday Life.* New York: Free Press, 1993.

Gladwell, Malcolm. "Dangerous Minds: Criminal Profiling Made Easy." *New Yorker*, November 12, 2007. https://www.newyorker.com/magazine/2007/11/12/dangerous-minds.

REFERENCES

Hunter, Colin. "Cold Reading: Confessions of a 'Psychic.'" Association for Science and Reason, August 8, 2007. http://www.scienceandreason.ca/skepticism /cold-reading-confessions-of-a-psychic/.

Hyman, Ray. "Cold Reading: How to Convince Strangers That You Know All About Them." *Skeptical Inquirer*, 1977. https://www.deceptionary.com/ftp /Hyman.pdf.

Konnikova, Maria. *The Confidence Game: Why We Fall for It . . . Every Time.* New York: Penguin, 2016.

Lilienfeld, Scott O., et al. *Fifty Great Myths of Popular Psychology: Shattering Widespread Misconceptions about Human Behavior.* Malden, MA: Wiley-Blackwell, 2010.

MacMillan, Thomas. "Can Criminal Profilers Really Get Inside the Head of a Killer?" Vulture, October 20, 2017. https://www.vulture.com/2017/10/mind hunter-criminal-profiling-really-work-like-this.html.

Matthews, Dylan. "Criminal Profiling Doesn't Work: TV Shows Should Maybe Stop Celebrating It." Vox, November 12, 2018. https://www.vox.com/future -perfect/2018/11/12/18044688/criminal-profilers-mindhunter-hannibal -criminal-minds.

McRaney, David. *You Are Not So Smart.* New York: Gotham, 2011.

Picker, Lenny. "Before There Was Harry Bosch, There Was Grace Humiston: PW Talks with Brad Ricca." *Publisher's Weekly*, November 11, 2016. https:// www.publishersweekly.com/pw/by-topic/authors/interviews/article/72002 -before-there-was-harry-bosch-there-was-grace-humiston-pw-talks-with -brad-ricca.html.

Ricca, Brad. *Mrs. Sherlock Holmes: The True Story of New York City's Greatest Female Detective and the 1917 Missing Girl Case That Captivated a Nation.* New York: St. Martin's, 2017.

Ricca, Brad. "Searching for Grace Humiston: Mrs. Sherlock Holmes." The History Reader, January 13, 2012. http://www.thehistoryreader.com/modern -history/grace-humiston/.

Rowland, Ian. *The Full Facts Book of Cold Reading.* London: Ian Rowland Limited, Sixth edition, 2015.

Wikipedia. "Barnum Effect." https://en.wikipedia.org/wiki/Barnum_effect.

Wikipedia. "Confirmation Bias." https://en.wikipedia.org/wiki/Confirmation _bias.

Wikipedia. "Mary Grace Quackenbos." https://en.wikipedia.org/wiki/Mary _Grace_Quackenbos.

Wikipedia. "Offender Profiling." https://en.wikipedia.org/wiki/Offender_pro filing.

Witkowski, Tomasz. "Are Criminal Profilers 'Any Better Than a Bartender?' Not Necessarily, Suggests Review of Forty Years of Relevant Research." *Research Digest* (blog), January 30, 2019. https://digest.bps.org.uk/2019/01/30/better -than-a-bartender-not-necessarily-suggests-review-of-40-years-of-research-on -criminal-profiling/.

REFERENCES

CHAPTER 2

Bellows, Alan. "Clever Hans the Math Horse." Damn Interesting, February 2007. https://www.damninteresting.com/clever-hans-the-math-horse/.

Brown, Erik. "Clever Hans—the Horse That Could Count." Medium, April 12, 2019. https://medium.com/lessons-from-history/clever-hans-the-horse-that-could-count-561cdd5a1eab.

Dare, Tim. "Clever Hans: Cueing and the Observer Effect." Future Learn, n.d. https://www.futurelearn.com/courses/logical-and-critical-thinking/0/steps/9163.

Epley, Nicholas. *Mindwise: Why We Misunderstand What Others Think, Believe, Feel, and Want*. New York: Knopf Doubleday, 2014.

Eyal, Tal, and Nicholas Epley. "How to Seem Telepathic: Enabling Mind Reading by Matching Construal." *Psychological Science* 21, no. 5 (2010): 700–705. https://journals.sagepub.com/doi/pdf/10.1177/0956797610367754.

Eyal, T., M. Steffel, and N. Epley. "Perspective Mistaking: Accurately Understanding the Mind of Another Requires Getting Perspective, Not Taking Perspective." *Journal of Personality and Social Psychology* 114, no. 4 (2018): 547–71. http://psycnet.apa.org/record/2018-13651-004.

Galinsky, Adam D., Cynthia S. Wang, and Gillian Ku. "Perspective-Takers Behave More Stereotypically." *Journal of Personality and Social Psychology* 95, no. 2 (2008): 404–19. https://pubmed.ncbi.nlm.nih.gov/18665710/.

Goman, Carol Kinsey. *The Silent Language of Leaders: How Body Language Can Help—or Hurt—How You Lead*. San Francisco: Jossey-Bass, 2011.

Hall, Judith A., Marianne Schmid Mast, and Tessa V. West. *The Social Psychology of Perceiving Others Accurately*. Cambridge: Cambridge University Press, 2016.

Hooper, Rowan. *Superhuman: Life at the Extremes of Our Capacity*. New York: Simon & Schuster, 2018.

Knapp, Mark L., Judith Hall, and Terrence G. Horgan. *Nonverbal Communication in Human Interaction* eighth edition. Boston: Wadsworth, Cengage Textbook, 2014.

Konnikova, Maria. *The Confidence Game: Why We Fall for It . . . Every Time*. New York: Penguin, 2016.

Murphy, Heather. "Why It Seems as If Everyone Is Always Angry with You." *New York Times*, April 24, 2018. https://www.nytimes.com/2018/04/24/science/reading-neutral-faces.html.

New York Times. "Berlin's Wonderful Horse." September 5, 1904. https://timesmachine.nytimes.com/timesmachine/1904/09/04/101396572.pdf.

New York Times. "'Clever Hans' Again." October 2, 1904. https://timesmachine.nytimes.com/timesmachine/1904/10/02/120289067.pdf.

New York Times. "Expert Commission Decides That the Horse Actually Reasons." 1904.

New York Times. "A Horse—and the Wise Men." July 23, 1911. https://timesmachine.nytimes.com/timesmachine/1911/07/23/104872007.pdf.

Pfungst, Oskar. *Clever Hans (The Horse of Mr. Von Osten): A Contribution to*

Experimental Animal and Human Psychology. Translated by Carl L. Rahn. 1911. https://www.gutenberg.org/files/33936/33936-h/33936-h.htm.

Samhita, Laasya, and Hans J. Gross. "The 'Clever Hans Phenomenon' Revisited." *Communicative and Integrative Biology* 6, no. 6 (2013). https://www.ncbi.nlm. nih.gov/pmc/articles/PMC3921203/.

Swann, William B., Jr., and Michael J. Gill. "Beliefs, Confidence, and the Widows Ademoski: On Knowing What We Know About Others." 107–25. https://labs. la.utexas.edu/swann/files/2017/05/Ademoski.pdf.

Swann, William B., Jr., and Michael J. Gill. "Confidence and Accuracy in Person Perception: Do We Know What We Think We Know About Our Relationship Partners?" *Journal of Personality and Social Psychology* 73, no. 4 (1997): 747–57. https://labs.la.utexas.edu/swann/files/2016/03/swann_gill97.pdf.

Todorov, Alexander. *Face Value: The Irresistible Influence of First Impressions.* Princeton, NJ: Princeton University Press, 2017.

Wikipedia. "Clever Hans." https://en.wikipedia.org/wiki/Clever_Hans.

Wikipedia. "Observer-Expectancy Effect." https://en.wikipedia.org/wiki/Observer -expectancy_effect.

CHAPTER 3

l1gouveia. "Hyperthymesia: Gift or Curse?" Do Good, November 4, 2013. https://l1gouveia.wordpress.com/2013/11/04/hyperthymesia-gift-or-curse/.

American Association for the Advancement of Science. "First Impressions Count When Making Personality Judgments, New Research Shows." *EurekAlert!*, November 3, 2009. https://www.eurekalert.org/news-releases/759765.

American Association for the Advancement of Science. "Personalities Judged by Physical Appearance Alone." *EurekAlert!*, December 10, 2009. https://www.eu-rekalert.org/news-releases/678601.

Biesanz, Jeremy C., et al. "Do We Know When Our Impressions of Others Are Valid? Evidence for Realistic Accuracy Awareness in First Impressions of Personality." *Social Psychological and Personality Science* 2, no. 5 (2011): 452–59. https://journals.sagepub.com/doi/pdf/10.1177/1948550610397211.

"The Boy Who Can't Forget (Superhuman Genius Documentary)." Real Stories, October 12, 2016. https://www.youtube.com/watch?v=9Bnu0UrgxBg.

Brandon, A. Ally, Erin P. Hussey, and Manus J. Donahue. "A Case of Hyperthymesia: Rethinking the Role of the Amygdala in Autobiographical Memory." *Neurocase* 19, no. 2 (2012): 166–81. https://www.ncbi.nlm.nih.gov/pmc/articles/PMC3432421/.

Cooperman, Jeannette. "The Boy Who Can't Forget." *St. Louis*, August 22, 2014. https://www.stlmag.com/news/the-boy-who-can%27t-forget/.

"Endless Memory, Part 1." *CBS News*, December 19, 2010. https://www.youtube. com/watch?v=2zTkBgHNsWM.

"Endless Memory, Part 2." *CBS News*, June 19, 2011. https://www.youtube.com/ watch?v=en23bCvp-Fw.

Epley, Nicholas. *Mindwise: Why We Misunderstand What Others Think, Believe, Feel, and Want.* New York: Knopf Doubleday, 2014.

REFERENCES

"Extraordinary Variations of the Human Mind: James McGaugh: Highly Superior Autobiographical Memory." University of California Television, July 12, 2017. https://www.youtube.com/watch?v=YDbFSiMg_nQ.

Fetchenhauer, Detlef, Ton Groothuis, and Julia Pradel. "Not Only States but Traits—Humans Can Identify Permanent Altruistic Dispositions in 20's." *Evolution and Human Behavior* 31, no. 2 (2010): 80–86. https://psycnet.apa.org/record/2009-16070-001.

Fowler, Katherine A., Scott O. Lilienfeld, and Christopher J. Patrick. "Detecting Psychopathy from Thin Slices of Behavior." *Psychological Assessment* 21, no. 1 (2009): 68–78. https://pubmed.ncbi.nlm.nih.gov/19290767/.

"The Gift of Endless Memory." *60 Minutes*, December 16, 2010. https://www.cbsnews.com/news/the-gift-of-endless-memory/.

Gilovich, Thomas. *How We Know What Isn't So: The Fallibility of Human Reason in Everyday Life*. New York: Free Press, 1993.

Gosling, Sam. *Snoop: What Your Stuff Says About You*. New York: Basic Books, 2009.

Gray, Keturah, and Katie Escherich. "Woman Who Can't Forget Amazes Doctors." *ABC News*, May 9, 2008. https://abcnews.go.com/Health/story?id=4813052&page=1.

Hall, Judith A., Marianne Schmid Mast, and Tessa V. West. *The Social Psychology of Perceiving Others Accurately*. Cambridge: Cambridge University Press, 2016.

Himmelfarb, Samuel. "Studies in the Perception of Ethnic Group Members: I. Accuracy, Response Bias, and Anti-Semitism." *Journal of Personality and Social Psychology* 4, no. 4 (1966): 347–55. https://psycnet.apa.org/record/1966-13126-001.

"Holding Grudges When You Remember Everything." *60 Minutes*, January 12, 2014. https://www.youtube.com/watch?v=HLotU3_taUc.

Hooper, Rowan. *Superhuman: Life at the Extremes of Our Capacity*. New York: Simon & Schuster, 2018.

"In Defense of Ignorance." *This American Life*, April 22, 2016. https://www.thisamericanlife.org/585/transcript.

Israel, David K. "Four People with Super Memory." *Mental Floss*, September 21, 2009. http://mentalfloss.com/article/30543/4-people-super-memory.

Knapp, Hall, and Horgan. *Nonverbal Communication in Human Interaction*.

Ko, Young Jin, and Jin Nam Choi. "Overtime Work as the Antecedent of Employee Satisfaction, Firm Productivity, and Innovation." *Journal of Organizational Behavior* 40, no. 3 (2019): 282–95. https://onlinelibrary.wiley.com/doi/full/10.1002/job.2328.

Konnikova, Maria. *The Confidence Game: Why We Fall for It . . . Every Time*. New York: Penguin, 2016.

Konnikova, Maria. *Mastermind: How to Think Like Sherlock Holmes*. New York: Penguin, 2013.

Kraus, Michael W., and Dracher Keltner. "Signs of Socioeconomic Status: A Thin-Slicing Approach." *Psychological Science* 20, no. 1 (2009): 99–106. https://pubmed.ncbi.nlm.nih.gov/19076316/.

REFERENCES

LePort, Aurora K. R., Shauna M. Stark, and James L. Mcgaugh. "Highly Superior Autobiographical Memory: Quality and Quantity of Retention over Time." *Frontiers in Psychology* 6 (January 2016). https://www.researchgate.net/publica tion/291391487_Highly_Superior_Autobiographical_Memory_Quality_and _Quantity_of_Retention_Over_Time.

LePort, Aurora K. R., et al. "Behavioral and Neuroanatomical Investigation of Highly Superior Autobiographical Memory (HSAM)." *Neurobiology of Learning and Memory* 98, no. 1 (2012): 78–92. https://www.sciencedirect.com/sci ence/article/pii/S1074742712000706.

LePort, Aurora K. R., et al. "A Cognitive Assessment of Highly Superior Autobiographical Memory." *Memory* 25, no. 2 (2017). https://www.tand fonline.com/doi/abs/10.1080/09658211.2016.1160126?scroll=top&need Access=true&journalCode=pmem20.

LePort, Aurora K. R., et al. "Highly Superior Autobiographical Memory: Quality and Quantity of Retention over Time." *Frontiers in Psychology*, January 21, 2016. https://www.frontiersin.org/articles/10.3389/fpsyg.2015.02017/full.

Little, Anthony C., and David I. Perrett. "Using Composite Images to Assess Accuracy in Personality Attribution to Faces." *British Journal of Psychology* 98, pt. 1 (February 2007): 111–26. https://pubmed.ncbi.nlm.nih.gov/17319053/.

Lorenzo, Genevieve L., Jeremy C. Biesanz, and Lauren J. Human. "What Is Beautiful Is Good and More Accurately Understood: Physical Attractiveness and Accuracy in First Impressions of Personality." *Psychological Science* 21, no. 12 (2010): 1777–82. https://pubmed.ncbi.nlm.nih.gov/21051521/.

Lount, Robert B., Jr., et al. "Getting Off on the Wrong Foot: The Timing of a Breach and the Restoration of Trust." *Personality and Social Psychology Bulletin* 34, no. 12 (2008): 1601–12. https://journals.sagepub.com/doi /10.1177/0146167208324512.

Macmillan, Amanda. "The Downside of Having an Almost Perfect Memory." *Time*, December 8, 2017. http://time.com/5045521/highly-superior -autobiographical-memory-hsam/.

Marcus, Gary. "Total Recall: The Woman Who Can't Forget." *Wired*, March 23, 2009. https://www.wired.com/2009/03/ff-perfectmemory/?currentPage=all.

McRobbie, Linda Rodriquez. "Total Recall: The People Who Never Forget." *Guardian*, February 8, 2017. https://www.theguardian.com/science/2017 /feb/08/total-recall-the-people-who-never-forget.

Naumann, Laura P., Simine Vazire, and Peter J. Rentfrow. "Personality Judgments Based on Physical Appearance." *Personality and Social Psychology Bulletin* 35, no. 12 (2009): 1661–71. https://journals.sagepub.com/doi/10 .1177/0146167209346309.

Patihis, Lawrence. "Individual Differences and Correlates of Highly Superior Autobiographical Memory." *Memory* 24, no. 7 (2016): 961–78. https://www.tandf online.com/doi/abs/10.1080/09658211.2015.1061011.

Pentland, Alex. *Honest Signals: How They Shape Our World*. Cambridge, MA: MIT Press, 2010.

REFERENCES

Price, Jill. *The Woman Who Can't Forget: The Extraordinary Story of Living with the Most Remarkable Memory Known to Science—a Memoir.* New York: Free Press, 2008.

Roberts, Amber. "The People Who Can Remember Every Single Day of Their Life." Vice, July 28, 2015. https://www.vice.com/en_us/article/xd7wxk/we-spoke -to-a-guy-who-remembers-almost-everything-about-his-life.

"Scientific Reports on Highly Superior Autobiographical Memory." Center for the Neurobiology of Learning and Memory, UC Irvine. http://cnlm.uci.edu/hsa /scientific-reports/.

Shafy, Samiha. "An Infinite Loop in the Brain." Translated by Christopher Sultan. *Spiegel International,* November 21, 2008. http://www.spiegel.de/international /world/the-science-of-memory-an-infinite-loop-in-the-brain-a-591972.html.

Spiegel, Alix. "When Memories Never Fade, the Past Can Poison the Present." *All Things Considered,* NPR, December 27, 2013. https://www.npr.org/sections /health-shots/2013/12/18/255285479/when-memories-never-fade-the-past-can -poison-the-present.

Thomson, Helen. "People Who Never Forget Their Past Could Have a Unique Kind of OCD." *New Scientist,* April 1, 2016. https://www.newscientist.com /article/2082771-people-who-never-forget-their-past-could-have-unique-kind -of-ocd/.

Thomson, Helen. *Unthinkable: An Extraordinary Journey Through the World's Strangest Brains.* New York: HarperCollins, 2019.

Thompson, Victoria. "He Never Forgets: Meet the Super-Memory Man." *ABC News,* March 13, 2009. https://abcnews.go.com/Nightline/story?id=7075443& page=1.

Todorov, Alexander. *Face Value: The Irresistible Influence of First Impressions.* Princeton, NJ: Princeton University Press, 2017.

Tsoulis-Reay, Alexa. "What It's Like to Remember Almost Everything That Has Ever Happened to You." *The Cut,* November 13, 2014. http://nymag.com/sci enceofus/2014/11/what-its-like-to-remember-almost-everything.html.

Wheeler, Sarah, Angela Book, and Kimberly Costello. "Psychopathic Traits and Perceptions of Victim Vulnerability." *Criminal Justice and Behavior* 36, no. 6 (2009): 635–48. https://journals.sagepub.com/doi/10.1177/0093854809 333958.

Wikipedia. "Confirmation Bias." https://en.wikipedia.org/wiki/Confirmation _bias.

Wikipedia. "Eidetic Memory." https://en.wikipedia.org/wiki/Eidetic_memory.

Wikipedia. "Hyperthymesia." https://en.wikipedia.org/wiki/Hyperthymesia.

Willis, Janine, and Alexander Todorov. "First Impressions: Making Up Your Mind After a 100-Ms Exposure to a Face." *Psychological Science* 17, no. 7 (2006): 592–98. https://journals.sagepub.com/doi/10.1111/j.1467-9280.2006 .01750.x.

Wyer, Natalie A. "You Never Get a Second Chance to Make a First (Implicit) Impression: The Role of Elaboration in the Formation and Revision of Implicit

Impressions." *Social Cognition* 28, no. 1 (2010): 1–19. https://psycnet.apa
.org/record/2010-04279-001.

Zander-Schellenberg, Thea, et al. "It Was Intuitive, and It Felt Good: A Daily Di-
ary Study on How People Feel When Making Decisions." *Cognition and Emotion* 33, no. 7 (2019): 1505–13. https://www.tandfonline.com/doi/full/10.1080
/02699931.2019.1570914.

CHAPTER 4

Alison, Laurence. ed. *The Forensic Psychologist's Casebook: Psychological Profiling
and Criminal Investigation*. Milton Park, UK: Taylor and Francis, 2005.

"Beyond Good Cop / Bad Cop: A Look at Real-Life Interrogations." *Fresh Air*,
NPR, December 5, 2013. https://www.npr.org/2013/12/05/248968150/beyond
-good-cop-bad-cop-a-look-at-real-life-interrogations.

Bogira, Steve. *Courtroom 302: A Year Behind the Scenes in an American Criminal
Courthouse*. New York: Knopf Doubleday, 2005.

Boon, Jon. "Carlos Kaiser: Fake Footballer Who Cheated a Living out of the
Game but Never Played in a Professional Match." *Sun*, July 19, 2018. https://
www.thesun.co.uk/sport/football/6798246/carlos-kaiser-farce-footballer
-documentary-brazil/.

Cole, Tim. "Lying to the One You Love: The Use of Deception in Romantic Relationships." *Journal of Social and Personal Relationships* 18, no. 1 (2001): 107–29.
https://journals.sagepub.com/doi/10.1177/0265407501181005.

DePaulo, B. M., and D. A. Kashy. "Everyday Lies in Close and Casual Relationships." *Journal of Personality and Social Psychology* 74, no. 1 (1998): 63–79.
https://psycnet.apa.org/record/1997-38342-005.

Etcoff, Nancy, et al. "Lie Detection and Language Comprehension." *Nature*, June
2000. https://www.researchgate.net/publication/12497273_Lie_detection_and
_language_comprehension.

Hall, Judith A., Marianne Schmid Mast, and Tessa V. West. *The Social Psychology
of Perceiving Others Accurately*. Cambridge: Cambridge University Press, 2016.

High-Value Detainee Interrogation Group. *Interrogation Best Practices*. Washington, DC: FBI, August 26, 2016. https://www.fbi.gov/file-repository/hig-report
-august-2016.pdf/view.

High-Value Detainee Interrogation Group. *Interrogation: A Review of the Science*.
Washington, DC: FBI, September 2016. "https://www.fbi.gov/file-repository
/hig-report-interrogation-a-review-of-the-science-september-2016.pdf/view.

Hirsch, Alan. "Going to the Source: The 'New' Reid Method and False Confessions." 2014. https://pdfs.semanticscholar.org/9f3f/d52ecc20cb9c988818403
d66664278e97352.pdf.

Jordan, Sarah, et al. "A Test of the Micro-expressions Training Tool: Does It Improve Lie Detection?" *Journal of Investigative Psychology and Offender Profiling* 16,
no. 3 (2019): 222–35. https://onlinelibrary.wiley.com/doi/10.1002/jip.1532.

Kassin, Saul M., et al. "Police-Induced Confessions: Risk Factors and Recom-
mendations." *Law and Human Behavior*, July 15, 2009. https://papers.ssrn.com
/sol3/papers.cfm?abstract_id=1483878.

REFERENCES

Katwala, Amit. "The Race to Create a Perfect Lie Detector—and the Dangers of Succeeding." *Guardian*, September 5, 2019. https://www.theguardian.com /technology/2019/sep/05/the-race-to-create-a-perfect-lie-detector-and-the -dangers-of-succeeding.

Kolker, Robert. "Nothing but the Truth." Marshall Project, May 24, 2016. https://www.themarshallproject.org/2016/05/24/nothing-but-the-truth.

Lilienfeld, Scott O., et al. *Fifty Great Myths of Popular Psychology: Shattering Widespread Misconceptions about Human Behavior.* Malden, MA: Wiley-Blackwell, 2010.

Leighty-Phillips, Tucker. "Superstar Who Couldn't Play the Game." Atlas Obscura, August 19, 2016. https://www.atlasobscura.com/articles/soccers-ultimate -con-man-was-a-superstar-who-couldnt-play-the-game.

Meissner, C. A., et al. "Developing an Evidence-Based Perspective on Interrogation: A Review of the U.S. Government's High-Value Detainee Interrogation Group Research Program." *Psychology, Public Policy, and Law* 23, no. 4 (2017): 438–57. https://psycnet.apa.org/record/2017-49224-003.

Nuwer, Rachel. ""What If We Knew When People Were Lying?"" BBC, March 25, 2019. https://www.bbc.com/future/article/20190324-what-if-we -knew-when-people-were-lying.

Phillips, Dom. "Confessions of Carlos Kaiser: Football's Biggest Conman." Yahoo Sport, July 23, 2018. https://uk.sports.yahoo.com/news/confessions-carlos -kaiser-football-biggest-110947116.html?guccounter=1.

Rollings, Grant. "Brazilian Footballer Enjoyed a Twenty-Six Year Run of Sex, Money, and Fame—Without Kicking a Ball." *Sun*, July 31, 2018. https://www .thesun.co.uk/sport/6900946/brazil-carlos-henrique-raposo/.

Rollings, Grant. "Inside the Life of Football Con Artist Carlos Henrique Raposo." news.com.au, August 2, 2018. https://www.news.com.au/sport/sports -life/inside-the-life-of-football-con-artist-carlos-henrique-raposo/news-story /fc356e7613d66ee69fba482306f4f88c.

Roy, Ayush. "Carlos Henrique 'Kaiser': The Story of Football's Greatest Conman." Sportskeeda, October 7, 2021. http://www.sportskeeda.com/football /carlos-henrique-kaiser-the-story-of-footballs-greatest-conman.

Schollum, Mary. *Investigative Interviewing: The Literature.* Office of the Commissioner of Police, Wellington, NZ, 2005. https://books.google.com/books /about/Investigative_Interviewing.html?id=7pPcMgAACAAJ.

Shea, Christopher. "The Liar's 'Tell': Is Paul Ekman Stretching the Truth?" *Chronicle Review*, October 10, 2014. https://www.chronicle.com/article/The -Liars-Tell/149261.

Smyth, Rob. "The Forgotten Story of . . . Carlos Kaiser, Football's Greatest Conman." *Guardian*, April 25, 2019. https://www.theguardian.com/football/blog /2017/apr/26/the-forgotten-story-of-carlos-kaiser-footballs-greatest-conman.

Starr, Douglas. "Do Police Interrogation Techniques Produce False Confessions?" *New Yorker*, December 1, 2013. https://www.newyorker.com/magazine /2013/12/09/the-interview-7.

Starr, Douglas. "Police Interrogation Techniques Are Bogus and Inaccurate."

REFERENCES

Aeon, February 9, 2016. https://aeon.co/ideas/standard-interrogation-techniques
-lead-to-false-confessions/.

"Toddlers Who Lie 'Will Do Better.'" BBC, May 17, 2010. https://www.bbc
.co.uk/news/10119297.

Tyers, Alan. "Kaiser! The Greatest Footballer to Never Play Football: Meet the
Legendary Brazilian Con-Man and Womanizer." *Telegraph*, July 25, 2018.
https://www.telegraph.co.uk/football/2018/07/25/kaiser-greatest-footballer
-never-play-football-meet-legendary/.

Vrij, Aldert. "Deception and Truth Detection When Analyzing Nonverbal and
Verbal Cues." *Applied Cognitive Psychology* 33, no. 2 (2019): 160–67. https://
onlinelibrary.wiley.com/doi/abs/10.1002/acp.3457.

Vrij, Aldert, Pär Anders Granhag, and Stephen Porter. "Pitfalls and Opportunities
in Nonverbal and Verbal Lie Detection." *Psychological Science in the Public Interest* 11, no. 3 (2010): 89–121. https://www.psychologicalscience.org/journals
/pspi/pspi_10_6.pdf.

Wikipedia. "Carlos Kaiser (Footballer)." Accessed . https://en.wikipedia.org/wiki
/Carlos_Kaiser_(footballer).

Wikipedia. "William Mouton Marston." Accessed . https://en.wikipedia.org/wiki
/William_Moulton_Marston.

Wray, Herbert. "When Thoughts Weigh Heavy: Outsmarting the Liars." April 4,
2011. Association for Psychological Science. https://www.psychologicalscience
.org/news/full-frontal-psychology/when-thought-weigh-heavy-outsmarting
-the-liars.html

CHAPTER 5

BEC Crew. "Harvard Physicists Just Proposed That Mystery Radio Bursts Are
Powering Alien Spaceships." *ScienceAlert*, May 11, 2017. https://www.science
alert.com/harvard-physicists-just-proposed-that-mysterious-cosmic-radio
-bursts-are-powering-alien-spaceships.

BEC Crew. "Scientists Are at a Loss to Explain This Mysterious Cosmic Radio Signal." *ScienceAlert*, May 11, 2017. https://www.sciencealert.com/scientists-are
-at-a-complete-loss-to-explain-this-mysterious-cosmic-radio-signal.

Bushwick, Sophie. "Mysterious Radio Bursts Are Indeed Coming from a Galaxy Far, Far Away." *Popular Science*, April 22, 2015. https://www.popsci.com
/cosmic-whodunnit-culprit-ismicrowave-ovens.

Butler, Jeffrey, Paola Giuliano, and Luigi Guiso. "The Right Amount of Trust."
Discussion Paper No. 4416. Institute for the Study of Labor, September 2009.
https://ftp.iza.org/dp4416.pdf.

Cole, Tim. "Lying to the One You Love: The Use of Deception in Romantic Relationships." *Journal of Social and Personal Relationships* 18, no. 1 (2001): 107–29.
https://journals.sagepub.com/doi/10.1177/0265407501181005.

Drake, Nadia. "Rogue Microwave Ovens Are the Culprits Behind Mysterious
Radio Signals." *National Geographic*, April 9, 2015. https://www.national
geographic.com/science/phenomena/2015/04/10/rogue-microwave-ovens-are
-the-culprits-behind-mysterious-radio-signals/.

REFERENCES

Gibney, Elizabeth. "Why Ultra-Powerful Radio Bursts Are the Most Perplexing Mystery in Astronomy." *Nature*, June 28, 2016, 610–12. https://www.nature.com/news/why-ultra-powerful-radio-bursts-are-the-most-perplexing-mystery-in-astronomy-1.20175.

Golub, Sarit A., Daniel T. Gilbert, and Timothy D. Wilson. "Anticipating One's Troubles: The Costs and Benefits of Negative Expectations." *Emotion* 9, no. 2 (2009): 277–81. https://pubmed.ncbi.nlm.nih.gov/19348540/.

Hall, Judith A., Marianne Schmid Mast, and Tessa V. West. *The Social Psychology of Perceiving Others Accurately*. Cambridge: Cambridge University Press, 2016.

HEASARC. "GR/FRB?" Picture of the Week. Last modified December 5, 2016. https://heasarc.gsfc.nasa.gov/docs/objects/heapow/archive/transients/frbgrb_swift.html.

Kaplan, Sarah. "Stumped for Years, Astronomers Find Source of Mysterious Signals—in Their Kitchen." *Washington Post*, May 6, 2015. https://www.washingtonpost.com/news/morning-mix/wp/2015/05/06/stumped-for-years-astronomers-find-source-of-mysterious-signals-in-their-kitchen/.

Knapton, Sarah. "Mystery 'Alien' Radio Signal Picked Up in Space." *Telegraph*, January 20, 2015. https://www.telegraph.co.uk/news/science/space/11357176/Mystery-alien-radio-signal-picked-up-in-space.html.

Konnikova, Maria. *The Confidence Game: Why We Fall for It . . . Every Time*. New York: Penguin, 2016.

Li, Jamy, and Mark Chignell. "Birds of a Feather: How Personality Influences Blog Writing and Reading." *International Journal of Human-Computer Studies* 68, no. 9 (2010): 589–602. https://www.sciencedirect.com/science/article/abs/pii/S1071581910000522.

Lingam, Manasvi, and Abraham Loeb. "Fast Radio Bursts from Extragalactic Light Sails." Draft, February 28, 2017. https://arxiv.org/pdf/1701.01109.pdf.

MacDonald, Fiona. "NASA Researchers Are Working on a Laser Propulsion System That Could Get to Mars in Three Days." *ScienceAlert*, February 22, 2016. https://www.sciencealert.com/nasa-scientists-are-investigating-a-propulsion-system-that-could-reach-mars-in-3-days.

Mandelbaum, Ryan F. "Mysterious 'Alien' Radio Signal: Here's What You Need to Know." Gizmodo, August 9, 2018. https://www.gizmodo.com.au/2018/08/mysterious-alien-radio-signal-heres-what-you-need-to-know/.

"Mysterious Cosmic Radio Burst Caught in Real Time." IFLScience. https://www.iflscience.com/space/world-first-cosmic-radio-burst-caught-real-time/.

Nuwer, Rachel. "What If We Knew When People Were Lying?" BBC, March 25, 2019. https://www.bbc.com/future/article/20190324-what-if-we-knew-when-people-were-lying.

"Origins of Mysterious Radio Wave Bursts Discovered." IFLScience. https://www.iflscience.com/space/astronomical-quest-leads-ovens/.

Pennebaker, James W. *The Secret Life of Pronouns: What Our Words Say About Us*. New York: Bloomsbury, 2013.

Pennebaker, James W. "Your Use of Pronouns Reveals Your Personality." *Harvard*

REFERENCES

Business Review, December 2011. https://hbr.org/2011/12/your-use-of-pronouns
-reveals-your-personality.

Pennebaker, James W., and Anna Graybeal. "Patterns of Natural Language Use: Disclosure, Personality, and Social Integration." *Current Directions in Psychological Science* 10, no. 3 (2001): 90–93. https://c3po.media.mit.edu/wp-content /uploads/sites/45/2016/01/Pennebaker-1999-Patterns-of-language-use-and -personality.pdf.

Petroff, Emily. "How We Found the Source of the Mystery Signals at The Dish." The Conversation, May 24, 2015. http://theconversation.com/how-we-found -the-source-of-the-mystery-signals-at-the-dish-41523.

Petroff, E., et al. "Identifying the Source of Perytons at the Parkes Radio Telescope." *Monthly Notices of the Royal Astronomical Society*, April 10, 2015. https:// arxiv.org/pdf/1504.02165.pdf.

The Phrase Finder. "The Meaning and Origin of the Expression: A Friend in Need Is a Friend Indeed." https://www.phrases.org.uk/meanings/a-friend-in -need.html.

Seaburn, Paul. "Lasers May Propel Craft to Mars in Three Days." Mysterious Universe, February 25, 2016. https://mysteriousuniverse.org/2016/02/lasers-may -propel-craft-to-mars-in-three-days/.

Seaburn, Paul. "Scientists Say Fast Radio Bursts May Power Alien Spaceships." Mysterious Universe, March 11, 2017. https://mysteriousuniverse.org/2017/03 /scientists-say-fast-radio-bursts-may-power-alien-spaceships/.

Starr, Michelle. "Parkes Observatory: Extraterrestrial Messages or Microwave Noodles." CNET, April 12, 2015. https://www.cnet.com/news/parkes-observatory -extraterrestrial-messages-or-microwave-noodles/.

Strom, Marcus. "PhD Student Emily Petroff Solves Astronomy Mystery." Daily Life, May 5, 2015. http://www.dailylife.com.au/dl-people/dl-entertainment /phd-student-emily-petroff-solves-astronomy-mystery-20150504-ggu3mu. html.

Stromberg, Joseph. "Radio Signals Puzzled Astrophysicists for Seventeen Years: They Were Coming from a Microwave Oven." Vox, May 5, 2015. https://www .vox.com/2015/5/5/8553609/microwave-oven-perytons.

Wikipedia. "Fast Radio Burst." https://en.wikipedia.org/wiki/Fast_radio_burst.

Wikipedia. "Parkes Observatory." https://en.wikipedia.org/wiki/Parkes_Obser vatory.

Wikipedia. "Solar Sail." https://en.wikipedia.org/wiki/Solar_sail.

Wilson, David. "The Cosmic Microwave Oven Background." Planetary Society, April 17, 2015. http://www.planetary.org/blogs/guest-blogs/2015/0417-the-cosmic -microwave-oven-background.html.

CHAPTER 6

Angier, Natalie. "Friendship's Dark Side: 'We Need a Common Enemy.'" *New York Times*, April 16, 2018. https://www.nytimes.com/2018/04/16/science /friendship-discrimination.html.

REFERENCES

Beck, Julie. "How Friends Become Closer." *Atlantic*, August 29, 2017. https://www.theatlantic.com/health/archive/2017/08/how-friends-become-closer/538092/.

Beck, Julie. "How Friendships Change in Adulthood." *Atlantic*, October 22, 2015. https://www.theatlantic.com/health/archive/2015/10/how-friendships-change-over-time-in-adulthood/411466/.

Christakis, Nicholas A. *Blueprint: The Evolutionary Origins of a Good Society.* New York: Little, Brown, 2019.

Clark, Taylor. *Nerve: Poise Under Pressure, Serenity Under Stress, and the Brave New Science of Fear and Cool.* New York: Little, Brown, 2011.

Collier, Peter. *Medal of Honor: Portraits of Valor Beyond the Call of Duty.* New York: Artisan, 2001.

Demır, Melıkşah, and Lesley A. Weitekamp. "I Am So Happy 'Cause Today I Found My Friend: Friendship and Personality as Predictors of Happiness." *Journal of Happiness Studies* 8 (2007): 181–211. https://link.springer.com/article/10.1007/s10902-006-9012-7.

Denworth, Lydia. *Friendship: The Evolution, Biology, and Extraordinary Power of Life's Fundamental Bond.* New York: W. W. Norton, 2020.

Feeney, Brooke C., and Nancy L. Collins. "New Look at Social Support: A Theoretical Perspective on Thriving Through Relationships." *Personality and Social Psychology Review* 19, no. 2 (2015): 113–47. https://www.ncbi.nlm.nih.gov/pmc/articles/PMC5480897/.

Flora, Carlin. *Friendfluence: The Surprising Ways Friends Make Us Who We Are.* New York: Knopf Doubleday, 2013.

Greif, Geoffrey L. *Buddy System: Understanding Male Friendships.* New York: Oxford University Press, 2008.

"Hector A. Cafferata, Eighty-Six, Dies; Given a Medal of Honor for Korean Heroics." *New York Times*, April 15, 2016. https://www.nytimes.com/2016/04/15/us/hector-a-cafferata-a-medal-of-honor-recipient-dies-at-86.html.

Holt-Lunstad, Julianne. "Fostering Social Connection in the Workplace." *American Journal of Health Promotion* 32, no. 5 (2018): 1307–12. https://journals.sagepub.com/doi/full/10.1177/0890117118776735a.

Hruschka, Daniel J. *Friendship: Development, Ecology, and Evolution of a Relationship.* Berkeley: University of California Press, 2010.

Lewis, C. S. *The Four Loves.* New York: HarperOne, 2017.

Mashek, Debra J., and Arthur Aron. *Handbook of Closeness and Intimacy.* Hove, UK: Psychology Press, 2004.

McKay, Brett. "Podcast #567: Understanding the Wonderful, Frustrating Dynamic of Friendship." *Art of Manliness*, last updated September 30, 2021. https://www.artofmanliness.com/articles/podcast-567-understanding-the-wonderful-frustrating-dynamic-of-friendship/.

Misurelli, Frank. "Marine Corps Medal of Honor Recipient Hector A. Cafferata Remembered as Humble Hero." U.S. Army, May 26, 2016. https://www.army.mil/article/168707/marine_corps_medal_of_honor_recipient_hector_a_cafferata_remembered_as_humble_hero.

REFERENCES

Pahl, Ray. *On Friendship*. New York: Polity, 2000.

Pakaluk, Michael, ed. *Other Selves: Philosophers on Friendship*. Cambridge, MA: Hackett, 1991.

Parker-Pope, Tara. "How to Be a Better Friend." *New York Times*, n.d. https://www.nytimes.com/guides/smarterliving/how-to-be-a-better-friend.

Powdthavee, Nattavudh. "Putting a Price Tag on Friends, Relative, and Neighbours: Using Surveys of Life Satisfaction to Value Social Relationships." *Journal of Socio-Economics* 37, no. 4 (2008): 1459–80. https://www.sciencedirect.com/science/article/abs/pii/S1053535707001205.

Radiolab. "An Equation for Good." New York Public Radio, December 14, 2010. https://www.wnycstudios.org/podcasts/radiolab/segments/103983-equation-good.

Rath, Tom. *Vital Friends: The People You Can't Afford to Live Without*. New York: Gallup, 2006.

Rawlins, William K. *Friendship Matters: Communication, Dialectics, and the Life Course*. New York: Aldine de Gruyter, 1992.

Rawlins, William K. *The Compass of Friendship: Narratives, Identities, and Dialogues*. Los Angeles: Sage.

Ruiz, Rebecca. "World's Friendliest Countries." *Forbes*, December 1, 2009. https://www.forbes.com/2009/11/30/worlds-friendliest-countries-lifestyle-travel-canada-bahrain-hsbc-chart.html?sh=c35dff465730.

Russ, Martin. *Breakout: The Chosin Reservoir Campaign, Korea 1950*. New York: Penguin, 2001.

Schudel, Matt. "Hector Cafferata, Medal of Honor Recipient in Korean War, Dies at Eighty-Six." *Washington Post*, April 14, 2016. https://www.washingtonpost.com/national/hector-cafferata-medal-of-honor-recipient-in-korean-war-dies-at-86/2016/04/14/9c7711a6-0259-11e6-b823-707c79ce3504_story.html.

Smith, Larry. *Beyond Glory: Medal of Honor Heroes in Their Own Words*. New York: W. W. Norton, 2004.

Tashiro, Ty. *Awkward: The Science of Why We're Socially Awkward and Why That's Awesome*. New York: HarperCollins, 2018.

Vernon, Mark. *The Meaning of Friendship*. London: Palgrave Macmillan, 2010.

Wikipedia. "Audie Murphy." https://en.wikipedia.org/wiki/Audie_Murphy#Decorations.

Wikipedia. "Hector A. Cafferata Jr." https://en.wikipedia.org/wiki/Hector_A._Cafferata_Jr.

Wikipedia. "List of Medal of Honor Recipients." https://en.wikipedia.org/wiki/List_of_Medal_of_Honor_recipients.

CHAPTER 7

Aron, Arthur, and Barbara Fraley. "Relationship Closeness as Including Other in the Self: Cognitive Underpinnings and Measures." *Social Cognition* 17, no. 2 (1999): 140–60. https://psycnet.apa.org/record/1999-03814-003.

Aron, Arthur, Elaine N. Aron, and Danny Smollan. "Inclusion of Other in the

REFERENCES

Self Scale and the Structure of Interpersonal Closeness." *Journal of Personality and Social Psychology* 63, no. 4 (1992): 596–612. https://psycnet.apa.org /record/1993-03996-001.

Aron, Arthur, et al. "The Self-Expansion Model of Motivation and Cognition in Close Relationships." In *The Oxford Handbook of Close Relationships*, edited by Jeffry Simpson and Lorne Campbell. Oxford: Oxford University Press, 2013. https://www.oxfordhandbooks.com/view/10.1093 /oxfordhb/9780195398694.001.0001/oxfordhb-9780195398694-e-005.

Christakis, Nicholas A. *Blueprint: The Evolutionary Origins of a Good Society*. New York: Little, Brown, 2019.

Denworth, Lydia. *Friendship: The Evolution, Biology, and Extraordinary Power of Life's Fundamental Bond*. New York: W. W. Norton, 2020.

Harman, Oren. *The Price of Altruism: George Price and the Search for the Origins of Kindness*. New York: W. W. Norton, 2011.

Hruschka, Daniel J. *Friendship: Development, Ecology, and Evolution of a Relationship*. Berkeley: University of California Press, 2010.

Jarrett, Christian. "Close Friends Become Absorbed into Our Self-Concept, Affecting Our Ability to Distinguish Their Faces from Our Own." *Research Digest* (blog), August 8, 2018. https://digest.bps.org.uk/2018/08/08/close-friends -become-absorbed-into-our-self-concept-affecting-our-ability-to-distinguish-their -faces-from-our-own/.

Mashek, Debra J., and Arthur Aron. *Handbook of Closeness and Intimacy*. Hove, UK: Psychology Press, 2004.

Mashek, Debra J., Arthur Aron, and Maria Boncimino. "Confusions of Self with Close Others." *Personality and Social Psychology Bulletin* 29, no. 3 (2003): 382– 92. https://pubmed.ncbi.nlm.nih.gov/15273015/.

Nehamas, Alexander. *On Friendship*. New York: Basic Books, 2016.

Pahl, Ray. *On Friendship*. New York: Polity, 2000.

Pakaluk, Michael, ed. *Other Selves: Philosophers on Friendship*. Cambridge, MA: Hackett, 1991.

Radiolab. "An Equation for Good." New York Public Radio, December 14, 2010. https://www.wnycstudios.org/podcasts/radiolab/segments/103983-equation -good.

Vernon, Mark. *The Meaning of Friendship*. London: Palgrave Macmillan, 2010.

Wikipedia. "Altruism." https://en.wikipedia.org/wiki/Altruism.

Wikipedia. "George R. Price." https://en.wikipedia.org/wiki/George_R._Price.

Wikipedia. "Self-Expansion Model." https://en.wikipedia.org/wiki/Self-expansion _model.

CHAPTER 8

American Associates. "New Study Debunks Dale Carnegie Advice to 'Put Yourself in Their Shoes.'" ScienceDaily, June 21, 2018. https://www.sciencedaily.com /releases/2018/06/180621000339.htm.

Anwar, Yasmin. "Easily Embarrassed? Study Finds People Will Trust You More."

REFERENCES

Berkeley News, September 28, 2011. https://news.berkeley.edu/2011/09/28/easily-embarrassed/.

Arnold, Carrie. "Why Are Dogs So Friendly? Science Finally Has an Answer." *National Geographic*, July 19, 2017. https://news.nationalgeographic.com/2017/07/dogs-breeds-pets-wolves-evolution/.

Beck, Julie. "How Friends Become Closer." *Atlantic*, August 29, 2017. https://www.theatlantic.com/health/archive/2017/08/how-friends-become-closer/538092/.

Beck, Julie. "How Friendships Change in Adulthood." *Atlantic*, October 22, 2015. https://www.theatlantic.com/health/archive/2015/10/how-friendships-change-over-time-in-adulthood/411466/.

Biography. "Dale Carnegie." https://www.biography.com/writer/dale-carnegie.

Brafman, Ori. *Click: The Forces Behind How We Fully Engage with People, Work, and Everything We Do*. New York: Currency, 2011.

Bruk, Anna, Sabine G. Scholl, and Herbert Bless. "Beautiful Mess Effect: Self-Other Differences in Evaluation of Showing Vulnerability." *Journal of Personality and Social Psychology* 115, no. 2 (2018): 192–205. https://psycnet.apa.org/record/2018-34832-002.

Carnegie, Dale. *How to Win Friends and Influence People*. New York: Simon & Schuster, 2009.

Crespi, Bernard J., and Peter L. Hurd. "Cognitive-Behavioral Phenotypes of Williams Syndrome Are Associated with Genetic Variation in the GTF21 Gene, in a Healthy Population." *BMC Neuroscience* 15, no. 127 (2014). https://bmcneurosci.biomedcentral.com/articles/10.1186/s12868-014-0127-1.

Denworth, Lydia. *Friendship: The Evolution, Biology, and Extraordinary Power of Life's Fundamental Bond*. New York: W. W. Norton, 2020.

Dobbs, David. "The Gregarious Brian." *New York Times*, July 8, 2007. https://www.nytimes.com/2007/07/08/magazine/08sociability-t.html.

Egg, Easter. You found another Golden Ticket, Charlie. Go here: https://www.bakadesuyo.com/easteregg.

Epley, Nicholas. *Mindwise: Why We Misunderstand What Others Think, Believe, Feel, and Want*. New York: Knopf Doubleday, 2015.

Feinberg, Matthew, Robb Willer, and Dacher Keltner. "Flustered and Faithful: Embarrassment as a Signal of Prosociality." *Journal of Personality and Social Psychology* 102, no. 1 (2012): 81–97. https://pdfs.semanticscholar.org/a75f/af6748be54be79a667ca803e23fe3c67b2a2.pdf.

Flora, Carlin. *Friendfluence: The Surprising Ways Friends Make Us Who We Are*. New York: Knopf Doubleday, 2013.

Frank, Robert H. *Under the Influence: Putting Peer Pressure to Work*. Princeton, NJ: Princeton University Press, 2020.

Gambetta, Diego. "Can We Trust Trust?" In *Trust: Making and Breaking Cooperative Relations*, 213–37. New York: Blackwell, 1988. https://philpapers.org/rec/GAMCWT.

Garfield, Robert. *Breaking the Male Code: Unlocking the Power of Friendship*. New York: Avery, 2016.

REFERENCES

Gosling, Sam. *Snoop: What Your Stuff Says About You.* New York: Basic Books, 2009.

Greif, Geoffrey L. *Buddy System: Understanding Male Friendships.* New York: Oxford University Press, 2008.

Hall, Jeffrey A. "How Many Hours Does It Take to Make a Friend?" *Journal of Social and Personal Relationships* 36, no. 4 (2018): 1278–96. https://journals .sagepub.com/doi/full/10.1177/0265407518761225.

Hruschka, Daniel J. *Friendship: Development, Ecology, and Evolution of a Relationship.* Berkeley: University of California Press, 2010.

Huang, Karen, et al. "Mitigating Malicious Envy: Why Successful Individuals Should Reveal Their Failures." Working Paper 18-080. Harvard Business School, 2018. https://www.hbs.edu/faculty/Publication%20Files/18 -080_56688b05-34cd-47ef-adeb-aa7050b93452.pdf.

Jarrett, Christian. "The 'Beautiful Mess' Effect: Other People View Our Vulnerability More Positively Than We Do." *Research Digest* (blog), August 2, 2018. https://digest.bps.org.uk/2018/08/02/the-beautiful-mess-effect-other-people -view-our-vulnerability-more-positively-than-we-do/.

Latson, Jennifer. *The Boy Who Loved Too Much: A True Story of Pathological Friendliness.* New York: Simon & Schuster, 2017.

Latson, Jennifer. "How a Real Genetic Disorder Could Have Inspired Fairy Tales." *Time,* June 20, 2017. https://time.com/4823574/mythology-williams -syndrome/.

Latson, Jennifer. "The Secret to Small Talk." *The Cut,* June 20, 2017. https:// www.thecut.com/2017/06/the-secret-to-small-talk.html.

Levine, Emma, and Taya R. Cohen. "You Can Handle the Truth: Mispredicting the Consequences of Honest Communication." *Journal of Experimental Psychology General* 147, no. 9 (2018): 1400–1429. https://www.researchgate.net /publication/327371514_You_can_handle_the_truth_Mispredicting_the _consequences_of_honest_communication.

Lukianoff, Greg, and Jonathan Haidt. *The Coddling of the American Mind: How Good Intentions and Bad Ideas Are Setting Up a Generation for Failure.* New York: Penguin, 2018.

Mashek, Debra J., and Arthur Aron. *Handbook of Closeness and Intimacy.* Hove, UK: Psychology Press, 2004.

McKay, Brett. "Podcast #567: Understanding the Wonderful, Frustrating Dynamic of Friendship." *Art of Manliness,* last updated September 30, 2021. https://www.artofmanliness.com/articles/podcast-567-understanding-th e-wonderful-frustrating-dynamic-of-friendship/.

MedLine Plus. "Williams Syndrome." https://ghr.nlm.nih.gov/condition/williams -syndrome.

Morris, Colleen A. "Introduction: Williams Syndrome." *American Journal of Medical Genetics: Part C, Seminars in Medical Genetics* 154C, no. 2 (2010): 203–8. https://www.ncbi.nlm.nih.gov/pmc/articles/PMC2946897/.

Moseley, Tolly. "What Happens When You Trust Too Much." *Atlantic,* May 12, 2014. https://www.theatlantic.com/health/archive/2014/05/going-to-work-with -williams-syndrome/361374/.

REFERENCES

Nizza, Mike. "A Simple B.F.F. Strategy, Confirmed by Scientists." *New York Times*, April 22, 2008. https://thelede.blogs.nytimes.com/2008/04/22/a-simple-bff-strategy-confirmed-by-scientists/.

"Oliver Sacks: The Mind Traveller—'Don't Be Shy, Mr Sacks.'" YouTube, September 19, 2016. https://www.youtube.com/watch?v=2J8YNyHIT64.

Pahl, Ray. *On Friendship*. New York: Polity, 2000.

Pakaluk, Michael, ed. *Other Selves: Philosophers on Friendship*. Cambridge, MA: Hackett, 1991.

Pattee, Emma. "How to Have Closer Friendships (and Why You Need Them)." *New York Times*, November 20, 2019. https://www.nytimes.com/2019/11/20/smarter-living/how-to-have-closer-friendships.html.

Pennebaker, James W., and Joshua M. Smyth. *Opening Up by Writing It Down: How Expressive Writing Improves Health and Eases Emotional Pain*, 3rd ed. New York: Guilford, 2016.

Riby, Deborah. "What Is Williams Syndrome?" The Conversation, May 13, 2014. https://theconversation.com/explainer-what-is-williams-syndrome-26142.

Robson, David. "What the World's Most Sociable People Reveal About Friendliness." *Atlantic*, June 3, 2019. https://www.theatlantic.com/health/archive/2019/06/williams-syndrome-and-human-evolution/590797/.

Rogers, Nala. "Rare Human Syndrome May Explain Why Dogs Are So Friendly." Inside Science, July 19, 2017. https://www.insidescience.org/news/rare-human-syndrome-may-explain-why-dogs-are-so-friendly.

Rouillard, Teresa. "Why My Daughter's Dreams Make My Heart Ache." The Mighty, April 22, 2015. https://themighty.com/2015/04/the-dreams-of-my-child-with-williams-syndrome/.

Santos, Andreia, Andreas Meyer-Lindenberg, and Christine Deruelle. "Absence of Racial, but Not Gender, Stereotyping in Williams Syndrome Children." *Current Biology* 20, no. 7 (2010): PR307–8. https://www.cell.com/current-biology/supplemental/S0960-9822(10)00144-2.

Smith, Emily Esfahani. "Your Flaws Are Probably More Attractive Than You Think They Are." *Atlantic*, January 9, 2019. https://www.theatlantic.com/health/archive/2019/01/beautiful-mess-vulnerability/579892/.

Society for Personality and Social Psychology. "Forget the Bling: High Status-Signaling Deters New Friendships." ScienceDaily, August 15, 2018. https://www.sciencedaily.com/releases/2018/08/180815105259.htm.

Spiegel, Alix. "A Genetic Drive to Love, yet Distanced by Differences." *Morning Edition*, May 3, 2010. https://www.npr.org/templates/story/story.php?storyId=126396171.

Spiegel, Alix. "A Life Without Fear." *Morning Edition*, April 26, 2010. https://www.npr.org/templates/story/story.php?storyId=126224885.

Spiegel, Alix. "When the 'Trust Hormone' Is out of Balance." *All Things Considered*, April 22, 2010. https://www.npr.org/templates/story/story.php?storyId=126141922.

Srivastava, Sanjay, et al. "The Social Costs of Emotional Suppression: A Prospective Study of the Author." *Journal of Personality and Social Psychology* 96, no. 4 (2009): 883–97. https://pdfs.semanticscholar.org/dea0/93ae5ebc11baff7e4c cff83939f2034b25c0.pdf.

University of California, San Diego. "Neurodevelopmental Model of Williams Syndrome Offers Insight into Human Social Brain." ScienceDaily, August 10, 2016. https://www.sciencedaily.com/releases/2016/08/160810141922 .htm.

Wikipedia. "How to Win Friends and Influence People." Accessed . https://en .wikipedia.org/wiki/How_to_Win_Friends_and_Influence_People.

Wikipedia. "Williams Syndrome." https://en.wikipedia.org/wiki/Williams _syndrome.

Williams Syndrome Association. "What Is Williams Syndrome?" https://williams -syndrome.org/what-is-williams-syndrome.

Worrall, Simon. "This Rare Medical Condition Makes You Love Everyone." *National Geographic*, July 15, 2017. https://www.nationalgeographic.com /news/2017/07/williams-health-love-genetics-books/.

Wikipedia. "Pratfall Effect." https://en.wikipedia.org/wiki/Pratfall_effect.

Wikipedia. "Signalling Theory." https://en.wikipedia.org/wiki/Signalling_theory.

Yale University. "Robots That Admit Mistakes Foster Better Conversation in Humans." ScienceDaily, March 9, 2020. https://www.sciencedaily.com /releases/2020/03/200309152047.htm.

Young, Emma. "The 'Liking Gap'—We Tend to Underestimate the Positive First Impression We Make on Strangers." *Research Digest* (blog), September 24, 2018. https://digest.bps.org.uk/2018/09/24/the-liking-gap-we-tend-to-underestimate -the-positive-first-impression-we-make-on-strangers/.

CHAPTER 9

Barker, Eric. "Are Ethical People Happier?" *Barking Up the Wrong Tree* (blog), November 2011. https://www.bakadesuyo.com/2011/11/are-ethical-people-happier/.

Bernstein, Albert J. *Am I The Only Sane One Working Here? 101 Solutions for Surviving Office Insanity.* New York: McGraw-Hill Education, 2009.

Bernstein, Albert J. *Emotional Vampires: Dealing with People Who Drain You Dry.* New York: McGraw-Hill Education, 2012.

Brunell, Amy B., and Mark S. Davis. "Grandiose Narcissism and Fairness in Social Exchanges." *Current Psychology* 35 (2016): 220–33. https://link.springer .com/article/10.1007/s12144-016-9415-5.

Bushman, Briahna Bigelow, and Julianne Holt-Lunstad. "Understanding Social Relationship Maintenance Among Friends: Why Don't We End Those Frustrating Friendships." *Journal of Social and Clinical Psychology* 28, no. 6 (2009): 749–78. https://psycnet.apa.org/record/2009-10225-005.

BYU University Communications. "BYU Study Shows Why 'Frenemies' Make Blood Pressure Rise." News, June 18, 2007. https://news.byu.edu/news /byu-study-shows-why-frenemies-make-blood-pressure-rise.

Caligor, Eve, Kenneth N. Levy, and Frank E. Yeomans. "Narcissistic Personality Disorder: Diagnostic and Clinical Challenges." *American Journal of Psychiatry*, April 30, 2015. https://ajp.psychiatryonline.org/doi/10.1176/appi.ajp.2014.14060723.

Chester, David S., C. Nathan DeWall, and Brian Enjaian. "Sadism and Aggressive Behavior: Inflicting Pain to Feel Pleasure." *Personality and Social Psychology Bulletin*, November 5, 2018. https://psyarxiv.com/cvgkb/.

Chopik, William J., and Kevin J. Grimm. "Longitudinal Changes and Historic Differences in Narcissism from Adolescence to Older Adulthood." *Psychology and Aging* 34, no. 8 (2019): 1109–23. https://psyarxiv.com/bf7qv/.

Christakis, Nicholas A. *Blueprint: The Evolutionary Origins of a Good Society*. New York: Little, Brown, 2019.

Christina L. Patton, Sarah Francis Smith, and Scott O. Lilienfeld. "Psychopathy and Heroism in First Responders: Traits Cut from the Same Cloth?" *Personality Disorders: Theory, Research, and Treatment* 9, no. 4 (2018): 354–68. https://psycnet.apa.org/record/2017-50493-001.

"Daniel Kahneman: Biographical." The Nobel Prize. Accessed . https://www.nobelprize.org/prizes/economic-sciences/2002/kahneman/biographical/.

Dobbs, David. "The Gregarious Brain." *New York Times*, July 8, 2007. https://www.nytimes.com/2007/07/08/magazine/08sociability-t.html.

Finkel, Eli J., et al. "The Metamorphosis of Narcissus: Communal Activation Promotes Relationship Commitment Among Narcissists." *Personality and Social Psychology Bulletin* 35, no. 10 (2009): 1271–84. https://journals.sagepub.com/doi/10.1177/0146167209340904.

Flora, Carlin. *Friendfluence: The Surprising Ways Friends Make Us Who We Are*. New York: Knopf Doubleday, 2013.

Forbes, Steve. "Kahneman: Lessons from Hitler's SS and the Danger in Trusting Your Gut." *Forbes*, June 24, 2013. https://www.forbes.com/sites/steveforbes/2013/01/24/nobel-prize-winner-daniel-kahneman-lessons-from-hitlers-ss-and-the-danger-in-trusting-your-gut/#8bf03cc156e7.

Garrett, Neil, et al. "The Brain Adapts to Dishonesty." *Nature Neuroscience* 19 (2016). https://www.nature.com/articles/nn.4426.

Gerven A. Van Kleef, and Paul A. M. Van Lange. "What Other's Disappointment May Do to Selfish People: Emotion and Social Value Orientation in a Negotiation Context." *Personality and Social Psychology Bulletin* 34, no. 8 (2008): 1084–95. https://psycnet.apa.org/record/2008-09895-006.

Giacomin, Miranda, and Christian H. Jordan. "Down-Regulating Narcissistic Tendencies: Communal Focus Reduces State Narcissism." *Personality and Social Psychology Bulletin* 40, no. 4 (2014): 488–500. https://journals.sagepub.com/doi/10.1177/0146167213516635.

Glass, Ira. "389: Frenemies." *This American Life*, September 11, 2009. https://www.thisamericanlife.org/389/transcript.

Hepper, Erica G., Claire M. Hart, and Constantine Sedikides. "Moving Narcissus: Can Narcissists Be Empathic?" *Personality and Social Psychology Bulletin* 40, no. 9 (2014): 1079–91. https://journals.sagepub.com/doi/abs/10.1177/0146167214535812.

REFERENCES

Hill, Patrick L., and Brent W. Roberts. "Narcissism, Well-Being, and Observer-Rated Personality Across the Lifespan." *Social Psychological and Personality Science* 3, no. 2 (2012): 216–23. https://journals.sagepub.com/doi/10.1177/1948550611415867.

Holt-Lunstad, Julianne, et al. "On the Importance of Relationship Quality: The Impact of Ambivalence in Friendships on Cardiovascular Functioning." *Annals of Behavioral Medicine* 33, no. 3 (2007): 278–90. https://www.ncbi.nlm.nih.gov/pubmed/17600455.

Kajonius, Petri J., and Therese Björkman. "Individuals with Dark Traits Have the Ability but Not the Disposition to Empathize." *Personality and Individual Differences* 155 (2020). https://www.sciencedirect.com/science/article/abs/pii/S0191886919306567.

Kalemi, Georgia, et al. "Narcissism but Not Criminality Is Associated with Aggression in Women: A Study Among Female Prisoners and Women Without a Criminal Record." *Frontiers in Psychiatry* 10 (February 2019). https://www.ncbi.nlm.nih.gov/pmc/articles/PMC6375288/.

Kaufman, Scott Barry. "Do Narcissists Know They Are Narcissists?" *HuffPost*, April 3, 2011. https://www.huffpost.com/entry/do-narcissists-know-they-_b_840894.

Konrath, Sara, Brad J. Bushman, and W. Keith Campbell. "Attenuating the Link Between Threatened Egotism and Aggression." *Psychological Science* 17, no. 11 (2006): 995–1001. https://pubmed.ncbi.nlm.nih.gov/17176433/.

Kupferschmidt, Kai. "She's the World's Top Empathy Researcher: But Colleagues Say She Bullied and Intimidated Them." *Science*, August 8, 2018. https://www.sciencemag.org/news/2018/08/she-s-world-s-top-empathy-researcher-colleagues-say-she-bullied-and-intimidated-them.

Lewis, Michael. *The Undoing Project: A Friendship That Changed Our Minds*. New York: W. W. Norton, 2016.

Malkin, Craig. *Rethinking Narcissism: The Secret to Recognizing and Coping with Narcissists*. New York: Harper Perennial, 2016.

McLean, Jamie. "Psychotherapy with a Narcissistic Patient Using Kohut's Self Psychology Model." *Psychiatry (Edgmont)* 4, no. 10 (2007): 40–47. https://www.ncbi.nlm.nih.gov/pmc/articles/PMC2860525/.

Michigan State University. "Me, Me, Me! How Narcissism Changes Throughout Life." ScienceDaily, December 10, 2019. https://www.sciencedaily.com/releases/2019/12/191210111655.htm.

Murphy, Ryan. "Psychopathy by U.S. State." SSRN, May 26, 2018. https://papers.ssrn.com/sol3/papers.cfm?abstract_id=3185182.

Ronningstam, Elsa. "Internal Processing in Patients with Pathological Narcissism or Narcissistic Personality Disorder: Implications for Alliance Building and Therapeutic Strategies." *Journal of Personality Disorders* 34 (suppl.) (March 2020): 80–103. https://pubmed.ncbi.nlm.nih.gov/32186980/.

Ronningstam, Elsa. "Narcissistic Personality Disorder: A Current Review." *Current Psychiatry Reports* 12, no. 1 (2010): 68–75. https://pubmed.ncbi.nlm.nih.gov/20425313/.

REFERENCES

Ronningstam, Elsa. "Pathological Narcissism and Narcissistic Personality Disorder: Recent Research and Clinical Implications." *Current Behavioral Neuroscience Reports* 3 (2016): 34–42. https://link.springer.com/article/10.1007/s40473-016-0060-y.

Ronningstam, Elsa, and Igor Weinberg. "Narcissistic Personality Disorder: Progress in Recognition and Treatment." *Focus: The Journal of Lifelong Learning in Psychiatry* 11, no. 2 (2013): 167–77. https://focus.psychiatryonline.org/doi/10.1176/appi.focus.11.2.167.

Rubens, Jim. *OverSuccess: Healing the American Obsession with Wealth, Fame, Power, and Perfection.* Austin, TX: Greenleaf Book Group, 2008.

Takru, Radhika. "Friends with Negatives." BrainBlogger, September 28, 2011. https://brainblogger.com/2011/09/28/friends-with-negatives/.

Tortoriello, Gregory K. William Hart, and Christopher J. Breeden. "Of Malevolence and Morality: Psychopathy Dimensions Are Conducive to Helping in Highly-Distressing Moral Dilemmas." *Personality and Individual Differences* 155 (2020). https://www.sciencedirect.com/science/article/abs/pii/S0191886919306981.

University of Colorado Denver. "Top Reasons for Facebook Unfriending." ScienceDaily, October 5, 2010. https://www.sciencedaily.com/releases/2010/10/101005121822.htm.

University of Copenhagen. "Psychologists Define the 'Dark Core of Personality.'" ScienceDaily, September 26, 2018. https://www.sciencedaily.com/releases/2018/09/180926110841.htm.

Vedantam, Shankar. "Daniel Kahneman on Misery, Memory, and Our Understanding of the Mind." *Hidden Brain*, March 12, 2018. https://www.npr.org/transcripts/592986190.

Weaver, Jonathan, and Jennifer K. Bosson. "I Feel Like I Know You: Sharing Negative Attitudes of Others Promotes Feelings of Familiarity." *Personality and Social Psychology Bulletin* 37, no. 4 (2011): 481–91. https://pubmed.ncbi.nlm.nih.gov/21296970/.

Weinberg, Igor, and Elsa Ronningstam. "Dos and Don'ts in Treatments of Patients with Narcissistic Personality Disorder." *Journal of Personality Disorders* 34 (suppl.) (March 2020): 122–42. https://pubmed.ncbi.nlm.nih.gov/32186986/.

Weir, Kirsten. "Fickle Friends: How to Deal with Frenemies." *Scientific American*, May 1, 2011. https://www.scientificamerican.com/article/fickle-friends/.

Wikipedia. "Frenemy." https://en.wikipedia.org/wiki/Frenemy.

CHAPTER 10

"About the Supreme Court." United States Courts. Accessed . https://www.uscourts.gov/about-federal-courts/educational-resources/about-educational-outreach/activity-resources/about.

Adams, Mason. "The Thirty-Fifth Anniversary of Falwell v. Flynt." *Roanoker*, October 29, 2019. https://theroanoker.com/magazine/features/the-35th-anniversary-of-falwell-v-flynt/.

Applebome, Peter. "Jerry Falwell, Moral Majority Founder, Dies at 73." *New

York Times, May 16, 2016. https://www.nytimes.com/2007/05/16/obituaries
/16falwell.html.

Denworth, Lydia. *Friendship: The Evolution, Biology, and Extraordinary Power of
Life's Fundamental Bond.* New York: W. W. Norton, 2020.

"Excerpts from the Testimony of Jerry Falwell." Famous Trials, December 4,
1984. https://famous-trials.com/falwell/1770-falwelltestimony.

"Falwell v. Flynt: 1984." https://law.jrank.org/pages/3390/Falwell-v-Flynt-1984
.html.

Flora, Carlin. *Friendfluence: The Surprising Ways Friends Make Us Who We Are.*
New York: Knopf Doubleday, 2013.

Flynt, Larry. "The Porn King and the Preacher." *Los Angeles Times*, May 20, 2007.
https://www.latimes.com/archives/la-xpm-2007-may-20-op-flynt20-story.html.

Flynt, Larry. *An Unseemly Man: My Life as a Pornographer, Pundit, and Social Out-
cast.* Beverly Hills, CA: Phoenix Books, 1996.

Forgas, Joseph P., and Roy F. Baumeister, eds. *The Social Psychology of Living Well.*
New York: Taylor and Francis, 2018.

Forman, Milos, dir. *The People vs. Larry Flynt.* Columbia Pictures, 1997.

"A Friend in Need Is a Friend Indeed." The Phrase Finder. Accessed . https://www
.phrases.org.uk/meanings/a-friend-in-need.html.

Galloway, Stephen. "Larry Flynt's Wild Life: Porn, Politics, and Penile Implants."
Hollywood Reporter, February 27, 2013. https://www.hollywoodreporter.com
/news/larry-flynts-wild-life-porn-424687.

Hoglund, Andy. "Flashback: Hustler Magazine Score First Amendment Vic-
tory Against Jerry Falwell." *Rolling Stone*, November 2017. https://www
.rollingstone.com/culture/culture-news/flashback-hustler-magazine-scores
-first-amendment-victory-against-jerry-falwell-128956/.

Horn, Dan. "How 1968 Helped Larry Flynt Build a Pornography Empire."
USA Today, July 13, 2018. https://www.usatoday.com/story/news/nation-now
/1968-project/2018/07/13/larry-flynt-and-1968-making-pornography-empire
/771604002/.

Hudson Union. "Larry Flynt & U.S. Supreme Court, & the Resignation of the
Speaker of the House." YouTube, May 5, 2011. https://www.youtube.com/watch?v
=payPtEiACF8.

Hustler Casino. "Larry Flynt on Jerry Falwell (Larry King 05/16/07) Part 2."
YouTube. https://www.youtube.com/watch?v=WgC12NzGiu4.

Hustler Magazine and Larry C. Flynt, Petitioners v. Jerry Falwell. Legal Information
Institute. Accessed . https://www.law.cornell.edu/supremecourt/text/485/46.

Khadjavi, Menusch, and Andreas Lange. "Prisoners and Their Dilemma." *Journal of Economic Behavior and Organization* 92 (August 2013): 163–75. https://
www.sciencedirect.com/science/article/abs/pii/S0167268113001522.

"Larry Flynt and Jerry Falwell." *Larry King Live*, CNN, January 10, 1997.
https://web.archive.org/web/20160817103157/http://www.cnn.com/SHOW
BIZ/9701/11/falwell.v.flynt/lkl.00.html.

Linder, Douglas O. "Ad Appearing in the November 1983 Issue of Hustler." Famous Trials. Accessed . https://famous-trials.com/falwell/1775-parodyad.

REFERENCES

Linder, Douglas O. "Excerpts from the Deposition Testimony of Larry Flynt." Famous Trials, December 5–6, 1984. https://famous-trials.com/falwell/1771-flynt deposition.

Linder, Douglas O. "Excerpts from the Testimony of Larry Flynt." Famous Trials, December 6, 1984. https://famous-trials.com/falwell/1772-flynttestimony.

Linder, Douglas O. "The Falwell vs. Flynt Trial: A Chronology." Famous Trials, October 31, 1983. https://famous-trials.com/falwell/1768-falwellchron ology.

Linder, Douglas O. "The Jerry Falwell v Larry Flynt Trial: An Account." Famous Trials. https://famous-trials.com/falwell/1779-account.

Millard, Drew. "The Pervert Who Changed America: How Larry Flynt Fought the Law and Won." Vice, December 11, 2016. https://www.vice.com/en_us/article/qkbzjx/larry-flynt-profile-2016.

Perry Como. "Larry Flynt vs Jerry Falwell Funny Deposition Footage from 06-15-1984." YouTube. https://www.youtube.com/watch?v=-bi6CycM3mE.

Smolla, Rodney. *Jerry Falwell v. Larry Flynt: The First Amendment on Trial*. New York: St. Martin's, 1988.

Thomas Jefferson Center for the Protection of Free Expression. "1997 Larry Flynt & Jerry Falwell Debate." https://www.youtube.com/watch?v=tLAOzn9x9Go.

United Press International. "Flynt Cleared of Libel but Must Pay $200,000." *New York Times*, December 9, 1984. https://www.nytimes.com/1984/12/09/us/flynt-cleared-of-libel-but-must-pay-200000.html.

Wikipedia. "Hustler Magazine v. Falwell." https://en.wikipedia.org/wiki/Hustler_Magazine_v._Falwell.

Wikipedia. "Jerry Falwell Sr." https://en.wikipedia.org/wiki/Jerry_Falwell_Sr.

Wikipedia. "Larry Flynt." https://en.wikipedia.org/wiki/Larry_Flynt.

Wikipedia. "The People vs. Larry Flynt." https://en.wikipedia.org/wiki/The_People_vs._Larry_Flynt.

Wiktionary. "A Friend in Need Is a Friend Indeed." https://en.wiktionary.org/wiki/a_friend_in_need_is_a_friend_indeed.

CHAPTER 11

Ansari, Aziz. *Modern Romance: An Investigation*. New York: Penguin, 2016.

Baumeister, Roy, Jessica A. Maxwell, and Geoffrey P. Thomas. "The Mask of Love and Sexual Gullibility." http://www.sydneysymposium.unsw.edu.au/2018/chapters/BaumeisterSSSP2018.pdf.

Botton, Alain de. "Why You Will Marry the Wrong Person." *New York Times*, May 28, 2016. https://www.nytimes.com/2016/05/29/opinion/sunday/why-you-will-marry-the-wrong-person.html.

Brooks, David. "The Nuclear Family Was a Mistake." *Atlantic*, March 2020. https://www.theatlantic.com/magazine/archive/2020/03/the-nuclear-family-was-a-mistake/605536/.

Brooks, David. *The Second Mountain: The Quest for a Moral Life*. New York: Random House, 2019.

REFERENCES

Buss, David M. *The Dangerous Passion: Why Jealousy Is as Necessary as Love and Sex*. New York: Free Press, 2000.

Buss, David M. *The Evolution of Desire*. New York: Basic Books, 2016.

Chapman, Bruce, and Cahit Guven. "Marital Status Is Misunderstood in Happiness Models." Deakin University Australia, Faculty of Business and Law, School Working Paper, January 2010. https://www.researchgate.net/publication/46459850_Marital_Status_is_Misunderstood_in_Happiness_Models.

Christakis, Nicholas A. *Connected: The Surprising Power of Our Social Networks and How They Shape Our Lives*. New York: Little, Brown, 2011.

Coontz, Stephanie. *Marriage, a History: How Love Conquered Marriage*. New York: Penguin, 2006.

Denworth, Lydia. *Friendship: The Evolution, Biology, and Extraordinary Power of Life's Fundamental Bond*. New York: W. W. Norton, 2020.

DePaulo, Bella. *Singled Out: How Singles Are Stereotyped, Stigmatized, and Ignored, and Still Live Happily Ever After*. New York: St. Martin's, 2007.

Druckerman, Pamela. *Lust in Translation: Infidelity from Tokyo to Tennessee*. New York: Penguin, 2008.

Finkel, Eli J. *The All-or-Nothing Marriage: How the Best Marriages Work*. New York: Penguin 2017.

Fisher, Helen. *Anatomy of Love: A Natural History of Mating, Marriage, and Why We Stray*. New York: W. W. Norton, 2016.

Fromm, Erich. *The Art of Loving*. New York: Open Road Media, 2013.

Gottman, John, *The Marriage Clinic: A Scientifically Based Marital Therapy*. New York: W. W. Norton, 1999.

Gottman, John, and Nan Silver. *The Seven Principles for Making Marriage Work*. New York: Harmony, 2015.

Gross-Loh, Christine. "The First Lesson of Marriage 101: There Are No Soul Mates." Pocket Worthy. https://getpocket.com/explore/item/the-first-lesson-of-marriage-101-there-are-no-soul-mates.

Hruschka, Daniel J. *Friendship: Development, Ecology, and Evolution of a Relationship*. Berkeley: University of California Press, 2010.

Human Relations Area Files. "Romantic or Disgusting? Passionate Kissing Is Not a Human Universal." https://hraf.yale.edu/romantic-or-disgusting-passionate-kissing-is-not-a-human-universal/.

Jones, Daniel. *Love Illuminated: Exploring Life's Most Mystifying Subject (with the Help of Fifty Thousand Strangers)*. New York: HarperCollins, 2014.

Kushner, David. "How Viagra Went from a Medical Mistake to a $3-Billion-Dollar-a-Year Industry." *Esquire*, August 21, 2018. https://www.esquire.com/lifestyle/health/a22627822/viagra-erectile-dysfunction-pills-history/.

Lawrence, Elizabeth M., et al. "Marital Happiness, Marital Status, Health, and Longevity." *Journal of Happiness Studies* 20 (2019): 1539–61. https://link.springer.com/article/10.1007/s10902-018-0009-9.

Lucas, Richard E. "Time Does Not Heal All Wounds: A Longitudinal Study of Reaction and Adaptation to Divorce." *Psychological Science* 16, no. 12 (2005): 945–50. https://journals.sagepub.com/doi/abs/10.1111/j.1467-9280.2005.01642.x.

REFERENCES

Michigan State University. "Health and Marriage: The Times They Are A Changin'." *ScienceDaily*, August 11, 2008. https://www.sciencedaily.com /releases/2008/08/080811070626.htm.

Niven, David. *One Hundred Simple Secrets of Great Relationships: What Scientists Have Learned and How You Can Use It*. New York: HarperCollins, 2009.

Ogas, Ogi, and Sai Gaddam. *A Billion Wicked Thoughts: What the Internet Tells Us About Sexual Relationships*. New York: Penguin, 2012.

Parker-Pope, Tara. *For Better: How the Surprising Science of Happy Couples Can Help Your Marriage Succeed*. New York: Penguin, 2011.

Perel, Esther. *The State of Affairs: Rethinking Infidelity*. New York: Harper, 2017.

Pinsker, Joe. "The Not-So-Great-Reason Divorce Rates Are Decreasing." *Atlantic*, September 2018. https://www.theatlantic.com/family/archive/2018/09 /millennials-divorce-baby-boomers/571282/.

Rusting, Ricki. "Can Marriage Make You Sick?" *Washington Post*, April 15, 2018. https://www.washingtonpost.com/national/health-science/can-marriage-make -you-sick/2018/04/13/df3599e6-1bdd-11e8-9de1-147dd2df3829_story.html.

Sample, Ian. "The Price of Love? Losing Two of Your Close Friends." *Guardian*, September 15, 2010. https://www.theguardian.com/science/2010/sep/15/price -love-close-friends-relationship.

Sternberg, Robert, and Karin Sternberg, eds. *The New Psychology of Love*, 2nd ed. Cambridge: Cambridge University Press, 2019.

Stutzer, Alois, and Bruno S. Frey. *Journal of Socio-Economics* 35, no. 2 (2006): 326–47. https://www.sciencedirect.com/science/article/abs/pii/S1053535705001745.

Tallis, Frank. *The Incurable Romantic and Other Tales of Madness and Desire*. New York: Basic Books, 2018.

Tallis, Frank. *Love Sick: Love as a Mental Illness*. New York: Da Capo Lifelong Books, 2005.

Tashiro, Ty. *The Science of Happily Ever After: What Really Matters in the Quest for Enduring Love*. New York: Harlequin Nonfiction, 2014.

Tennov, Dorothy. *Love and Limerence: The Experience of Being in Love*. Lanham, MD: Scarborough House, 1999.

Waite, Linda J., et al. "Does Divorce Make People Happy? Findings from a Study of Unhappy Marriages." Institute for American Values, January 2002. https://www.researchgate.net/publication/237233376_Does_Divorce_Make _People_Happy_Findings_From_a_Study_of_Unhappy_Marriages.

Wargo, Eric. "Life's Ups and Downs May Stick." *Observer*, May 1, 2007. https:// www.psychologicalscience.org/observer/lifes-ups-and-downs-may-stick.

Wikipedia. "Chinese Ghost Marriage." https://en.wikipedia.org/wiki/Chinese _ghost_marriage.

Wikipedia. "Sildenafil." https://en.wikipedia.org/wiki/Sildenafil.

CHAPTER 12

Apostolou, Menelaos, and Yan Wang. "The Challenges of Keeping an Intimate Relationship: An Evolutionary Examination." *Evolutionary Psychology*, July 2020. https://journals.sagepub.com/doi/full/10.1177/1474704920953526.

REFERENCES

Barelds, Dick P. H., and Pieternel Dijkstra. "Positive Illusions About a Partner's Physical Attractiveness and Relationship Quality." *Personal Relationships*, June 5, 2009. https://onlinelibrary.wiley.com/doi/abs/10.1111/j.1475 -6811.2009.01222.x.

Barker, Eric. "How to Have a Great Relationship—Five New Secrets from Research." *Barking Up the Wrong Tree* (blog), October 2014. https://www .bakadesuyo.com/2014/10/how-to-have-a-great-relationship-2/.

Bergreen, Laurence. *Casanova: The World of a Seductive Genius.* New York: Simon & Schuster, 2016.

Buss, David M. *The Dangerous Passion: Why Jealousy Is as Necessary as Love and Sex.* New York: Free Press, 2000.

Buss, David M. *The Evolution of Desire.* New York: Basic Books, 2016.

Childs, J. Rives. *Casanova: A New Perspective.* London: Constable, 1989.

Coontz, Stephanie. *Marriage, a History: How Love Conquered Marriage.* New York: Penguin, 2006.

Crockett, Zachary. "What Death Row Inmates Say in Their Last Words." Priceonomics, March 4, 2016. https://priceonomics.com/what-death-row-inmates-say -in-their-last-words/.

Diener, Ed. *Happiness: Unlocking the Mysteries of Psychological Wealth.* Malden, MA: Wiley-Blackwell, 2008.

Eisenberg, Michael L., et al. "Socioeconomic, Anthropomorphic, and Demographic Predictors of Adult Sexual Activity in the United States: Data from the National Survey of Family Growth." *Journal of Sexual Medicine* 7, no. 1, pt. 1 (2010): 50–58. https://www.ncbi.nlm.nih.gov/pmc/articles/PMC4081028/.

Felmlee, Diane. "From Appealing to Appalling: Disenchantment with a Romantic Partner." *Sociological Perspectives* 44, no. 3 (2001): 263–80. https://www .researchgate.net/publication/240760673_From_Appealing_to_Appalling _Disenchantment_with_a_Romantic_Partner.

Finkel, Eli J. *The All-or-Nothing Marriage: How the Best Marriages Work.* New York: Penguin, 2017.

Fisher, Helen. *Anatomy of Love: A Natural History of Mating, Marriage, and Why We Stray.* New York: W. W. Norton, 2016.

Fisher, Helen E. *Why We Love.* New York: Henry Holt, 2004.

Fisher, Helen E., et al. "Intense, Passionate, Romantic Love: A Natural Addiction? How the Fields That Investigate Romance and Substance Abuse Can Inform Each Other." *Frontiers in Psychology* 10, no. 7 (2016). https://pubmed.ncbi.nlm .nih.gov/27242601/.

Fisher, Helen, Arthur Aron, and Lucy L. Brown. "Romantic Love: An fMRI Study of a Neural Mechanism for Mate Choice." *Journal of Comparative Neurology 493, no. 1* (2005): 58–62. https://pubmed.ncbi.nlm.nih.gov/16255001/.

Fradera, Alex. "While Your Deliberate 'Monogamy Maintenance Strategies' Probably Won't Keep You Faithful, Your Automatic Psychological Biases Just Might." *Research Digest* (blog), August 31, 2018. https://digest.bps.org.uk/2018/08/31 /while-your-deliberate-monogamy-maintenance-strategies-probably-wont -keep-you-faithful-your-automatic-psychological-biases-just-might/.

REFERENCES

Gottman, John M. *The Marriage Clinic: A Scientifically Based Marital Therapy.* New York: W. W. Norton, 1999.

Gottman, John, and Nan Silver. *The Seven Principles for Making Marriage Work.* New York: Harmony, 2015.

Gottman, John Mordechai, with Nan Silver. *Why Marriages Succeed or Fail: And How You Can Make Yours Last.* New York: Simon & Schuster, 1994.

Hruschka, Daniel J. *Friendship: Development, Ecology, and Evolution of a Relationship.* Berkeley: University of California Press, 2010.

Jones, Daniel. *Love Illuminated: Exploring Life's Most Mystifying Subject (with the Help of Fifty Thousand Strangers).* New York: HarperCollins, 2014.

Lewis, Thomas H., Fari Amini, and Richard Lannon. *A General Theory of Love.* New York: Vintage, 2001.

Maner, Jon K., David Aaron Rouby, and Gian C. Gonzaga. "Automatic Inattention to Attractive Alternatives: The Evolved Psychology of Relationship Maintenance." *Evolution and Human Behavior* 29, no. 5 (2008): 343–49.

Murray, Sandra L., and John G. Holmes. "A Leap of Faith? Positive Illusions in Romantic Relationships." *Personality and Social Psychology Bulletin* 23, no. 6 (1997): 586–604. https://journals.sagepub.com/doi/10.1177/0146167297236003.

Murray, Sandra L., et al. "Tempting Fate or Inviting Happiness? Unrealistic Idealization Prevents the Decline of Marital Satisfaction." *Psychological Sciences* 22, no. 5 (2011): 619–26. https://www.ncbi.nlm.nih.gov/pmc/articles/PMC4094166/.

Niven, David. *One Hundred Simple Secrets of Great Relationships: What Scientists Have Learned and How You Can Use It.* New York: HarperCollins, 2009.

O'Leary, K. Daniel, et al. "Is Long-Term Love More Than a Rare Phenomenon? If So, What Are Its Correlates?" *Social and Psychological and Personality Science* 3, no. 2 (2012): 241–49. https://journals.sagepub.com/doi/abs/10.1177/1948550611417015.

O'Neill, Tracy. "Podcast #152: Casanova: Seduction and Genius in Venice." New York Public Library, February 21, 2017. https://www.nypl.org/blog/2017/02/20/podcast-152-casanova-seduction-and-genius-venice.

Parker-Pope, Tara. *For Better: How the Surprising Science of Happy Couples Can Help Your Marriage Succeed.* New York: Penguin, 2011.

Perel, Esther. *The State of Affairs: Rethinking Infidelity.* New York: Harper, 2017.

Regan, Pamela C. *The Mating Game: A Primer on Love, Sex, and Marriage.* Los Angeles: Sage, 2017.

Song, Hongwen, et al. "Improving Relationships by Elevating Positive Illusion and the Underlying Psychological and Neural Mechanisms." *Frontiers in Human Neuroscience* 12, no. 526 (2019). https://www.ncbi.nlm.nih.gov/pmc/articles/PMC6336892/.

Sternberg, Robert. *Cupid's Arrow: The Course of Love Through Time.* Cambridge: Cambridge University Press, 1998.

Sternberg, Robert, and Karin Sternberg, eds. *The New Psychology of Love,* 2nd ed. Cambridge: Cambridge University Press, 2019.

Tallis, Frank. *The Incurable Romantic and Other Tales of Madness and Desire.* New York: Basic Books, 2018.

REFERENCES

Tallis, Frank. *Love Sick: Love as a Mental Illness*. New York: Da Capo Lifelong Books, 2005.

Tennov, Dorothy. *Love and Limerence: The Experience of Being in Love*. Lanham, MD: Scarborough House.

University of California–Los Angeles. "Should I Marry Him? If You're Having Doubts, Don't Ignore Them, Psychology Study Suggests." ScienceDaily, September 13, 2012. https://www.sciencedaily.com/releases/2012/09/120913173324.htm.

Wikipedia. "Giacomo Casanova." https://en.wikipedia.org/wiki/Giacomo_Casanova.

Wikipedia. "Lovesickness." https://en.wikipedia.org/wiki/Lovesickness.

Wikipedia. "Lovestruck." https://en.wikipedia.org/wiki/Lovestruck.

Wikipedia. "Sense and Sensibility." https://en.wikipedia.org/wiki/Sense_and_Sensibility#Title.

Yamada, Junko, Mie Kito, and Masaki Yuki. "Passion, Relational Mobility, and Proof of Commitment: A Comparative Socio-Ecological Analysis of an Adaptive Emotion in a Sexual Market." *Evolutionary Psychology*, October 2017. https://journals.sagepub.com/doi/full/10.1177/1474704917746056.

CHAPTER 13

Athitakis, Mark. "Edgar Allan Poe's Hatchet Jobs." *Humanities* 38, no. 4 (2017). https://www.neh.gov/humanities/2017/fall/feature/edgar-allan-poe%E2%80%99s-hatchet-jobs.

Baker, Levi, and James K. McNulty. "Shyness and Marriage: Does Shyness Shape Even Established Relationships?" *Personality and Social Psychology Bulletin* 36, no. 5 (2010): 665–76. https://www.ncbi.nlm.nih.gov/pmc/articles/PMC4112747/.

Barker, Eric. "What Determines Whether a Marriage Succeeds or Fails?" *Barking Up the Wrong Tree* (blog), December 2011. https://www.bakadesuyo.com/2011/12/what-determines-whether-a-marriage-succeeds-o/.

Beck, Aaron T. *Love Is Never Enough: How Couples Can Overcome Misunderstandings, Resolve Conflicts, and Solve Relationship Problems Through Cognitive Therapy*. New York: HarperCollins, 1989.

Bernstein, Elizabeth. "Divorcé's Guide to Marriage: Study Reveals Five Common Themes Underlie Most Divorces." *Wall Street Journal*, July 24, 2012. https://www.wsj.com/articles/SB10000872396390444025204577544951717564114.

Brooks, David. *The Second Mountain: The Quest for a Moral Life*. New York: Random House, 2019.

Botton, Alain de. *The Course of Love: A Novel*. New York: Simon & Schuster, 2017.

Botton, Alain de. *On Love: A Novel*. New York: Grove/Atlantic, 2006.

Botton, Alain de. "Why You Will Marry the Wrong Person." *New York Times*, May 28, 2016. https://www.nytimes.com/2016/05/29/opinion/sunday/why-you-will-marry-the-wrong-person.html.

Collins, Paul S. "Seven Things You Probably Didn't Know About Edgar Allan Poe." *HuffPost*, October 26, 2014. https://www.huffpost.com/entry/edgar-allan-poe-facts_b_5698360.

REFERENCES

Diener, Ed. *Happiness: Unlocking the Mysteries of Psychological Wealth*. Malden, MA: Wiley-Blackwell, 2009.

Encyclopedia Virginia. "Poe, Edgar Allan (1809–1849)." https://www.encyclope diavirginia.org/poe_edgar_allan_1809-1849#start_entry.

Epstein, Robert. "Fall in Love and Stay That Way." *Scientific American*, January 2010. https://www.scientificamerican.com/article/how-science-can-help -love/.

Finkel, Eli J. *The All-or-Nothing Marriage: How the Best Marriages Work*. New York: Penguin, 2017.

Fromm, Erich. *The Art of Loving*. New York: Open Road Media, 2013.

Gilbert, Susan. "Married with Problems? Therapy May Not Help." *New York Times*, April 19, 2005. https://www.nytimes.com/2005/04/19/health/psychology /married-with-problems-therapy-may-not-help.html.

Gilovich, Thomas. *How We Know What Isn't So: The Fallibility of Human Reason in Everyday Life*. New York: Free Press, 1993.

Gottman, John. *The Man's Guide to Women: Scientifically Proven Secrets from the Love Lab About What Women Really Want*. New York: Rodale, 2016.

Gottman, John M. *The Marriage Clinic: A Scientifically Based Marital Therapy*. New York: W. W. Norton, 1999.

Gottman, John M. *The Science of Trust: Emotional Attunement for Couples*. New York: W. W. Norton, 2011.

Gottman, John, and Joan DeClaire. *The Relationship Cure: A Five Step Guide to Strengthening Your Marriage, Family, and Friendships*. New York: Harmony, 2002.

Gottman, John, and Nan Silver. *The Seven Principles for Making Marriage Work*. New York: Harmony, 2015.

Gottman, John M., and Nan Silver. *What Makes Love Last? How to Build Trust and Avoid Betrayal*. New York: Simon & Schuster, 2013.

Gottman, John Mordechai, with Nan Silver. *Why Marriages Succeed or Fail: And How You Can Make Yours Last*. New York: Simon & Schuster, 1994.

Gottman, John M., Julie Schwartz Gottman, and Joan DeClaire. *Ten Lessons to Transform Your Marriage: America's Love Lab Experts Share Their Strategies for Strengthening Your Relationship*. New York: Harmony, 2007.

Iyengar, Sheena. *The Art of Choosing*. New York: Twelve, 2011.

Jackson, Kevin. "The Great Bad Writer." *Prospect*, February 22, 2012. https:// www.prospectmagazine.co.uk/magazine/the-great-bad-writer-edgar-allan-poe -raven-cusack.

Jones, Daniel. *Love Illuminated: Exploring Life's Most Mystifying Subject (with the Help of Fifty Thousand Strangers)*. New York: HarperCollins, 2014.

Lehrer, Jonah. *A Book About Love*. New York: Simon & Schuster, 2017.

Markman, Howard, Scott Stanley, and Susan L. Blumberg. *Fighting for Your Marriage: A Deluxe Revised Edition of the Classic Best-seller for Enhancing Marriage and Preventing Divorce*. San Francisco: Jossey-Bass, 2010.

Maxwell, Jessica A., and Andrea L. Meltzer. "Kiss and Make Up? Examining the Co-occurrence of Conflict and Sex." *Archives of Sexual Behavior* 49 (2020): 2883–92. https://rd.springer.com/article/10.1007/s10508-020-01779-8.

REFERENCES

Mitchell, Stephen A. *Can Love Last? The Fate of Romance over Time*. New York: W. W. Norton, 2003.

Myers, Jane E., Jayamala Madathil, and Lynne R. Tingle. "Marriage Satisfaction and Wellness in India and the United States: A Preliminary Comparison of Arranged Marriages and Marriages of Choice." *Journal of Counseling & Development* 83, no. 2 (2005): 183–90. https://onlinelibrary.wiley.com/doi/abs/10.1002/j.1556-6678.2005.tb00595.x.

Niven, David. *The Simple Secrets for Becoming Healthy, Wealthy, and Wise: What Scientists Have Learned and How You Can Use It*. New York: HarperOne, 2009.

Niven, David. *One Hundred Simple Secrets of Great Relationships: What Scientists Have Learned and How You Can Use It*. New York: HarperCollins, 2009.

Ohio State University. "Conflict Levels Don't Change Much over Course of Marriage." ScienceDaily, August 15, 2011. https://www.sciencedaily.com/releases/2011/08/110815101538.htm.

Parker-Pope, Tara. *For Better: How the Surprising Science of Happy Couples Can Help Your Marriage Succeed*. New York: Penguin, 2011.

Parker-Pope, Tara. "The Happy Marriage Is the 'Me' Marriage." *New York Times*, December 31, 2020. https://www.nytimes.com/2011/01/02/weekinreview/02parkerpope.html.

Perel, Esther. *Mating in Captivity: Unlocking Erotic Intelligence*. New York: HarperCollins e-books, 2009.

Perel, Esther. *The State of Affairs: Rethinking Infidelity*. New York: Harper, 2017.

Poe, Edgar Allan. "The Philosophy of Composition." Last updated September 5, 2011. https://www.eapoe.org/works/essays/philcomp.htm.

Poe, Edgar Allan. "The Philosophy of Composition." *Graham's Magazine* 28, no. 4 (April 1846): 163–67.

Poe, Edgar Allan. "The Raven." Poetry Foundation. Accessed . https://www.poetryfoundation.org/poems/48860/the-raven.

Pruette, Lorine. "A Psycho-Analytical Study of Edgar Allan Poe." *American Journal of Psychology* 31, no. 4 (1920): 370–402. https://www.jstor.org/stable/1413669?seq=1#metadata_info_tab_contents.

Regan, Pamela C. *The Mating Game: A Primer on Love, Sex, and Marriage*. Los Angeles: Sage, 2017.

Scheibehenne, Benjamin, Jutta Mata, and Peter M. Todd. "Older but Not Wiser—Predicting a Partner's Preference Gets Worse with Age." *Journal of Consumer Psychology* 21, no. 2 (2011): 184–91. https://psycnet.apa.org/record/2011-17293-011.

Seligman, Martin E. P. *Flourish: A Visionary New Understanding of Happiness and Well-Being*. New York: Atria Books, 2012.

Simonton, Dean Keith. *Greatness: Who Makes History and Why*. New York: Guilford, 1994.

Sternberg, Robert. *Cupid's Arrow: The Course of Love Through Time*. Cambridge: Cambridge University Press, 1998.

Tallis, Frank. *The Incurable Romantic and Other Tales of Madness and Desire*. New York: Basic Books, 2018.

REFERENCES

Tallis, Frank. *Love Sick: Love as a Mental Illness*. New York: Da Capo Lifelong Books, 2005.

Tierney, John. *The Power of Bad*. New York: Penguin, 2019.

University of Rochester. "Do Open Relationships Really Work?" Science-Daily, October 29, 2019. https://www.sciencedaily.com/releases/2019/10/191029182513.htm.

University of Tennessee at Knoxville. "How Happy Couples Argue: Focus on Solvable Issues First." ScienceDaily, September 16, 2016. https://www.science daily.com/releases/2019/09/190916114014.htm.

Velella, Rob. "The Many Names of Poe." *American Literary Blog*, January 7, 2010. https://americanliteraryblog.blogspot.com/2010/01/many-names-of-poe.html.

Waite, Linda J., et al. "Does Divorce Make People Happy? Findings from a Study of Unhappy Marriages." Institute for American Values, January 2002. https://www.researchgate.net/publication/237233376_Does_Divorce_Make_People _Happy_Findings_From_a_Study_of_Unhappy_Marriages.

"War over Being Nice." *Seph* (blog), September 19, 2018. https://josephg.com /blog/war-over-being-nice/.

Wikipedia. "Age of Enlightenment." https://en.wikipedia.org/wiki/Age_of_En lightenment.

Wikipedia. "Couples Therapy." https://en.wikipedia.org/wiki/Couples_therapy #History.

Wikipedia. "Edgar Allan Poe." https://en.wikipedia.org/wiki/Edgar_Allan _Poe.

Wikipedia. "The Philosophy of Composition." https://en.wikipedia.org/wiki/The _Philosophy_of_Composition.

Wikipedia. "The Raven." https://en.wikipedia.org/wiki/The_Raven.

Wikipedia. "Romanticism." https://en.wikipedia.org/wiki/Romanticism.

CHAPTER 14

Acevedo, Bianca P., et al. "Neural Correlates of Long-Term Intense Romantic Love." *Social Cognitive and Affective Neuroscience* 7, no. 2 (2012): 145–59. https://pubmed.ncbi.nlm.nih.gov/21208991/.

Aron, Arthur, and Elaine Aron. *The Heart of Social Psychology: A Backstage View of a Passionate Science*. Lexington, MA: Lexington Books, 1986.

Aron, Arthur, et al. "The Self-Expansion Model of Motivation and Cognition in Close Relationships." In *The Oxford Handbook of Close Relationships*, edited by Jeffry Simpson and Lorne Campbell. Oxford: Oxford University Press, 2013. https://www.oxfordhandbooks.com/view/10.1093 /oxfordhb/9780195398694.001.0001/oxfordhb-9780195398694-e-005.

Barker, Eric. "Does Discussing Abortions and STD's Make for a Better First Date?" *Barking Up the Wrong Tree* (blog), February 2012. https://www.bakadesuyo .com/2012/02/does-discussing-abortions-and-stds-make-for-a/.

Barker, Eric. "How to Have a Great Relationship—Five New Secrets from Research." *Barking Up the Wrong Tree* (blog), October 2014. https://www.bakadesuyo .com/2014/10/how-to-have-a-great-relationship-2/.

REFERENCES

Baumeister, Roy, and Sara R. Wotman. *Breaking Hearts: The Two Sides of Unrequited Love*. New York: Guilford, 1992.

Baumeister, Roy F., et al. "The Mask of Love and Sexual Gullibility." In *The Social Psychology of Gullibility*, edited by Joseph P. Forgas and Roy F. Baumeister. New York: Routledge, 2019. https://www.taylorfrancis.com/chapters/edit/10.4324/9780429203787-2/mask-love-sexual-gullibility-roy-baumeister-jessica-maxwell-geoffrey-thomas-kathleen-vohs.

Beck, Aaron. *Love Is Never Enough: How Couples Can Overcome Misunderstandings, Resolve Conflicts, and Solve Relationship Problems Through Cognitive Therapy*. New York: Harper Perennial, 1989.

Botton, Alain de. *The Course of Love: A Novel*. New York: Simon & Schuster, 2017.

Brooks, David. *The Second Mountain: The Quest for a Moral Life*. New York: Random House, 2019.

Bühler, Janina Larissa, et al. "Does Michelangelo Care About Age? An Adult Life-Span Perspective on the Michelangelo Phenomenon." *Journal of Social and Personal Relationships* 36, no. 4 (2019): 1392–1412. https://journals.sagepub.com/doi/full/10.1177/0265407518766698.

Busby, Dean M., Veronica Hanna-Walker, and Chelom E. Leavitt. "A Kiss Is Not a Kiss: Kissing Frequency, Sexual Quality, Attachment, and Sexual and Relationship Satisfaction." *Sexual and Relationship Therapy*, January 31, 2020. https://www.tandfonline.com/doi/abs/10.1080/14681994.2020.1717460.

Buss, David M. *The Dangerous Passion: Why Jealousy Is as Necessary as Love and Sex*. New York: Free Press, 2000.

Cao, Chao, et al. "Trends in Sexual Activity and Associations with All-Cause and Cause-Specific Mortality Among US Adults." *Journal of Sexual Medicine* 17, no. 10 (2020): 1903–13. https://www.sciencedirect.com/science/article/abs/pii/S174360952030669X.

Carrère, S., et al. "Predicting Marital Stability and Divorce in Newlywed Couples." *Journal of Family Psychology* 14, no. 1 (2000): 42–58. https://pubmed.ncbi.nlm.nih.gov/10740681/.

Coontz, Stephanie. "For a Better Marriage, Act Like a Single Person." *New York Times*, February 10, 2018. https://www.nytimes.com/2018/02/10/opinion/sunday/for-a-better-marriage-act-like-a-single-person.html.

Drigotas, S. M., et al. "Close Partner as Sculptor of the Ideal Self: Behavioral Affirmation and the Michelangelo Phenomenon." *Journal of Personal and Social Psychology* 77, no. 2 (1999): 293–323. https://pubmed.ncbi.nlm.nih.gov/10474210/.

Druckerman, Pamela. *Lust in Translation: Infidelity from Tokyo to Tennessee*. New York: Penguin, 2008.

Dunn, Elizabeth W., et al. "Misunderstanding the Affective Consequences of Everyday Social Interactions: The Hidden Benefits of Putting One's Best Face Forward." *Journal of Personality and Social Psychology* 92, no. 6 (2007): 990–1005. https://pubmed.ncbi.nlm.nih.gov/17547484/.

Finkel, Eli J. *The All-or-Nothing Marriage: How the Best Marriages Work*. New York: Penguin, 2017.

REFERENCES

Fisher, Helen E. *Why We Love*. New York: Henry Holt, 2004.

Forgas, Joseph P., and Roy F. Baumeister, eds. *The Social Psychology of Living Well*. New York: Taylor and Francis, 2018.

Gottman, John M. *The Marriage Clinic: A Scientifically Based Marital Therapy*. New York: W. W. Norton, 1999.

Gottman, John M. *The Science of Trust: Emotional Attunement for Couples*. New York: W. W. Norton, 2011.

Gottman, John, and Joan DeClaire. *The Relationship Cure: A Five Step Guide to Strengthening Your Marriage, Family, and Friendships*. New York: Harmony, 2002.

Gottman, John, and Nan Silver. *The Seven Principles for Making Marriage Work*. New York: Harmony, 2015.

Gottman, John, and Nan Silver. *What Makes Love Last? How to Build Trust and Avoid Betrayal*. New York: Simon & Schuster, 2013.

Gottman, John Mordechai, with Nan Silver. *Why Marriages Succeed or Fail: And How You Can Make Yours Last*. New York: Simon & Schuster, 1994.

Gottman, John M., Julie Schwartz Gottman, and Joan DeClaire. *Ten Lessons to Transform Your Marriage: America's Love Lab Experts Share Their Strategies for Strengthening Your Relationship*. New York: Harmony, 2007.

Hagspiel, Stefan. "The Man with a Thirty Second Memory." YouTube, December 29, 2006. https://www.youtube.com/watch?v=WmzU47i2xgw.

Harris, Sam. *Lying*. Four Elephants, 2013.

Harvey-Jenner, Catriona. "The Woman with Amnesia Whose True Story May Have Inspired Fifty First Dates." *Cosmopolitan*, January 19, 2017. https://www.cosmopolitan.com/uk/reports/news/a48933/michelle-philpots-amnesia-true-story-50-first-dates/.

Hazell, Ward. "Ten People with Amnesia Who Literally Lost Their Minds." Listverse, January 17, 2019. https://listverse.com/2019/01/17/10-people-with-amnesia-who-literally-lost-their-minds/.

Hicks, Angela M., and Lisa M. Diamond. "How Was Your Day? Couples' Affect When Telling and Hearing Daily Events." *Personal Relationships* 15, no. 2 (2008): 205–28. https://onlinelibrary.wiley.com/doi/abs/10.1111/j.1475-6811.2008.00194.x.

Hira, Shreena N., and Nickola C. Overall. "Improving Intimate Relationships: Targeting the Partner Versus Changing the Self." *Journal of Social and Personal Relationships* 28, no. 5 (2011): 610–33. https://journals.sagepub.com/doi/10.1177/0265407510388586.

Inbar, Michael. "'Groundhog Day' for Real: Woman Is Stuck in 1994." Today, August 16, 2010. https://www.today.com/news/groundhog-day-real-woman-stuck-1994-1C9017393.

Jarrett, Christian. "Try Something New Together—Research Shows Engaging in 'Self-Expanding Activities' Rekindles the Sexual Desire of Long-Term Couples." *Research Digest* (blog), February 14, 2019. https://digest.bps.org.uk/2019/02/14/try-something-new-together-research-shows-engaging-in-self-expanding-activities-rekindles-the-sexual-desire-of-long-term-couples/.

REFERENCES

Johnson, Matthew D., and Franz J. Neyer. "(Eventual) Stability and Change Across Partnerships." *Journal of Family Psychology* 33, no. 6 (2019): 711–21. https://psycnet.apa.org/record/2019-10172-001.

Jones, Daniel. *Love Illuminated: Exploring Life's Most Mystifying Subject (with the Help of Fifty Thousand Strangers)*. New York: HarperCollins, 2014.

Kirshenbaum, Sheril. *The Science of Kissing: What Our Lips Are Telling Us*. New York: Grand Central, 2011.

Levy, Andrew. "The Woman Who Wakes Up Thinking Its 1994 Every Morning and Then Forgets Everything the Next Day Due to a Car Crash Injury." *Daily Mail*, June 10, 2010. https://www.dailymail.co.uk/health/article-1285535/Two -car-crashes-leave-Michelle-Philpots-24-hour-memory.html.

Lewis, Thomas H., Fari Amini, and Richard Lannon. *A General Theory of Love*. New York: Vintage, 2001.

Mashek, Debra J., and Arthur Aron. *Handbook of Closeness and Intimacy*. Hove, UK: Psychology Press, 2004.

McRaney, David. "Misattribution of Arousal." You Are Not So Smart, July 7, 2011. https://youarenotsosmart.com/2011/07/07/misattribution-of-arousal/.

Mitchell, Stephen A. *Can Love Last? The Fate of Romance over Time*. New York: W. W. Norton, 2003.

Murray, Samuel, and Peter Finocchiaro. "These Confabulations Are Guaranteed to Improve Your Marriage! Toward a Teleological Theory of Confabulation." PsyArXiv Preprints, May 25, 2020. https://psyarxiv.com/huywk/.

Niven, David. *One Hundred Simple Secrets of Great Relationships: What Scientists Have Learned and How You Can Use It*. New York: HarperCollins, 2009.

Parker-Pope, Tara. *For Better: How the Surprising Science of Happy Couples Can Help Your Marriage Succeed*. New York: Penguin, 2011.

Parker-Pope, Tara. "The Happy Marriage Is the 'Me' Marriage." *New York Times*, December 31, 2020. https://www.nytimes.com/2011/01/02/weekinreview /02parkerpope.html.

Pennebaker, James. *The Secret Life of Pronouns: What Our Words Say About Us*. New York: Bloomsbury, 2013.

Perel, Esther. *Mating in Captivity: Unlocking Erotic Intelligence*. New York: HarperCollins e-books, 2009.

Perel, Esther. *The State of Affairs: Rethinking Infidelity*. New York: Harper, 2017.

Roper, Matt. "The Real Groundhog Day: Rare Disorder Wipes Women's Memory Clean Every Twenty-Four Hours." *Mirror*, January 27, 2012. https://www .mirror.co.uk/news/weird-news/the-real-groundhog-day-rare-disorder-227866.

Rusbult, Caryl, Eli J. Finkel, and Madoka Kumashiro. "The Michelangelo Phenomenon." *Current Directions in Psychological Science* 18, no. 6 (2009): 305–9.

Sacks, Oliver. "The Abyss: Music and Amnesia." *New Yorker*, September 24, 2007. https://www.newyorker.com/magazine/2007/09/24/the-abyss.

Sagarin, Brad J., et al. "Hormonal Changes and Couple Bonding in Consensual Sadomasochistic Activity." *Archives of Sexual Behavior* 38, no. 2 (2009): 186–200. https://pubmed.ncbi.nlm.nih.gov/18563549/.

Seider, Benjamin, et al. "We Can Work It Out: Age Differences in Relational

REFERENCES

Pronouns, Physiology, and Behavior in Marital Conflict." *Psychology and Aging* 24, no. 3 (2009): 604–13. https://pubmed.ncbi.nlm.nih.gov/19739916/.

Sexton, James. *If You're in My Office, It's Already Too Late: A Divorce Lawyer's Guide to Staying Together.* New York: Macmillan, 2018.

Smith, Anthony, et al. "Sexual and Relationship Satisfaction Among Heterosexual Men and Women: The Importance of Desired Frequency of Sex." *Journal of Sex and Marital Therapy* 37, no. 2 (2011): 104–15. https://www.tandfonline.com/doi/abs/10.1080/0092623X.2011.560531.

Sternberg, Robert. *Cupid's Arrow: The Course of Love Through Time.* Cambridge: Cambridge University Press, 1999.

Sternberg, Robert. *Love Is a Story: A New Theory of Relationships.* Chosen Books, Oxford: Oxford University Press, 1998.

Sternberg, Robert, and Karin Sternberg, eds. *The New Psychology of Love*, 2nd ed. Cambridge: Cambridge University Press, 2019.

Tallis, Frank. *Love Sick: Love as a Mental Illness.* New York: Da Capo Lifelong Books, 2005.

Tierney, John. *The Power of Bad.* New York: Penguin, 2019.

Tsapelas, Irene, Arthur Aron, and Terri Orbuch. "Marital Boredom Now Predicts Less Satisfaction Nine Years Later." *Psychological Science* 20, no. 5 (2009): 543–45. https://psycnet.apa.org/record/2009-06873-004.

u/BlueOrange. "TIL I learned of Michelle Philpots, the real life inspiration behindthe movie 50 first dates. Her memory is wiped clean everyday, and she has been stuck in 1994 for 25 years." Reddit, August 16, 2019, 2:02:22. https://www.reddit.com/r/todayilearned/comments/crcfsj/til_i_learned_of_michelle_philpots_the_real_life/.

University of Alberta. "Changing Partners Doesn't Change Relationship Dynamics." ScienceDaily, August 27, 2019. https://www.sciencedaily.com/releases/2019/08/190827123518.htm.

University of California–Riverside. "Research Affirms the Power of 'We.'" ScienceDaily, October 5, 2018. https://www.sciencedaily.com/releases/2018/10/181005111455.htm.

Wikipedia. "Amnesia." https://en.wikipedia.org/wiki/Amnesia.

Wikipedia. "Anterograde Amnesia." https://en.wikipedia.org/wiki/Anterograde_amnesia.

Wikipedia. "Clive Wearing." https://en.wikipedia.org/wiki/Clive_Wearing.

Wikipedia. "*Memento* (film)—Scientific Response." https://en.wikipedia.org/wiki/Memento_(film)#Scientific_response.

Wikipedia. "Michelangelo Phenomenon." https://en.wikipedia.org/wiki/Michelangelo_phenomenon.

Wikipedia. "Procedural Memory." https://en.wikipedia.org/wiki/Procedural_memory.

Wikipedia. "Transient Global Amnesia." https://en.wikipedia.org/wiki/Transient_global_amnesia.

Wright, Robert. *The Moral Animal: Why We Are the Way We Are: The New Sci-*

ence of Evolutionary Psychology. New York: Knopf Doubleday, Vintage Books, 1995.

Zachary. "This Woman's Rare Form of Amnesia Makes Her Forget Everything Before 1994." Shared, December 22, 2017. https://www.shared.com/woman-with-rare-form-of-amnesia/.

CHAPTER 15

Bradley, Robert. *Husband-Coached Childbirth: The Bradley Method of Natural Childbirth*, 5th ed. New York: Bantam, 2008.

Gottman, John. *The Man's Guide to Women: Scientifically Proven Secrets from the Love Lab About What Women Really Want*. New York: Rodale, 2016.

Rome News-Tribune. "50 Years Ago in Rome News-Tribune." September 18, 2010.

CHAPTER 16

Achor, Shawn. *The Happiness Advantage: The Seven Principles of Positive Psychology That Fuel Success and Performance at Work*. New York: Currency, 2010.

Alberti, Fay Bound. *A Biography of Loneliness: The History of an Emotion*. Oxford: Oxford University Press, 2019.

Alberti, Fay Bound. "One Is the Loneliest Number: The History of a Western Problem." *Aeon*, September 12, 2018. https://aeon.co/ideas/one-is-the-loneliest-number-the-history-of-a-western-problem.

Baumeister, Roy F. *The Cultural Animal: Human Nature, Meaning, and Social Life*. New York: Oxford University Press, 2005.

Cacioppo, John T., and William Patrick. *Loneliness: Human Nature and the Need for Social Connection*. New York: Norton, 2009.

Cacioppo, John T., Louise C. Hawkley, and Gary G. Berntson. "The Anatomy of Loneliness." *Current Directions in Psychological Science* 12, no. 3 (2003): 71–74. https://www.jstor.org/stable/20182842?seq=1.

Chen, Zhansheng, et al. "When Hurt Will Not Heal: Exploring the Capacity to Relive Social and Physical Pain." *Psychological Science* 19, no. 8 (2008): 789–95. https://pubmed.ncbi.nlm.nih.gov/18816286/.

Csikszentmihalyi, Mihaly. *Finding Flow: The Psychology of Engagement with Everyday Life*. New York: Basic Books, 1998.

DePaulo, Bella. *Singled Out: How Singles Are Stereotyped, Stigmatized, and Ignored, and Still Live Happily Ever After*. New York: St. Martin's, 2007.

Diamond, Jared. *The World Until Yesterday: What Can We Learn from Traditional Societies?* New York: Penguin, 2013.

Finkel, Michael. "The Strange and Curious Tale of the Last True Hermit." *GQ*, August 4, 2014. https://www.gq.com/story/the-last-true-hermit.

Finkel, Michael. *The Stranger in the Woods: The Extraordinary Story of the Last True Hermit*. New York: Knopf Doubleday, 2017.

Forgas, Joseph P., and Roy F. Baumeister, eds. *The Social Psychology of Living Well*. New York: Taylor and Francis, 2018.

REFERENCES

Friedrich, Lena. "The Hermit—the True Legend of the North Pond Hermit." Vimeo, April 10, 2020. https://vimeo.com/406217619.

Gawande, Atul. "Hellhole." *New Yorker*, March 23, 2009. https://www.new yorker.com/magazine/2009/03/30/hellhole.

Gottman, John, and Nan Silver. *What Makes Love Last? How to Build Trust and Avoid Betrayal*. New York: Simon & Schuster, 2013.

Haney, Craig. "Mental Health Issues in Long-Term Solitary and 'Supermax' Confinement." *Crime and Delinquency* 49, no. 1 (2003): 124–56. https://www .researchgate.net/publication/249718605_Mental_Health_Issues_in_Long -Term_Solitary_and_Supermax_Confinement.

Hari, Johann. *Lost Connections: Uncovering the Real Causes of Depression—and the Unexpected Solutions*. New York: Bloomsbury, 2018.

Harris, Michael. *Solitude: In Pursuit of a Singular Life in a Crowded World*. New York: St. Martin's, 2017.

Holt-Lunstad, Julianne. "Why Social Relationships Are Important for Physical Health: A Systems Approach to Understanding and Modifying Risk and Protection." *Annual Review of Psychology* 69 (January 2018): 437–58. https:// pubmed.ncbi.nlm.nih.gov/29035688/.

Insel, Thomas R. "Is Social Attachment an Addictive Disorder? *Physiology and Behavior* 79 (August 2003): 351–57. https://pubmed.ncbi.nlm.nih.gov /12954430/.

Junger, Sebastian. *Tribe: On Homecoming and Belonging*. New York: Grand Central, 2016.

Kemp, Andrew Haddon, Juan A. Arias, and Zoe Fisher. "Social Ties, Health, and Wellbeing: A Literature Review and Model." In *Neuroscience and Social Science: The Missing Link*, edited by Augustín Ibáñez, Luca Sedeño, and Adolfo M. Garcia. Cham, Switzerland: Springer International, 2018. https://www .researchgate.net/publication/317616735_Social_Ties_Health_and_Wellbeing _A_Literature_Review_and_Model.

Khazan, Olga. "How Loneliness Begets Loneliness." *Atlantic*, April 2017. https://www.theatlantic.com/health/archive/2017/04/how-loneliness-begets -loneliness/521841/.

Klinenberg, Eric. *Going Solo: The Extraordinary Rise and Surprising Appeal of Living Alone*. New York: Penguin, 2013.

Latson, Jennifer. *The Boy Who Loved Too Much: A True Story of Pathological Friendliness*. New York: Simon & Schuster, 2017.

Lilienfeld, Scott O., et al. *Fifty Great Myths of Popular Psychology: Shattering Widespread Misconceptions about Human Behavior*. Malden, MA: Wiley-Blackwell, 2010.

Massachusetts General Hospital. "Social Connection Is the Strongest Protective Factor for Depression." ScienceDaily, August 14, 2020. https://www.science daily.com/releases/2020/08/200814131007.htm.

Massachusetts Institute of Technology. "A Hunger for Social Contact." ScienceDaily, November 23, 2020. https://www.sciencedaily.com/releases/2020/11 /201123120724.htm.

REFERENCES

Murthy, Vivek H. *Together: The Healing Power of Human Connection in a Sometimes Lonely World*. New York: Harper Wave, 2020.

Olds, Jacqueline, and Richard S. Schwartz. *The Lonely American: Drifting Apart in the Twenty-First Century*. Boston: Beacon, 2010.

Pinker, Susan. *The Village Effect: How Face-to-Face Contact Can Make Us Healthier and Happier*. Toronto: Random House of Canada, 2014.

Powdthavee, Nattavudh. "Putting a Price Tag on Friends, Relatives, and Neighbours: Using Surveys of Life Satisfaction to Value Social Relationships." *Journal of Socio-Economics* 37, no. 4 (2008): 1459–80. https://www.sciencedirect.com/science/article/abs/pii/S1053535707001205.

Seelye, Katharine Q. "'Boo Radley' of the Woods? Not to All Maine Neighbors." *New York Times*, June 12, 2013. https://www.nytimes.com/2013/06/12/us/hermit-in-maine-is-legend-to-some-thief-to-others.html.

Self, Will, et al. "'Would That All Journeys Were on Foot': Writers on the Joys of Walking." *Guardian*, September 18, 2018. https://www.theguardian.com/cities/2018/sep/18/would-that-all-journeys-were-on-foot-writers-on-the-joy-of-walking.

Shenk, Joshua Wolf. "What Makes Us Happy?" *Atlantic*, June 2009. https://www.theatlantic.com/magazine/archive/2009/06/what-makes-us-happy/307439/.

Simonton, Dean Keith. *The Wiley Handbook of Genius*. Chichester, UK: Wiley Blackwell, 2014.

Stevens, Jenny. "The Friend Effect: Why the Secret of Health and Happiness Is Surprisingly Simple." *Guardian*, May 23, 2018. https://www.theguardian.com/society/2018/may/23/the-friend-effect-why-the-secret-of-health-and-happiness-is-surprisingly-simple.

Stockholm University. "Trust in Others Predicts Mortality in the United States." ScienceDaily, October 25, 2018. https://www.sciencedaily.com/releases/2018/10/181025103318.htm.

Storr, Will. *Selfie: How We Became So Self-Obsessed and What It's Doing to Us*. New York: Harry N. Abrams, 2019.

Storr, Anthony. *Solitude: A Return to the Self*. New York: Free Press, 2005.

Vincent, David. *A History of Solitude*. Cambridge, UK: Polity, 2020.

Walton, Gregory M., et al. "Mere Belonging: The Power of Social Connections." *Journal of Personality and Social Psychology* 102, no. 3 (2012): 513–32. https://pubmed.ncbi.nlm.nih.gov/22023711/.

Whitehead, Nadia. "People Would Rather Be Electrically Shocked Than Left Alone with Their Thoughts." *Science*, July 3, 2014. https://www.sciencemag.org/news/2014/07/people-would-rather-be-electrically-shocked-left-alone-their-thoughts.

Wikipedia. "Christopher Thomas Knight." https://en.wikipedia.org/wiki/Christopher_Thomas_Knight.

Wikipedia. "Solitary Confinement." https://en.wikipedia.org/wiki/Solitary_confinement.

Worrall, Simon. "Why the North Pond Hermit Hid from People for Twenty-Seven Years." *National Geographic*, April 8, 2017. https://www.nationalgeographic.com/news/2017/04/north-pond-hermit-maine-knight-stranger-woods-finkel/.

Yeginsu, Ceylan. "U.K. Appoints a Minister for Loneliness." *New York Times*, January 17, 2018. https://www.nytimes.com/2018/01/17/world/europe/uk-britain-loneliness.html.

CHAPTER 17

Alberti, Fay Bound. *A Biography of Loneliness: The History of an Emotion*. Oxford: Oxford University Press, 2019.

Alter, Adam. *Irresistible: The Rise of Addictive Technology and the Business of Keeping Us Hooked*. New York: Penguin, 2017.

American Association for the Advancement of Science. "Empathy: College Students Don't Have as Much as They Used To." *EurekAlert!*, May 28, 2010. https://www.eurekalert.org/pub_releases/2010-05/uom-ecs052610.php.

Beck, Julie. "Married to a Doll: Why One Man Advocates Synthetic Love." *Atlantic*, September 6, 2013. https://www.theatlantic.com/health/archive/2013/09/married-to-a-doll-why-one-man-advocates-synthetic-love/279361/.

Beusman, Callie. "My Sensual Journey into Japan's $90 Million Fake Anime Boyfriend Market." Vice, March 18, 2016. https://www.vice.com/en_us/article/qkg74b/my-sensual-journey-into-japans-90-million-fake-anime-boyfriend-market.

Bruni, Luigino, and Luca Stanca. "Watching Alone: Relational Goods, Television, and Happiness." *Journal of Economic Behavior and Organization* 65, nos. 3–4 (2008): 506–28. https://www.sciencedirect.com/science/article/abs/pii/S0167268106002095.

Cortez, C. A. "Mediated Interpersonal Communication: The Role of Attraction and Perceived Homophily in the Development of Parasocial Relationships." PhD diss., University of Iowa, 1993. https://elibrary.ru/item.asp?id=5801038.

Crist, Ry. "Dawn of the Sexbots." CNET, August 10, 2017. https://www.cnet.com/news/abyss-creations-ai-sex-robots-headed-to-your-bed-and-heart/.

Denworth, Lydia. *Friendship: The Evolution, Biology, and Extraordinary Power of Life's Fundamental Bond*. New York: W. W. Norton, 2020.

Derrick, Jaye L. "Energized by Television: Familiar Fictional Worlds Restore Self-Control." *Social Psychological and Personality Science* 4, no. 3 (2013): 299–307. https://journals.sagepub.com/doi/abs/10.1177/1948550612454889.

Derrick, Jaye L., Shira Gabriel, and Kurt Hugenberg. "Social Surrogacy: How Favored Television Programs Provide the Experience of Belonging." *Journal of Experimental Social Psychology* 45, no. 2 (2009): 352–62. https://www.sciencedirect.com/science/article/abs/pii/S0022103108002412.

DeSteno, David. *Emotional Success: The Power of Gratitude, Compassion, and Pride*. New York: Houghton Mifflin Harcourt, 2019.

Dormehl, Luke. "Realdoll Is Building a Fleet of AI-Powered Sex Robots with Customizable Personalities." Digital Trends, February 3, 2017. https://www.digitaltrends.com/cool-tech/realdoll-sex-robot-ai/.

Eyal, Keren, and Jonathan Cohen. "When Good Friends Say Goodbye: A Parasocial Breakup Study." *Journal of Broadcasting and Electronic Media* 50, no. 3 (2006): 502–23. https://www.tandfonline.com/doi/abs/10.1207/s15506878jobem5003_9.

Frey, Bruno S., Christine Benesch, and Alois Stutzer. "Does Watching TV Make

REFERENCES

Us Happy?" *Journal of Economic Psychology* 28, no. 3 (2007): 283–313. https://psycnet.apa.org/record/2007-07718-001.

Giles, David. *Illusions of Immortality: A Psychology of Fame and Celebrity*. London: Macmillan Education, 2000.

Glascock, Taylor. "The Japanese Gamers Who Prefer to Date Videogame Characters." *Wired*, October 28, 2015. https://www.wired.com/2015/10/loulou-daki-playing-for-love/.

Halpern, Jake. *Fame Junkies: The Hidden Truths Behind America's Favorite Addiction*. Boston: HMH Books, 2007.

Hampton, Keith N., Chul-joo Lee, Eun Ja Her. "How New Media Affords Network Diversity: Direct and Mediated Access to Social Capital Through Participation in Local Social Settings." *New Media and Society* 13, no. 7 (2011): 1031–49. https://journals.sagepub.com/doi/10.1177/1461444810390342.

Hari, Johann. *Lost Connections: Uncovering the Real Causes of Depression—and the Unexpected Solutions*. New York: Bloomsbury, 2018.

Harris, Michael. *Solitude: In Pursuit of a Singular Life in a Crowded World*. New York: St. Martin's, 2017.

Hegarty, Stephanie. "Why I 'Married' a Cartoon Character." BBC, August 17, 2019. https://www.bbc.com/news/stories-49343280.

Hirayama, Maki. "Developments in Information Technology and the Sexual Depression of Japanese Youth since 2000." *International Journal of the Sociology of Leisure* 2 (2019): 95–119. https://link.springer.com/article/10.1007/s41978-019-00034-2.

Lutz, Ashley. "Meet the Men Who Gave Up Dating in Favor of Life-Sized Dolls." *Insider*, May 16, 2012. https://www.businessinsider.com/meet-the-men-who-gave-up-dating-for-life-sized-dolls-2012-5.

Katayama, Lisa. "Love in 2-D." *New York Times*, July 21, 2009. https://www.nytimes.com/2009/07/26/magazine/26FOB-2DLove-t.html.

Khademi, Casey Ali. "The Cultural Reconstruction of Fame: How Social Media and Reality Television Have Reshaped America's Definition of 'Famous.'" PhD diss., Stanford University, March 2015. https://comm.stanford.edu/mm/2016/07/Casey-Khademi-MA-Thesis.pdf.

Khazan, Olga. "How Loneliness Begets Loneliness." *Atlantic*, April 2017. https://www.theatlantic.com/health/archive/2017/04/how-loneliness-begets-loneliness/521841/.

Koike, Mayu, et al. "What Factors Attract People to Play Romantic Video Games?" *PLOS One* 15, no. 4 (2020). https://www.ncbi.nlm.nih.gov/pmc/articles/PMC7162468/.

Kushlev, Kostadin, et al. "Smartphones Reduce Smiles Between Strangers." *Computers in Human Behavior* 91 (February 2019): 12–16. https://www.sciencedirect.com/science/article/abs/pii/S0747563218304643.

Lather, Julie, and Emily Moyer-Guse. "How Do We React When Our Favorite Characters Are Taken Away? An Examination of a Temporary Parasocial Breakup." *Mass Communication and Society* 14, no. 2 (2011): 196–215. https://www.tandfonline.com/doi/abs/10.1080/15205431003668603.

REFERENCES

Lindstrom, Martin. *Brandwashed: Tricks Companies Use to Manipulate Our Minds and Persuade Us to Buy.* New York: Currency, 2011.

Liu, Dong, et al. "Digital Communication Media Use and Psychological Well-Being: A Meta-Analysis." *Journal of Computer-Mediated Communication* 24, no. 5 (2019): 259–73. https://academic.oup.com/jcmc/article/24/5/259/5583692.

Lowry, Rachel. "Meet the Lonely Japanese Men in Love with Virtual Girlfriends." *Time,* September 15, 2015. https://time.com/3998563/virtual-love-japan/.

Maheshwari, Surabhika. "Children of Famous Parents: An Exploratory Study." *World Academy of Science, Engineering and Technology* 47 (2008): 350–59. https://citeseerx.ist.psu.edu/viewdoc/download?doi=10.1.1.193.1528&rep=rep1&type=pdf.

Marche, Stephen. "Is Facebook Making Us Lonely?" *Atlantic,* May 2012. https://www.theatlantic.com/magazine/archive/2012/05/is-facebook-making-us-lonely/308930/.

Marsh, Jenni. "The Rise of Romance Gaming: Is the Perfect Boyfriend Inside Your Phone?" CNN, November 1, 2017. https://www.cnn.com/2016/11/21/asia/romance-gaming-japan/index.html.

Murthy, Vivek H . *Together: The Healing Power of Human Connection in a Sometimes Lonely World.* New York: Harper Wave, 2020.

Naquin, Charles E., Terri R. Kurtzberg, and Liuba Y. Belkin. "E-Mail Communication and Group Cooperation in Mixed Motive Contexts." *Social Justice Research* 21 (2008): 470–89. https://link.springer.com/article/10.1007/s11211-008-0084-x.

Niemiec, Christopher P., Richard M. Ryan, and Edward L. Deci. "The Path Taken: Consequences of Attaining Intrinsic and Extrinsic Aspirations in Post-College Life." *Journal of Research in Personality* 73, no. 3 (2009): 291–306. https://www.ncbi.nlm.nih.gov/pmc/articles/PMC2736104/.

Nishimura-Poupee, Karyn. "No Sad Endings for Japan's Virtual Romance Fans." Phys Org, February 11, 2017. https://phys.org/news/2017-02-sad-japan-virtual-romance-fans.html.

Noser, Amy, and Virgil Zeigler-Hill. "Self-Esteem Instability and the Desire for Fame." *Self and Identity* 13, no. 6 (2014): 701–13. https://www.tandfonline.com/doi/abs/10.1080/15298868.2014.927394.

Ohanesian, Liz. "Japanese Romance Apps Hit the U.S., and They're Amazing." *LA Weekly,* July 7, 2014. https://www.laweekly.com/japanese-romance-apps-hit-the-u-s-and-theyre-amazing/.

Olds, Jacqueline, and Richard S. Schwartz. *The Lonely American: Drifting Apart in the Twenty-First Century.* Boston: Beacon, 2010.

Pinker, Susan. *The Village Effect: How Face-to-Face Contact Can Make Us Healthier and Happier.* Toronto: Random House of Canada, 2014.

Potter, Ned. "More Facebook Friends, Fewer Real Ones, Says Cornell Study." *ABC News,* November 7, 2011. https://abcnews.go.com/Technology/facebook-friends-fewer-close-friends-cornell-sociologist/story?id=14896994.

REFERENCES

Prinstein, Mitch. *Popular: Finding Happiness and Success in a World That Cares Too Much About the Wrong Kinds of Relationships*. New York: Penguin, 2017.

Putnam, Robert. *Bowling Alone: The Collapse and Revival of American Community*. New York: Simon & Schuster, 2000.

Rockwell, D., and D. C. Giles. "Being a Celebrity: A Phenomenology of Fame." *Journal of Phenomenological Psychology* 40, no. 2 (2009): 178–210. https://psycnet.apa.org/record/2009-21140-003.

Rosenblatt, Gideon. "Unrequited Love in the Time of Technology." Vital Edge, February 5, 2015. https://www.the-vital-edge.com/unrequited-love/.

Schwartz, Barry. *Paradox of Choice: Why More Is Less*. New York: Ecco, 2003.

Scott Barry Kaufman (@sbkaufman). "The thirst for power is an attempt to escape from loneliness. However, power is never as satisfying as love. (Baumeister & Leary, 1995)." Twitter, June 30, 2017, 8:41 P.M. https://mobile.twitter.com/sbkaufman/status/880994842221752320.

"Sex Dolls That Talk Back." *New York Times*, June 11, 2015. https://www.nytimes.com/2015/06/12/technology/robotica-sex-robot-realdoll.html?_r=0.

Storr, Will. *Selfie: How We Became So Self-Obsessed and What It's Doing to Us*. New York: Harry N. Abrams, 2018.

Tarantola, A. "Realdoll Invests in AI for Future Sexbots That Move, and Talk Dirty." Engadget, June 13, 2013. https://www.engadget.com/2015-06-12-realdoll-robots-ai-realbotix.html.

Thompson, Clive. *Coders: The Making of a New Tribe and the Remaking of the World*. New York: Penguin, 2019.

Turkle, Sherry. *Alone Together: Why We Expect More from Technology and Less from Each Other*. New York: Basic Books, 2012.

Turkle, Sherry. *Reclaiming Conversation: The Power of Talk in a Digital Age*. New York: Penguin, 2016.

Uhls, Y. T., and P. M. Greenfield. "The Value of Fame: Preadolescent Perceptions of Popular Media and Their Relationship to Future Aspirations." *Developmental Psychology*, December 19, 2011. Advance online publication. doi:10.1037/a0026369.

University of Maryland. "Cellphone Use Linked to Selfish Behavior." ScienceDaily, February 14, 2012. https://www.sciencedaily.com/releases/2012/02/120214122038.htm.

University of Rochester. "Achieving Fame, Wealth, and Beauty Are Psychological Dead Ends, Study Says." ScienceDaily, May 19, 2009. https://www.sciencedaily.com/releases/2009/05/090514111402.htm.

Young, Emma. "Different Kinds of Loneliness—Having Poor Quality Relationships Is Associated with Greater Distress Than Having Too Few." *Research Digest* (blog), February 2, 2019. https://digest.bps.org.uk/2019/02/20/different-kinds-of-loneliness-having-poor-quality-relationships-is-associated-with-a-greater-toll-than-having-too-few/.

Wichita State University. "People Lie More When Texting, Study Finds." ScienceDaily, January 26, 2012. https://www.sciencedaily.com/releases/2012/01/120125131120.htm.

REFERENCES

CHAPTER 18

"An Audience with . . . Ted Kaptchuk." *Nature Reviews Drug Discovery* 7 (July 2008): 554. https://www.nature.com/articles/nrd2629.

Baumeister, Roy F. *The Cultural Animal: Human Nature, Meaning, and Social Life.* New York: Oxford University Press, 2005.

Blanchflower, David G., and Andrew J. Oswald. "Well-Being over Time in Britain and the USA." Working Paper No. 7487. National Bureau of Economic Research, January 2000. https://www.nber.org/papers/w7487.

Bregman, Rutger. *Humankind: A Hopeful History.* Translated by Elizabeth Manton and Eric Moore. New York: Little, Brown, 2020.

Cacioppo, John T., and William Patrick. *Loneliness: Human Nature and the Need for Social Connection.* New York: Norton, 2009.

Cahalan, Susannah. *The Great Pretender: The Undercover Mission That Changed Our Understanding of Madness.* New York: Grand Central, 2019.

Caluori, Reto. "Even Psychological Placebos Have an Effect." *Informationsdienst Wissenschaft,* February 5, 2019. https://idw-online.de/de/news710065.

Charles, S. J., et al. "Blocking Mu-Opiod Receptors Inhibits Social Bonding in Rituals." *Biology Letters* 16 (2020). https://royalsocietypublishing.org/doi/10.1098/rsbl.2020.0485.

Christian Science Monitor. "The Ten Happiest Jobs." https://www.csmonitor.com/Photo-Galleries/In-Pictures/The-10-happiest-jobs/(photo)/382926.

Colla, Judith, et al. "Depression and Modernization: A Cross-Cultural Study of Women." *Social Psychiatry and Psychiatric Epidemiology* 41, no. 4 (2006): 271–79. https://pubmed.ncbi.nlm.nih.gov/16520885/.

Crockett, Molly J., et al. "Harm to Others Outweighs Harm to Self." *Proceedings of the National Academy of Sciences* 111, no. 448 (2014): 17320–25. https://www.pnas.org/content/111/48/17320.short.

Dartmouth College. "Our Brains Are Obsessed with Being Social." ScienceDaily, May 16, 2018. https://www.sciencedaily.com/releases/2018/05/180516162533.htm.

Denworth, Lydia. *Friendship: The Evolution, Biology, and Extraordinary Power of Life's Fundamental Bond.* New York: W. W. Norton, 2020.

Feinberg, Cara. "The Placebo Phenomenon." *Harvard Magazine,* January–February 2013. https://harvardmagazine.com/2013/01/the-placebo-phenomenon.

Finniss, Damien G., et al. "Placebo Effects: Biological, Clinical, and Ethical Advances." *Lancet* 375, no. 9715 (2010): 686–95. https://www.ncbi.nlm.nih.gov/pmc/articles/PMC2832199/.

Gaab, Jens, et al. "Effects and Components of Placebos with a Psychological Treatment Rationale—Three Randomized-Controlled Studies." *Scientific Reports* 9, no. 1421 (2019). https://www.nature.com/articles/s41598-018-37945-1.

Greenberg, Gary. "What If the Placebo Effect Isn't a Trick?" *New York Times Magazine,* November 7, 2018. https://www.nytimes.com/2018/11/07/magazine/placebo-effect-medicine.html.

Hare, Brian, and Vanessa Woods. *Survival of the Friendliest: Understanding Our*

Origins and Rediscovering Our Common Humanity. New York: Random House, 2020.

Hari, Johann. *Chasing the Scream: The First and Last Days of the War on Drugs.* New York: Bloomsbury, 2019.

Hari, Johann. *Lost Connections: Uncovering the Real Causes of Depression—and the Unexpected Solutions.* New York: Bloomsbury, 2018.

Hidaka, Brandon H. "Depression as a Disease of Modernity: Explanations for Increasing Prevalence." *Journal of Affective Disorders* 140, no. 3 (2012): 205–14. https://pubmed.ncbi.nlm.nih.gov/22244375/.

Insel, Thomas R. "Is Social Attachment an Addictive Disorder?" *Physiology & Behavior* 79, no. 3 (2003): 351–7. https://pubmed.ncbi.nlm.nih.gov/12954430/.

Junger, Sebastian. *Tribe: On Homecoming and Belonging.* New York: Grand Central, 2016.

Kaptchuk, Ted J. "About." https://www.tedkaptchuk.com/.

Kaptchuk, Ted J. "The Placebo Effect in Alternative Medicine: Can the Performance of a Healing Ritual Have Clinical Significance?" *Annals of Internal Medicine* 136, no. 11 (2002): 817–25. https://pubmed.ncbi.nlm.nih.gov/12044130/.

Kaptchuk, Ted. "Placebo Effects Make Good Medicine Better." TEDMED. https://www.tedmed.com/talks/show?id=299407.

Kaptchuk, Ted J., and Franklin G. Miller. "Open Label Placebo: Can Honestly Prescribed Placebos Evoke Meaningful Therapeutic Benefits?" *BMJ*, October 2, 2018. https://pubmed.ncbi.nlm.nih.gov/30279235/.

Kirsch, Irving. "Antidepressants and the Placebo Effect." *Zeitschrift für Psychologie* 222, no. 3 (2014): 128–34. https://www.ncbi.nlm.nih.gov/pmc/articles/PMC4172306/.

Kirsch, Irving, and Guy Sapirstein. "Listening to Prozac but Hearing Placebo: A Meta-analysis of Antidepressant Medication." *Prevention and Treatment* 1, no. 2 (1998). https://psycnet.apa.org/record/1999-11094-001.

Lowe, Derek. "Expensive Placebos Work Better." *Science*, January 29, 2015. https://blogs.sciencemag.org/pipeline/archives/2015/01/29/expensive_placebos_work_better.

Miller, Franklin G., and Ted J. Kaptchuk. "The Power of Context: Reconceptualizing the Placebo Effect." *Journal of the Royal Society of Medicine* 101, no. 5 (2008): 222–25. https://www.ncbi.nlm.nih.gov/pmc/articles/PMC2376272/.

Miller, Franklin G., Luana Colloca, and Ted J. Kaptchuk. "The Placebo Effect: Illness and Interpersonal Healing." *Perspectives in Biology and Medicine* 52, no. 4 (2009): 518. https://www.ncbi.nlm.nih.gov/pmc/articles/PMC2814126/.

Murthy, Vivek H. *Together: The Healing Power of Human Connection in a Sometimes Lonely World.* New York: Harper Wave, 2020.

Ohio State University. "Why Some Friends Make You Feel More Supported Than Others." ScienceDaily, October 7, 2020. https://www.sciencedaily.com/releases/2020/10/201007085609.htm.

Olds, Jacqueline, and Richard S. Schwartz. *The Lonely American: Drifting Apart in the Twenty-First Century.* Boston: Beacon, 2010.

REFERENCES

Olson, Jay A., et al. "Super Placebos: A Feasibility Study Combining Contextual Factors to Promote Placebo Effects." PsyArXiv Preprints, December 26, 2020. https://psyarxiv.com/sh4f6/.

Pinker, Susan. *The Village Effect: How Face-to-Face Contact Can Make Us Healthier and Happier.* Toronto: Random House of Canada, 2014.

Porot, Nicolas, and Eric Mandelbaum. "The Science of Belief: A Progress Report." *WIREs Cognitive Science* 12, no. 2 (2021): e1539. https://wires.onlinelibrary.wiley.com/doi/10.1002/wcs.1539.

Prioleau, Leslie, Martha Murdock, and Nathan Brody. "An Analysis of Psychotherapy Versus Placebo Studies." *Behavioral and Brain Sciences* 6, no. 2 (1983): 275–85. https://www.cambridge.org/core/journals/behavioral-and-brain-sciences/article/abs/an-analysis-of-psychotherapy-versus-placebo-studies/08C6F3704103BE1DE8737138D61BE66B.

Quinones, Sam. *Dreamland: The True Tale of America's Opiate Epidemic.* New York: Bloomsbury, 2015.

Robinson, Paul H., and Sarah M. Robinson. *Pirates, Prisoners, and Lepers: Lessons from Life Outside the Law.* Lincoln, NE: Potomac Books, 2015.

Snyder, C. Richard, ed. *Handbook of Hope: Theory, Measures, and Applications.* Cambridge, MA: Academic, 2000.

Solnit, Rebecca. *A Paradise Built in Hell: The Extraordinary Communities That Arise in Disaster.* New York: Penguin, 2010.

Specter, Michael. "The Power of Nothing." *New Yorker*, December 12, 2012. https://www.newyorker.com/magazine/2011/12/12/the-power-of-nothing.

Sternberg, Robert, and Judith Glück, eds. *The Cambridge Handbook of Wisdom.* Cambridge: Cambridge University Press, 2019.

Storr, Will. *Selfie: How We Became So Self-Obsessed and What It's Doing to Us.* New York: Harry N. Abrams, 2018.

Suttie, Jill. "Why Americans Struggle to Be Happy." *Greater Good Magazine*, October 26, 2015. https://greatergood.berkeley.edu/article/item/why_americans_struggle_to_be_happy.

University of Michigan Health System. "Placebo Power: Depressed People Who Respond to Fake Drugs Get the Most Help from Real Ones." ScienceDaily, September 30, 2015. https://www.sciencedaily.com/releases/2015/09/150930140131.htm.

Wai-lan Yeung, Victoria, Andrew Greers, and Simon Man-chun Kam. "Merely Possessing a Placebo Analgesic Reduced Pain Intensity: Preliminary Findings from a Randomized Trial." *Current Psychology* 38 (2019): 194–203. https://link.springer.com/article/10.1007/s12144-017-9601-0.

Wehrwein, Peter. "Astounding Increase in Antidepressant Use by Americans." *Harvard Health Blog*, October 20, 2011. https://www.health.harvard.edu/blog/astounding-increase-in-antidepressant-use-by-americans-201110203624.

Weissman, Myrna M., et al. "The Changing Rate of Major Depression: Cross-National Comparisons." *JAMA* 268, no. 21 (1992): 3098–105. https://jamanetwork.com/journals/jama/article-abstract/401629.

REFERENCES

Wikipedia. "Inclusion of the Ingroup in the Self." https://en.wikipedia.org /wiki/Self-expansion_model#Inclusion_of_the_ingroup_in_the_self.

Wikipedia. "Placebo." https://en.wikipedia.org/wiki/Placebo.

Wikipedia. "Rumspringa." https://en.wikipedia.org/wiki/Rumspringa.

Wikipedia. "Ted Kaptchuk." https://en.wikipedia.org/wiki/Ted_Kaptchuk.

CHAPTER 19

Christakis, Nicholas A. *Blueprint: The Evolutionary Origins of a Good Society*. New York: Little, Brown, 2019.

Cozolino, Louis. *The Neuroscience of Human Relationships: Attachment and the Developing Social Brain*, 2nd ed. New York: W. W. Norton, 2014.

Finkel, Michael. *The Stranger in the Woods: The Extraordinary Story of the Last True Hermit*. New York: Knopf Doubleday, 2017.

Robinson, Paul H., and Sarah M. Robinson. *Pirates, Prisoners, and Lepers: Lessons from Life Outside the Law*. Lincoln, NE: Potomac Books, 2015.

CONCLUSION

Baumeister, Roy F., and Mark R. Leary. "The Need to Belong: Desire for Interpersonal Attachments as a Fundamental Human Motivation." *Psychological Bulletin* 117, no. 3 (1995): 497–529. https://psycnet.apa.org/record /1995-29052-001.

Baumeister, Roy F., and William von Hippel. "Why Nature Selected Human Minds to Use Meaning." *Evolutionary Studies in Imaginative Culture* 4, no. 1 (2020): 1–18. https://www.jstor.org/stable/10.26613/esic.4.1.158?seq=1.

Freling, Traci H. "When Poignant Stories Outweigh Cold Hard Facts: A Metaanalysis of the Anecdotal Bias." *Organizational Behavior and Human Decision Processes* 160 (2020): 51–67. https://www.sciencedirect.com/science/article /abs/pii/S0749597819301633.

Hu, Caitlin. "An Italian Doctor Explains 'Syndrome K,' the Fake Disease He Invented to Save Jews from the Nazis." Quartz, July 8, 2016. https:// qz.com/724169/an-italian-doctor-explains-syndrome-k-the-fake-disease-he -invented-to-save-jews-from-the-nazis/.

"Italian Doctor Who Fooled Nazis." *BBC News*, last updated December 3, 2004. http://news.bbc.co.uk/2/hi/europe/4066105.stm.

Lambert, Nathaniel M., et al. "To Belong Is to Matter: Sense of Belonging Enhances Meaning in Life." *Personality and Social Psychology Bulletin* 39, no. 11 (2013): 1418–27. https://journals.sagepub.com/doi/abs/10.1177 /0146167213499186.

Wikipedia. "Fatebenefratelli Hospital." https://en.wikipedia.org/wiki/Fatebenefra telli_Hospital.

Wikipedia. "Giovanni Borromeo." https://en.wikipedia.org/wiki/Giovanni_Bor romeo.

ABOUT THE AUTHOR

When I write, I feel like an armless, legless man with
a crayon in his mouth.

—KURT VONNEGUT

ERIC BARKER stopped paying attention in physics class when they finished discussing car crashes, and lost interest in biology after they covered sex. Despite this, he writes about science. He attended the University of Pennsylvania, a school that prides itself on turning self-absorbed brats into educated adults. He then moved to Hollywood, a town that prides itself on turning educated adults into self-absorbed brats. His blog, *Barking Up the Wrong Tree*, presents evidence-based answers and expert insight on how to be awesome at life. Over 500,000 people have subscribed to its newsletter. His first book, *Barking Up the Wrong Tree*, was a *Wall Street Journal* bestseller and has been translated into more than eighteen languages. Eric has given talks at MIT, Yale, Google, United States Central Command (CENTCOM), NASDAQ, and the Olympic Training Center. He has done all manner of fancy, impressive things . . . but enough about him: how are *you*?